REINCARNATION AS A SCIENTIFIC CONCEPT

REINCARNATION AS A SCIENTIFIC CONCEPT

Scholarly Evidence for Past Lives

DR. K. S. RAWAT
AND TITUS RIVAS, M.A., M.SC.

WHITE CROW

www.whitecrowbooks.com

Dedicated to all scholars contributing to reincarnation research
and in remembrance of Dr. Ian Stevenson (1918-2007)

Published in the United States of America and the United Kingdom by
White Crow Books; an imprint of White Crow Productions Ltd.

For information, contact White Crow Books by e-mail: info@whitecrowbooks.com.

Cover Design by Astrid@Astridpaints.com
Interior design by Velin@Perseus-Design.com

Paperback: ISBN: 978-1-78677-127-8
eBook: ISBN: 978-1-78677-128-5

Non-Fiction / Body, Mind & Spirit / Reincarnation / Parapsychology

www.whitecrowbooks.com

"Our knowledge can only be finite, while our ignorance must necessarily be infinite".

~ **Karl Popper**

"It is not more surprising to be born twice than once; everything in nature is resurrection".

~ **Voltaire**

"By making the right use of those things remembered from the former life, by constantly perfecting himself in the mysteries, a man becomes truly perfect".

~ **Plato**

"You cannot say of the soul, it shall be, or is about to be, or is to be hereafter. It is without birth".

~ **Bhagavad-Gita**

"Science also tells us that all our cells and atoms and molecules are ever-changing, and there is nothing in our bodies that was with us seven years before. During our lifetime, our bodies, our minds and our personality undergo radical changes. However, even with all these changes, on some level we remain the same person. Spirit or soul is what seems to provide this continuity".

~ **Arya Bhushan**

"There is this doubt: When a man dies, some say that he lives on, yet others say that he does not; I wish to know for certain what the truth is".

~ **Nachiketa, Kathopanishad**

"If a man dies, will he live again?"

~ **Job 14:14**

"Who was I in my last birth and who I would be in my next one?"

~ **Jain saint, Acharang Sutra**

"You and I,
O Arjuna
Have lived many lives.
I remember them all;
You do not remember".

~ **Krishna, Bhagavad-Gita**

"It may be remarked that David Hume's proposition that evidence of miracles – that is, events that violate natural laws – should never justify our setting aside massively evidenced natural laws was answered by St. Augustine more than a millennium before Hume was born when the saint said that miracles are not a contradiction of nature's laws but only of what we believe to be nature's laws".

~ **Archie Roy, *The Eager Dead***

"When Galileo expounded the theory that it was the Earth which rotated on its axis and revolved round the Sun, he was persecuted because such facts were against the views of organized religion. The same happened to the Albigenses and the Cathars, who believed and talked about reincarnation. As this view endangered the then accepted religious beliefs, the papacy waged a crusade against them, confiscating their property, proscribing their literature and persecuting them.

This, perhaps, shows that whether it is religion or science, whenever any new thought is presented beyond the accepted theories and beliefs, it tends to be resisted, ridiculed, or put down. Today it is science that has become the established religion, which evaluates everything on the basis of known scientific theories, and what can be demonstrated in a laboratory … ".

~ **Arya Bhushan**

PRAISE FOR
REINCARNATION AS A SCIENTIFIC CONCEPT

~

"If you want to read one book that will give you a complete overview of impressive research into reincarnation presented with open-minded objectivity and scholarly accuracy, look no further. While it covers many aspects of the topic, it remains wonderfully readable and fascinating in detail.

As a bonus, both of the authors bring to the table enthusiasm generated by their personal research, Dr. Rawat from an Eastern, and Titus Rivas from a Western perspective. Together they have created a masterpiece that shows that the reincarnation hypothesis may now be taken as scientifically (in the sense of scholarly) "acceptable" if not yet "proved" to the satisfaction of all".

~ Victor and Wendy Zammit
co-authors of the Friday Afterlife Report.

"Unless reincarnation is already mundane to you, you will be amazed, and quite possibly convinced by this book and the cases it features. The co-authors minute detail demonstrate how some children's utterances, behaviours and physical marks defy any other explanation. But Rawat and Rivas also point out that the great strength of the evidence of reincarnation is the sheer number of investigated cases, and how in their thousands they show the common patterns you would expect of a genuine natural phenomenon.

Even veterans of academic reincarnation literature will likely find something new and striking in Rawat's many mentions of his unpublished cases. Readers with a penchant for philosophy will find Rivas's philosophical explorations of reincarnation and consciousness interesting.
Altogether, a fascinating read".

~ Karen M. Wehrstein

"For many Westerners, just reading or hearing about reincarnation makes their hair stand on end or causes them to totally close off their minds. They consider reincarnation an exotic, naïve, meaningless and even ridiculous belief that shows the ignorance of our early ancestors.

"However, the authors of this book examine and continue the scientific investigative work of Dr. Ian Stevenson and many other researchers, and add their own investigations to this tradition, and thus they show that reincarnation is a well-founded belief.

"One thing that stands out is the masterful way in which the authors offer a science-based explanation for the amnesia (memory loss) in respect to past lives that characterizes most of us. Amnesia (memory loss), or rather the inability to remember a past life, is the main reason why those who don't believe in reincarnation reject this concept.

"I have had the privilege and honour of collaborating in the translation of this book for a future Spanish language edition, and therefore needed to meticulously analyze its contents; I can highly recommend this book both for the neophyte and the expert in the field".

~ **Eduardo Jorge Fulco**

"I find *Reincarnation as a Scientific Concept: Scholarly Evidence for Past Lives* one of the very best books on this topic currently available. It is a quite readable and convincingly written text: comprehensive and thorough. Every person interested in reincarnation should have it on their bookcase".

~ **Rudolf Smit,** Editor of "Terugkeer naar Levenslicht" (Return to the Light of Life), quarterly journal of IANDS the Netherlands, and IANDS Flanders.

"The authors Rivas and Rawat have managed to gather in this book all the serious information available today on the phenomenon of reincarnation and submit it to a rigorous analysis. From the cases of Stevenson and Tucker to those investigated by the authors themselves in India and Europe, an intellectually solid and exciting edifice is built step by step. The result is also well placed in its context: what is said today about reincarnation in religions and philosophical currents, and the possible alternative hypotheses. In short, a must-have book for anyone who wants to confront the scientific evidence for reincarnation, and what this impressive phenomenon tells us about our true nature".

~ Alejandro Agudo, physicist.

ACKNOWLEDGEMENTS

〜

Thirty years ago, in 1991, Dr. Adela Amado of Tetragrama organized an international conference on survival and reincarnation research in the "Palau de la Música" (a large conference hall) of Valencia, Spain. This was where we first met and discussed what we each felt constitutes good evidence for reincarnation and related issues. Since we agreed on many subjects, we decided to write a book together. Dr. Rawat visited the Netherlands in 1998, and within a few weeks we finished a raw version of the original e-book. By our good fortune we were even able to combine this project with a joint study of a Dutch case in Amsterdam.

Dr. Rawat's visit led to a no longer available e-book published by Writers Publisher (Vancouver) in 2006, under the title Reincarnation: *The Scientific Evidence is Building*.
This new book is loosely inspired by it.

In addition to Adela Amado, we would like to thank the following people for inspiring, assisting or supporting us:

Eben Alexander, Mary Rose Barrington, Jon Beecher, Ariadne Belmer, Rob Berntsen, Arya Bhushan, Abhijat van Bilsen, Carol Bowman, Niels Brummelman, Chris Canter, Chris Carter, Jenny Cockell, René van Delft, Anny Dirven, Dominique Elkerbout, Gesa Dröge, Marcel Engeringh, Maria Fernandes Rodrigues, Hans Gerding, Tilly Gerritsma, Bob Good, John Gregg, Roman Gruijters, Jyoti Gupta, Erlendur Haraldsson, Dieter Hassler, Musa van den Heuvel, Simon van den Heuvel, Roland Hoedemaekers, Jan Holden, Ignacio Minaya

Sánchez, Ria Husken-Karsten, Antoine Janssen, Thomas Jones, Bharti Khandelwal, Richard Krebber, Han Kuik, Bikram Lalbahadoersing, Adil Lamalmi, David Lorimer, Ohkado Masayuki, Jim Matlock, Robert Mays, Suzanne Mays, Jo Meevis, Fred Melssen, Antonia Mills, Vitor Moura Visoni, Peter Mulacz, Alian Namaki, Alan Patterson, Guy Lyon Playfair, Mesut Polat, Jamuna Prasad, Smita Premchander, Toon Pruyn, Bharat Rawat, Jai Rawat, Vidya Rawat, Pierre Rezus, Esteban Rivas, José Rivas Rivas, Corrie Rivas-Wols, Archie Roy, Amir Saberifar, Elly Sablerolles, B. Shamsukha, Lian Sidorov, Júlio César de Siqueira Barros, Rudolf H. Smit, Roy Stemman, Bert Stoop, Ian Stevenson, Eliane Torres de Moura, Jim Tucker, Stephan Vollenberg, Donald West, Pieter van Wezel, and Arnold Ziegelaar.

Kirti Swaroop Rawat, Indore (Madhya Pradesh, India)
Titus Rivas, Nijmegen (The Netherlands)

Spring 2021

xiv

CONTENTS

~

1

INTRODUCTION

~

From time immemorial humankind has been trying to decipher the Book of Life. Unfortunately for us, the first and last pages are missing: Where do we come from? Where shall we go? The question eventually comes down to: What are we?

Are we a conglomeration of physical forces, or are we a "soul," a "psyche," or an "Atman"[1]? Is it true that "From dust we came and to dust we shall return" with nothing of us existing prior to our present life? Or: Were we in existence prior to the birth of our physical body, and shall we survive after its death?

Reincarnation

The idea of reincarnation appears to be as old as human thought. References are found in the Rig Veda of India, which is considered to be one of the oldest scriptures in the world. Surprisingly, Wendy Doniger O'Flaherty, editor of the book *Karma and Rebirth in Classical Indian Tradition*, states in a chapter dealing with the subject: "The theory of rebirth does not appear in the Vedas ...". (Pp. 268).

---

[1] Some Sanskritists hold that Atman is derived from a verbal root, *an*, meaning to breathe, the vital principle.

O'Flaherty is not alone in this view. J.N. Farquhar (*An Outline of the Religious Literature of India*, 1920) is quoted by Wilhelm Halbfass (*Karma and Rebirth in Classical Indian Traditions*, Editor Wendy Doniger O'Flaherty, Pp. 268) saying: "There is not a trace of transmigration in the hymns of Vedas". Lord Raglan has also opined that "the earliest Sanskrit scripture, the Rig Vedas contain no mention of reincarnation". (Lord Raglan: *Death and Birth: A Study in Comparative Religion*, 1945, Pp. 35).

Even Albert Schweitzer has written: "The hymns of the Rig Veda knew nothing as yet of a cycle of rebirths" (Albert Schweitzer, 1960, Bombay: Wilco Publishing House, Pp. 55). However, we do believe that some of the hymns clearly refer to the idea of reincarnation:

> When after death all the fire elements dissolve amongst themselves, the Jiva Atma[2] (Individual Soul) remains and this Jivatma takes to itself a new body. (10/16/5).

> We pray in the name of the God of fire who will be pleased and shall give us a rebirth on this earth where we may again get father and mother. (1/24/2).

Rig Veda references are also found in various hymns of Artharveda and Yajurveda. Later on, the idea was much elaborated in various Upanishads like the Kathopanishad, Brihadaranyaka, Prishna and Kenopanishad.

Reincarnation is a cardinal principle of Hindu religion. Every Hindu scripture has references to it. The same is true of Buddhism, Jainism and Sikhism, though these differ on many points from the view held by Hinduism. Despite differences, it is remarkable that "almost every country of the East accepts the doctrine (of rebirth) as too obvious to need proof" (Christmas Humphreys: *Buddhism*, 1951, Pp. 103).

It would be wrong to presume that the idea of reincarnation prevailed only in Eastern religions and philosophies. There have been numerous early advocates of reincarnation in the West too. Long before Christianity, belief in reincarnation was widespread in various European cultures.

Many African and Native American ancestors believed in reincarnation and so did a number of so-called "primitive" communities

---

[2] Jivatma(n) = Jiva Atma(n), individual soul.

and tribes in various parts of the globe. Australian Aborigines may be counted as firm believers to this day:

> [In Central Australia] the belief is firmly rooted that the human soul undergoes an endless series of reincarnations, the living men and women of one generation being nothing but the spirits of their ancestors come to life again. [In some parts of Queensland] they believe that every person's spirit undergoes a series of reincarnations.
> (Sir J.G. Frazer, *The Golden Bough* 1911, Pp. 36).

Among the Basala of Northern Rhodesia (present day Zambia), the birth name given to a child is always one that has been borne by some ancestor, and there is a ceremony to ascertain which ancestor has been reincarnated in a child. Similar beliefs are found in many other parts of the world. Certain customs illustrate this clearly: Among a tribe in Florida (USA),

> ... pregnant women were accustomed to go and meet funeral processions in the hope of receiving within themselves the soul of the deceased for the benefit of children by the road side so that their souls might enter the bodies of passing women and be born again. (Bertholet, D. Alfred, *The Transmigration of Souls*, 1909, Pp. 24-25).

The Calabarians of West Africa buried their dead in their houses. The soul of a dead man thus buried was thought to pass into the child next born in the house. In New Zealand, tribal priests stand before a newborn child and repeat a long list of ancestral names until the child sneezes or cries out at one of them. The ancestor is thus found whose soul is reincarnated in the child and after whom the child is then named. Similarly, in Little Popo (Togo) in former colonial West Africa, a custom prevails in which the parents of newborn children consult an oracle to find whether the soul on the mother's side or father's side is reincarnated in the child, and which soul it is.

This led Christmas Humphreys (1901-1983) to make the following remarks on reincarnation:

Western writers have traced its presence in the legends and indigenous ideas of nearly every country in the world. It is to be found in most of the greatest minds of Europe and America, from Plato to Origen, from Blake to Schopenhauer, from Goethe, Boehme, Kant and Swedenborg[3] to Browning, Emerson, Walt Whitman, and leading minds of the Western world today (Ibid.).

Among the Greeks, Pythagoras is the most famous exponent of the doctrine of reincarnation (metempsychosis). In fact, he asserted that he himself had passed through four previous lives in human form. He was even able to locate the shield, hung in the temple of the Goddess Hera, which he had used during his former life as Euphorbus at the siege of Troy, where Menelaus killed him. The Greek poet Pindar believed that the soul must pass through at least three earthly lives before it could escape the necessity of reincarnation. The philosopher Empedocles wrote about himself: "in former lives I have been a boy and a girl".

According to Plato, the soul self-selected its new position in life in accordance with the character it had acquired during its former existence, so that the soul was "symmetrical" with the body that clothed it.

Herodotus states that the Egyptians "were the first to teach that the human soul is immortal and at the death of the body enters into the form of an animal, which is born at the moment and after passing through all the creatures of land, sea and air, which cycle it completes in 3000 years, when it enters once more into a human body at birth". He also believed that the Greeks had "borrowed this doctrine from the Egyptians". (*Phaedrus*, 245.) The papyrus known as the *Book of the Dead* gives an interesting impression of Egyptian views.

Given that many people think that there have never been any influential doctrines about reincarnation in the so-called monotheistic religions, it is remarkable to find that in their common source – Judaism – there have been major reincarnationist currents that still survive today. As Rabbi Yonassan Gershom has pointed out, these are the mystical traditions of Kabbalah and Hasidism. Actually, many Jews believe in the reality of reincarnation and see no contradiction between this doctrine and their religion.

---

[3] In fact, Emanuel Swedenborg did not believe in reincarnation and explained claimed memories of previous lives by an influence from memories of discarnate spirits.

Is the idea of reincarnation compatible with Christian orthodoxy? What were Christ's views about it? Though Christ never taught the idea of reincarnation directly, he never denied it; nor did he ever say that it was false. In the book of John there is an interesting passage where we read:

> [As Jesus] passed by, he saw a man blind from his birth. And my disciples asked him: "Rabbi, who sinned, this man or his parents, that he was born blind?" (John 9:2).

Since a child could not have sinned in this life, the idea of pre-existence is implied in the question put to Jesus. It also indicates that the idea of reincarnation was prevalent among the Jews of the time. In reply, Jesus clearly had "the opportunity to condemn reincarnation and warn all Christians it was untrue or pernicious, but he did not" (Cranston and Williams, *Reincarnation: A new horizon in science, religion and society*, 1984, Pp. 207-8).

Following the Gospel of John (8:55-58), Jesus was taunted by the Israelites for setting himself up as greater than Abraham.

He replied: "Your father Abraham recognized that he was to see my day; he saw it and was glad".

The Israelites were astounded. They further asked: "You are not fifty years old, and have you seen Abraham?"

Jesus replied emphatically: "Truly, truly, I say to you: before Abraham was, I am" (John 8:58).

Again, the disciples asked Jesus, "Why do the scribes say that first Elijah does come, and he is to restore all things; but I tell you that Elijah has already come, and they did not know him. But did to him whatsoever they pleased ..". The disciples understood that he was speaking to them of John the Baptist. (Matt. 17:10-13; Mark 9:9-13).

"It would be hard to put into clearer language the idea that John the Baptist was a reincarnation of Elijah," comments Rev. Leslie D. Weatherhead (Weatherhead, Rev. Leslie D. *The Case for Reincarnation*, 1955, second revised and enlarged edition, 1960; fourth impression, 1963, Pp. 4).

According to several sources, to some early church fathers the idea of reincarnation seemed consistent with the Old and New Testament and complementary to the idea of personal salvation. The chief architect of the first systematic theology of Christianity, Origen, would have declared in his *De Principiis*: "Every soul comes into this world strengthened by the victories or weakened by the defeats of its previous life". Origen's position would have been officially condemned three centuries later.

However, other sources dispute this, saying that Origen did not believe in reincarnation.

Be that as it may, by the early Middle Ages reincarnation certainly seems to have become a heretical notion that was incompatible with official doctrines of the Roman Catholic Church.

A general view about Islam is that it also does not subscribe to the doctrine of reincarnation because some of its adherents had chosen to interpret passages of the Koran with an eye to limiting or denying anything relating to reincarnation. Those who deny it do that according to their own opinions or the written opinions of others, and believe in reaching Heaven or Paradise only. To them there is no subsequent return.

Still, some Islamic or semi-Islamic currents do indeed believe in reincarnation: for example, the Alevis in Turkey, and the Druze (or Druse) in Lebanon, Syria and Israel. In support of their belief, they cite passages from the Koran (Al-Qur'an), which appear to refer to rebirth:

> **Al-Qur'an**, (Al-Baqara [The Cow])
> How can ye reject the faith in Allah? – Seeing that ye were without life, and He gave you life; then will He cause you to die, and will again bring you to life; and again to Him will ye return.
> Surah 2.28

> **Al-Qur'an**, (Nooh [Noah])
> And Allah has produced you from the earth growing (gradually), and in the End He will return you into the (earth), and raise you forth.
> Surah 71.17, 18

There are people all over the world who do not believe in rebirth and are not part of – or influenced by – Christian or Muslim orthodoxy: "These few exceptions," writes Dr. Stevenson, "however, subtract little from the generalization that nearly everyone outside the range of orthodox Christianity, Judaism, Islam and science – the last being a secular religion for many people – believe in reincarnation".

We should not forget that there have always been unorthodox versions or "heretic" forms of the dominating ideologies in the Western world, such as that of the Cathars, who did indeed believe in reincarnation.

As to the literary scene throughout the world, Prof. Geddes MacGregor's observation seems quite appropriate:

> Preoccupation with the reincarnational theme has been so widespread among notable writers, it might be easier to make an inventory of authors who show no interest in it than to make a list of those who do.

Since the 1960s, the Western world has become more sympathetic towards rebirth and reincarnation, yet a diminishing number still think they are "exotic" notions, or profess to know nothing about them. Gurus who teach some versions of the Hindu doctrines about reincarnation and karma, such as Paramahansa Yogananda, Maharishi Mahesh Yogi or Bhagwan Sri Rajneesh (Osho), gather a considerable number of Western followers who accept those doctrines.

Long before these there had already been the "esoterical" Western teachings of occultists such as Helena Petrovna Blavatsky (Founder of the Theosophical Society), and anthroposophist Rudolf Steiner, both of whom included reincarnation in their philosophies.

During the early twentieth century, the teachings of Edgar Cayce, an American trance medium and prophet who gave 14,306 "readings" to people seeking help and advice, also received a lot of attention. Reincarnation became a central tenet of the teachings and, although Cayce was a devout Christian, he came to accept the messages he received.

Organizations such as the Association for Research and Enlightenment (ARE) and the Edgar Cayce Foundation continue his legacy and have done a lot to promote the concept of reincarnation. Currently a sizable number of people in the West who identify as "New Age," accept that humans have more than one life. New Age enthusiasts are not isolated, and many of them belong to mainstream churches.

Of course, counting noses can never be recommended as a means for verifying any belief. Even if a belief were universal, it would not necessarily mean that it is a fact. The truth or falsity of an idea can be determined only by empirical evidence for or against, using scientific methods. In other words, there must be evidence that support reincarnation, not just a belief that it exists.

Or as Arya Bhushan commented:

Swami Vivekananda once advised, "Do not believe in what you have heard," and the great Buddha said, "Do not believe in doctrines because they have been handed down to you through generations; do not believe in anything because it is followed blindly by many; do not believe because some old sage makes a statement; do not believe in truths to which you have become attached by habit; do not believe merely on the authority of your teachers and elders. Have deliberation and analyze, and when the result agrees with reason and conduces to the good of one and all, accept it and live up to it."

Compare reincarnation with Darwin's theory of evolution. There are many convergent sources of evidence that together make this theory very plausible.

So too, in reincarnation research, no one case proves everything. Yet, as we shall see, the combined effect of properly investigated evidence, in our view, makes it nearly impossible to argue against its existence.

Definition

Before going any further we must define the term "reincarnation". Our primary definition of reincarnation is: The phenomenon of a surviving component of human personality taking birth after its physical death, in a human form, and on this planet.

We have deliberately avoided naming the component of human personality that is supposed to survive its physical death. We use the word "human" in connection with both present and previous birth, since our primary focus here is on human reincarnation. Any evidence involving the reincarnation from or to other species is to be evaluated in the light of reincarnation within homo sapiens. In other words, we do not wish to imply that cases involving animals could never be acceptable as evidence or that the concept of reincarnation is any less plausible for animals.

In some scriptures, reference is made to birth in some "other world" or "planet". Obviously this cannot be verified – hence the limitation to "birth on this planet".

There are certain other terms that have been used as synonyms or have a somewhat different connotation. One such term is "transmigration," which has been less generally used in ancient European literature. The essential difference is that the concept of transmigration implies that a human "soul" may also be transferred to the body of some non-human animal.

Yet, transmigration is not a single creed having the same meaning to all those who believe in it. It takes a number of strikingly different forms in different cultures. Some of these are:

(1) The soul of the deceased person goes into some animal that is seen near his or her corpse.
(2) A person might possibly be able to choose the creature into which his soul shall go.
(3) A tribe, or each clan within a tribe, has its own special kind of animal, into which the souls of all members go after death.
(4) Kings and chiefs have a special kind of animal into which their souls go, while the soul of commoners go into some inferior animal, or into none.
(5) The souls of the dead pass through a succession of different animals.

The Greeks used a different term: "Metempsychosis" which simply means the entry of a person's soul (or "psyche") into a new body. The Greeks used yet another term "palingenesis" which is derived from the Greek word "palin" meaning back or again and "genesis" meaning origin or production. "Reembodiment" has also been used in some European scriptures.

These terms have a simple connotation of being born again, which is almost the same as what the Sanskrit word "Punarjanma" means.

The Question of Survival

Obviously, we are dealing with something that presupposes the survival of at least part of our personality beyond physical death; if absolutely nothing survives the death of our bodies, there can be nothing to be reborn. On the other hand, if reincarnation is plausible, this automatically implies survival of a soul or spiritual element.

Survival is thus an essential precondition for the hypothesis of reincarnation. Is there any empirical evidence favouring the more general survival hypothesis itself?

So far as the question of survival is concerned, evidence from scientific research by psychical investigators all over the world suggests that some part of the personality does survive after the physical death of the human body[4]. This research includes studies on apparitions, communication with the dead, out-of-body experiences (OBEs) and near-death experiences (NDEs). Data has now been collected for more than 115 years (Lommel et al, 2001, 2010; Parnia et al, 2001; Rivas, 2003, 2004; Sabom, 1998; Smit, 2003, 2008; Cook, Greyson & Stevenson, 1998; Rivas, 2008; Smit, 2008; Smit & Rivas, 2010; Carter, 2010; Rivas & Dirven, 2010; Rivas, Dirven, & Smit, 2016).

H.H. Price stated in 1959, "Still, it is assumed by the majority of modern western educated people that in some form or other the materialistic conception of human personality must be the right one". This sort of situation is due to the fact that most of the studies conducted by disciplined investigators using standard scholarly methodology (on the subjects of apparitions, communication with the dead, etc. mentioned above) are still not widely popular.

Similarly, the present situation seems remarkably similar to the position in 1966 when W.G. Roll wrote with regard to the survival question:

> Scientists today face a situation not unlike the one that confronted members of the Royal Society 300 years ago when a Dutch shopkeeper Antonie van Leeuwenhoek claimed to have found a world of life in a drop of water. It seemed as impossible then that life could exist in so small a scale as it seems now that it might exist beyond the grave.

That might remind one of the words of Sri Aurobindo:

> Human thought in the generality of men is no more than a rough and crude acceptance of unexamined ideas. Our mind is a sleepy

---

[4] One of us, Titus Rivas, interviewed, together with Anny Dirven and Rudolf H. Smit (2008), the male nurse TG involved in the well-known Dutch case of a patient who during an out-of-body experience perceived what happened to his dentures while his brain – according to orthodox neuroscience – could not have supported any type of consciousness. Smit and Rivas (2010) presented and defended their findings in this case study for the *Journal of Near-Death Experiences*.

or careless sentry and allows anything to pass the gates, which seems to it decently garbed or wears a plausible appearance or can mumble anything that resembles some familiar password. Especially is this so in subtle matters, those remote from the concrete facts of our physical life and environment. Even men who will reason carefully and acutely in ordinary matters and those who consider vigilance against error an intellectual or a practical duty, are yet content with the most careless stumbling when they get upon higher and more difficult ground. Where precision and subtle thinking are most needed, there they are most impatient of it and averse to the labour demanded of them. Men can manage fine thoughts about palpable things, but to think subtle is too great a strain on the grossness of our intellects; so we are content with making a dab at the truth, like the painter who threw his brush at his picture when he could not get the effect he desired. We mistake the smudge that results for the perfect form of a verity. (*The Problem of Rebirth*, Pp. 11.)

A great deal of what all of us believe about the existence of soul, life after death, reincarnation and theory of karma are carbon copies of what our parents, teachers and preachers believed. Their own beliefs, in turn, might have been carbon copies of their predecessors. While growing up we accept these ideas as facts whereas they may all be, at best, romanticized versions of the actual truth. It is extremely difficult for us to shed these ideas like masks, particularly if what we were told appears plausible.

Generally, people adopt one of two strategies upon encountering a new idea: often they accept and add to their fund of knowledge only ideas which are in accordance with those they had already or which agree with the interpretations they have given to their own life experiences. Interestingly enough, even ideas, which challenge one's cherished beliefs and yet are in some way harmonious with our wishes or expectations, may be accepted.

Alternatively, putting all their own wishes and expectations aside, they may examine and critically evaluate a new idea on the basis of evidence, and then modify their fund of knowledge accordingly. The success of modern materialistic science in putting the entire "heaven of pleasures" at our doorstep has gradually induced a new way of looking at old beliefs. This new way of looking is that of "verifiability" of any given proposition. Secondly, many people have started believing, though quite erroneously, that science has proved that there is no soul or spirit, no survival, no reincarnation.

True scientists do not reject ideas out-of-hand without fully testing the known facts. Scientists question and try to demonstrate what is, or is not, factual. It is clearly more difficult to prove or disprove facts that are less tangible.

Research into past life memories seems to provide particularly good evidence for an immortal soul. John Gliedman in Science Digest (July 1982) in an essay entitled "Scientists in Search of the Soul" wrote:

> From Berkeley to Paris and from London to Princeton, prominent scientists from fields as diverse as neuro-physiology and quantum physics are coming out of the closet and admitting their belief in the possibility, at least, of such unscientific entities as the immortal human spirit.

Sir Karl Popper also postulated "the existence of a non-material conscious mind" that influences ponderable matter. Intellectual minds are increasingly receptive to possibilities and "folklore" they used to discard out-of-hand as mere superstition.

2

INVESTIGATIONS: PAST AND PRESENT

~

Though the idea of reincarnation is very old, the history of its scientific investigation is still very new.

The earliest known case of a child's recalling his past life in which any semblance of investigation is apparent, occurred about 300 years ago. It is described in a book *Khulasa Tarikh* (1753) written by Munshi Subhan Rai. The extracts from this book with regards to this case are as follows:

In the 40th year of the reign of the Emperor Aurangzeb Alamgir, there was a village headman named Rawat Sukha Ram in the village Bakr. Someone who bore enmity to him, [one day] after overpowering him, wounded him in the back and at the root of the ear. Due to these injuries, Rawat died. A few months later a son was born to his son-in-law named Ram Das. This boy bore marks of injuries on his back and at the root of his ear. News spread that Rawat Sukha Ram, who had died after being injured, had reincarnated. And this boy, when he grew up started saying, 'I am Rawat Sukha'. He gave the correct address and other information, which were found [to be] correct. When the Emperor heard about this strange incident, he summoned the child to his court and personally satisfied himself about these facts.

This account does not mention any details with regard to the information given by the child, nor the manner in which the Emperor satisfied himself about the truth of the boy's claims about his past life as Rawat Sukha Ram. Still, in this case we note the first documented reference to two important features, which are found repeatedly in reincarnation studies conducted all over the world. These two recurring features are "violent death" and "birthmarks" which appear in the same relative location as the previous wounds.

In 1897, Lafcadio Hearn published a book on some cases in Japan, *Gleanings in Buddha Fields* (Houghton Mifflin, Boston). In Chapter 10 titled "The Rebirth of Katsugoro" Hearn presents "the translation of an old Japanese document dating back to the early part of the present [i.e., the 19th] century". The document narrates the case of a Japanese boy named Katsugoro (Japan: 30) from 1820:

> At the age of seven he first articulated his recalls of a previous life (though he claimed that he could remember everything till the age of four) and said that he was the son of a farmer called Kyubei and his mother was Shidzu. They all lived in Hodokubo. He gave his own name as Tozo. He also said that when he had been five years of age Kyubei had died and a man called Hanshiro took his place in the household. Tozo, he said, died of smallpox at the age of six. He could also recall the details of his burial and the appearance of his former parents. When taken to Hodokubo he recognized the house owned by Hanshiro and his wife Shidzu and some other places related to Tozo. Pointing toward a shop and a tree he said that they not been there before which was correct. About sixteen statements by Katsugoro matched with facts. The couple were convinced that the boy Katsugoro had been Tozo. There are numerous affidavits testifying this case. The case was studied by a special Japanese commission, the findings of which were kept in Japanese state archives.

In 1898, a book *The Soul of a People* by Fielding Hall was published. In this book, when describing the life of the Burmese in the 22nd chapter, The Potter's Wheel, he wrote:

> Many children, the Burmese will tell you, remember their former lives. As they grow older the memories die away and they forget,

but to the young children they are very clear. I have seen many such (Pp. 295 Macmillan and Co. Ltd. edition, London, 1928).

In one chapter, Hall writes about a man and his wife having been reborn as twins. He describes at great length a meeting with a little girl of seven who told him "all about her former life when she was a man".

'I was married four times,' she said. 'Two wives died, one I divorced; one was living when I died, and is living still. The one I divorced was a dreadful woman. See,' – pointing to a scar on her shoulder – 'this was given to me once in a quarrel. She took up a chopper and cut me like this.' [...] The mark was a birthmark, and I was certain that it corresponded exactly with one that had been given to the man by his wife in just such a quarrel as the one the little girl described (Ibid., Pp. 304).

These cases also display certain characteristics similar to those studied by later investigators.

In 1924, Gabriel Delanne published a remarkable compilation, consisting largely of an anthology of case reports gathered from diverse sources along with his own comments.

The credit for the earliest investigation of cases of reincarnation goes to Dr. R.B. Shyam Sunder Lal of Kisangarh in Rajasthan, founder of the *A Former Life Association*. We know at least about four such cases through an article that Dr Lal published in a French magazine, *Revue Métapsychique*, July/August 1924. Entitled *Cas apparents de réminiscences de vies antérieures (Apparent Cases of Past-Life Memory)*. This article presented four cases investigated by Dr. Lal and his team. One of the cases is that of Prabhu. Significantly, in this case, a written record of what Prabhu said about his previous life was made before any attempt at verifying his claims was undertaken.

Another important monograph of reincarnation cases was published by K.K.N. Sahay, a lawyer of Bareilly (Uttar Pradesh, India) in 1927. This booklet, entitled R*eincarnation: Verified Cases of Rebirth After Death*, consists of reports of seven cases, which he had investigated. In two cases, those of Jagdish Chandra and Bishan Chand Kapoor, a written record was made of the subjects' statements about their previous lives.

In 1936, a 26-page booklet was published, which presented a report of a single case – the case of Shanti Devi Mathur of Delhi. This booklet contains the report of a committee of fifteen eminent people specially constituted for the purpose of the verification of Shanti Devi's claim to be one Lugdi Bai of Mathura – a town at a distance of 145 kms from Delhi that she had never visited in her then – present life. It also contains a statement of the cousin of Shanti's husband in her alleged past life. He was the first person to meet Shanti and question her about the life of Lugdi Bai. His statement lists all the questions that he posed and the answers, which Shanti gave to them.

Dr. Indra Sen, a prominent philosopher, was perhaps the first who studied the Shanti Devi case scientifically. He first published an article in a Hindi magazine *Chitrapat*, 4th July 1936. Another paper, "Shanti Devi Further Investigated," was published in the *Proceedings of the Indian Philosophical Congress* in 1937. Shanti Devi was frequently interviewed throughout her life. Dr. Rawat had the good fortune to study this case until just before Shanti Devi's death. We shall return to it later.

Dr. B.L. Atreya, professor and head of the Departments of Philosophy, Psychology and Indian Philosophy and Religion at Banares Hindu University, was keenly interested in psychic phenomena. He was also honorary research director of the Institute of Philosophy, Psychology and Psychical Research of Dehradun. A collection of his addresses, papers and radio talks was published in 1952 entitled *An Introduction to Parapsychology* (Collected Papers on Psychical Research). A revised edition was printed in 1957. In this book, in a section subtitled "Memory of past lives," Dr. Atreya narrated details of a reincarnation investigation in India of a boy named Parmod.

In 1959, S.C. Bose, published reports of 14 cases (some of them he personally studied) in a book written in Bengali. The title of this book was *Jatismar Katha: A Book on Reincarnation* (translated into English in 1960). Of his major findings he notes, especially, that cases of reincarnation show certain common features. Common characteristics in almost all cases of reincarnated children include the following:

1. Such children begin to express the incidents of their previous life almost as soon as they start talking.
2. They continue to remember their past lives for a few more years after which the memory gradually fades.
3. Generally, there is no change of sex from one life to another. In one case alone a girl recalled that she was a boy in her past life.

4. There may be a link between a person's being spiritually advanced and his ability to recall his past life. (Most of Bose's subjects were known to be highly spiritually minded people in their respective previous births).
5. Subjects who could recall what happened during the period between death and the next birth were extremely rare, with Shanti Devi being the only exception.

These common features can universally be observed in reincarnation investigations to the present day.

In the early fifties another Bengali gentleman, Hemendra Nath Banerjee, wanted to study scientifically the cases of children reported to have recalled their past lives. His zeal led him to establish the *Seth Sohan Lal Memorial Institute of Parapsychology* at Sri Ganganagar (Rajasthan, India) in 1957. Here he started to study cases of reincarnation in a rigorous and systematic way. Besides conducting experimental studies of other psychic phenomena, such as extra-sensory perception and psychokinesis, this institution was the first to publish a journal of parapsychology in India.

The *Indian Journal of Parapsychology* lists among its contributors the names of leading authorities in the field: Gardner Murphy, Karlis Osis, Gertrude R. Schmeidler, Nandor Fodor, and, and Dr. Ian Stevenson to name but a few. Various symposia, seminars and conferences were held under the joint auspices of the institute and universities in India.

Initially, Banerjee studied cases of reincarnation in India only. In 1962 he studied the case of a child called Ismail in Istanbul. In 1963, the University of Rajasthan, acting upon the advice of the State Governor, opened a Department of Parapsychology and appointed Banerjee as its Director. This allowed Banerjee to visit various European, American and other countries, to continue his studies.

He coined a new term for the remembrances of a past life: Extra Cerebral Memory (ECM). He wrote:

I prefer to call the alleged cases of reincarnation as the cases of extra cerebral memory (ECM). The claims of memories of previous life by the subject appear to be independent of the cerebrum, which is supposed to be the main repository of memory, and the cerebrum of the person with whom the memories are associated is destroyed with the death of the person.

Banerjee visited and collected information with regard to these "ECM" cases in various parts of the world. For reasons unknown, the department was closed in 1971.

Banerjee and his wife ultimately settled in San Diego. Here he became executive and research director of the *Center for Para-analytical Studies*. Besides several articles, he authored two books on reincarnation in the US, entitled *Americans Who Have Been Reincarnated* and *Lives Unlimited*.

Dr. Ian Stevenson of the University of Virginia in Charlottesville has done the largest systematic and scientific studies on reincarnation-type cases in India.

Initially, Dr. Stevenson and Banerjee worked together on many cases in India. But personal and professional acrimony tore them apart in 1964. Despite widespread and possibly well-founded serious doubts about Banerjee's scientific integrity, we shall refer to his works, although never as the only source for a particular case.

In 1960 Stevenson published "The Evidence for Survival from Claimed Memories of Former Incarnations" in the *Journal of the American Society for Psychical Research*. In this paper Stevenson reviewed and analysed cases already published by others alongside one, which he himself had investigated – the case of Henriette Weisz-Roos. In the first part he surveyed the type of evidence in favour of the reincarnation hypothesis and described some instances of past life recalls. In the second part he discussed various alternative explanations with regard to these instances.

This was the first paper that Stevenson ever published on reincarnation research. Many were to follow. His *Twenty Cases Suggestive of Reincarnation*, which was first edited in Volume 26 (1966) of the Proceedings of the American Society for Psychical Research, has become a classic in the field, and was published in book form in 1974 by the Virginia University Press. Since then it has been translated into many languages and has undoubtedly contributed a great deal to the status of reincarnation research as a serious and respectable scholarly endeavour.

Twenty Cases, as it is often abbreviated, contains seven cases in India, three in Sri Lanka (formerly Ceylon), two cases in Brazil, seven among the Tlingit Indians of Southeastern Alaska, and one case in Lebanon. The evidential strength of each individual case presented in this book may differ, but the book contains several cases with written records made before verification of the child's statements.

After the publication of his *Evidence for Survival*, Stevenson and his team collected files on about 3000 cases of the reincarnation type from all over the world.

In 1967 he was appointed Carlson Professor of Psychiatry at the University of Virginia. He wrote several volumes on his cases: a series consisting of four volumes called *Cases of the Reincarnation Type* and two books about cases which showed some kind of xenoglossy (paranormal knowledge of a language someone has not learned in this life, at least not to that extent): *Xenoglossy* (in 1974) and *Unlearned Language* (in 1984).

In 1987 he wrote a book aimed at a general public, *Children Who Remember Previous Lives* (revised edition: 2000). This was followed in 1997 by an extensive book entitled *Reincarnation and Biology*. It presents many cases involving birthmarks and birth defects that may relate to the cause of death in a previous life. It is summarized in the book *Where Reincarnation and Biology Intersect*, also published in 1997. This was followed in 2003 by his book, *European Cases of the Reincarnation Type*.

It has been suggested that Dr. Ian Stevenson was simply looking for cases whose features matched those found by former researchers. However, this would really mean that he must have deliberately deceived the whole scientific community. Dr. Stevenson's research methodology is so thorough that any assumed bias could not be due to methodological naiveté. Therefore, any supposed bias could only be a conscious, fraudulent one. There is absolutely no foundation for such a criticism.

Ian Stevenson received much co-operation from native researchers in the countries wherein the cases were found. Dr. Jamuna Prasad assisted Stevenson during his earlier visits.

After 1964, when Banerjee and Stevenson separated, Dr. Prasad remained with Stevenson as his main assistant and chief interpreter in India. Later, this role was taken over by Dr. Satwant Pasricha, who obtained her PhD at the University of Bengalore. She was the Associate Professor of Clinical Psychology at the National Institute of Mental Health and Neurosciences, Bangalore until her retirement in 2010. Since the 1970s, she has authored articles for various journals, mostly in collaboration with Dr. Stevenson but also on her own. She has published a book based on her doctoral studies entitled *Claims of Reincarnation: An Empirical Study of Cases in India*. In 1985, the late Dr. Stevenson offered to study some cases jointly with Dr. K.S. Rawat in India. In the late 1980s they occasionally collaborated on research.

Although Ian Stevenson is still generally considered to have been a parapsychologist, he actually objected to using this term. Dr. Stevenson thought parapsychology, as it had developed, was "doomed" due to its one-sided emphasis on statistical, experimental studies. He preferred to be regarded as a qualified psychiatrist who was active in the field of psychical research, just like other scholars who have studied paranormal phenomena. He stressed the importance of case studies in a natural setting and was not in favour of using hypnotic experiments to evoke memories of previous lives.

The cases that Stevenson collected resemble the general pattern found in older cases studied by other researchers. Features of this pattern include similarities such as the age at which children remember their previous lives, the age at which their memories start fading, the strong emotions that children usually show when talking about these memories, birthmarks and birth defects possibly related to the end of the previous incarnation, and so on.

Similarly, some of Stevenson's colleagues have become known through their work with him. Hernani Guimaraes Andrade (Brazil), Reşat Bayer (Turkey), Jürgen Keil (Germany/Australia) and Godwin Samararatne (Sri Lanka) all studied cases of reincarnation and published their own reports.

Vitor Moura Visoni is also still active as an enthusiastic reincarnation researcher, working in Brazil. One of the cases he studied is that of Lílian Sarago. Other independent researchers in Asia are Ohkado Masayuki of Japan and Changzhen Li in China.

Europe's history of reincarnation investigation is more mixed. We should first mention some serious cases of hypnotism studied by researchers such as Albert de Rochas, Arnall Bloxham and American hypnotist Morey Bernstein who rekindled the European interest in regression. These have been followed by many popular and sometimes sensationalist books, often based on romantic claims about previous lives. An overview of European studies is given in Stevenson's book *European Cases of the Reincarnation Type*. It discusses many well-known cases, such as those of Henriette Weisz-Roos, Alessandrina Samoná and Edward Ryall.

One controversial story that has never received sufficient scholarly attention concerns the experiences of Dr. Arthur Guirdham. This British psychiatrist claimed that one of his patients had recurrent dreams about the persecutions of the Cathars in Southern France and that she showed paranormal knowledge of the period. Later on he discovered several other people close to him who all seemed to share the same memories, which he documented in his book *The Cathars and Reincarnation*.

The serious study of reincarnation in young children by Europeans may be said to have begun with the investigation of the case of Shanti Devi by the Swedish writer S. Lönnerstrand in the 1950s. Another important scholar in the field is the late Icelandic professor of psychology Erlendur Haraldsson who has done some important studies in Sri Lanka and Lebanon.

Also very important for his work in the field is the British historian Ian Wilson who published a book in 1982 entitled: *Reincarnation? The Claims Investigated* (later republished under different titles) in which he discusses and rejects evidence that was supposed to have been provided by several well-known hypnotic cases. It was just one year later when the British authors Peter and Mary Harrison published a somewhat popular but serious book on English cases, entitled *Children That Time Forgot*, which, unfortunately, seems to have escaped scholarly attention, although Stevenson included one of their cases, that of Carl Edon, in his *European Cases of the Reincarnation Type*.

In 1994 Roy Stemman launched a specialized international journal for reincarnation research, *Reincarnation International* in London, renamed *Life & Soul* magazine in 1999.

At the turn of the century, the late Mary Rose Barrington conducted a study into the well-known British case of Jenny Cockell, although she generally preferred a possession hypothesis for reincarnation type-cases. She also participated in an international investigation of the case of Iris Farczády, a Hungarian, alongside Peter Mulacz, Zsolt Banhegyi and Titus Rivas (2005).

In 1996, Titus Rivas established the *Athanasia Foundation*, which focuses on the study of survival and reincarnation. By then, he and his brother Esteban Rivas, both members of the Dutch Foundation for the Scientific Study of Reincarnation / FSSR had published several serious reports on Dutch cases in Dutch journals of parapsychology and in the *Journal of the Society for Psychical Research*.

In 2000 Titus Rivas published a book on his research entitled *Parapsychologisch onderzoek naar reïncarnatie en leven na de dood* ~(*Parapsychological Research into Reincarnation and Life After Death*) and in 2003 and 2004 he published two articles about nine Dutch cases in the *Journal of Scientific Exploration* and *The Paranormal Review*, along with numerous Dutch articles about the field.

Another notable researcher from the Netherlands is Dr. Joanne Klink, a Christian theologian who collected letters written by parents about unusual statements and behaviour of their children that might relate to a previous life. In 1990 she published a Dutch book about these letters, *Vroeger toen ik groot was*. It has not yet been translated into English, though a German edition was published a few years ago. Although her collection may not have been studied thoroughly, it suggests that classical cases of reincarnation also occur in the Netherlands.

Yet another Dutch researcher, author and psychotherapist Hans ten Dam, is known for his survey of the literature about reincarnation, *Een Ring van Licht*, translated into English as *Exploring Reincarnation*. More recently, Dutch journalist Michiel Hegener published an interesting overview of reincarnation research, "Leven op herhaling".

Swedish psychiatrist Dr. Nils-Olof Jacobson mentions several Northern European cases of possible past life memories in his standard work *Liv äfter döden?* Dr. Adrian Parker and Dr. Annekatrin Puhle jointly investigated the interesting Swedish case of Jesper Bood who recalled a previous life as a Scottish fisherman.

In Germany, retired technical engineer Dr. Dieter Hassler has been active in the field since 1996. He investigated several cases in German-speaking countries, and he's been working on serious books on reincarnation and survival research.

In the USA, no one has done as much work in the field as Dr. Ian Stevenson. Such American scholars as Dr. Emily Cook add (now known as Dr. Emily Williams Kelly), Dr. Antonia Mills and Dr. Jim Tucker assisted him while he was alive. Apart from Stevenson's assistants, we do not know of any other American academics researching spontaneous cases, although several hypnotherapists have made interesting claims. They include Dr. Helen Wambach, Morey Bernstein and Linda Tarazi.

Since 2000 there have been at least two interesting new names connected to case reports. One is Carol Bowman, who wrote two books entitled *Children's Past Lives* and *Return from Heaven*. She and her husband Steve established an important website including a forum where people can share their experiences.[5] Bowman was also involved in an American case that received a lot of publicity: the case of James Leininger who recalled a life as a young American pilot who was shot down by the Japanese during World War II.

---

[5] www.carolbowman.com

The second is that of Rabbi Yonassan Gershom who published two books on subjects with possible memories of the Holocaust; *Beyond the Ashes* and *From Ashes to Healing*. Some of the cases contained enough verifiable data to enable the identification of a previous personality.

Apart from these, there are more and more Western authors who claim to have verifiable memories of a previous life. Some of these seem to be really interesting, such as Angela Grubbs and Jeffrey Keene.

In 2017 Erlendur Haraldsson and James (Jim) Matlock published their excellent book, *I Saw a Light and Came Here* (Haraldsson & Matlock, 2017).

In 2019, Jim Matlock's book, *Signs of Reincarnation: Exploring Beliefs, Cases, and Theory* was published. Signs of Reincarnation, is also the name of his interesting discussion group on Facebook, which is run by Matlock and some very knowledgeable moderators such as Iris Giesler (now retired) and Karen Wehrstein.

Signs of Reincarnation is bound to become a classic academic book on reincarnation research. It is very rigorous and discusses the history, methodology, prominent investigators, and main empirical findings of the field at a scholarly level. Even readers who are well acquainted with serious research into cases of past life memories will learn new things from it: such as that by now there are around 1700 solved cases of young children who remember a previous life, and that phobias related to the past incarnation occur relatively frequently. Additionally, Matlock analyses universal and culture-specific patterns in *cases of the reincarnation type*.

There are cases in *Signs of Reincarnation* that have received little coverage elsewhere, such as the American case of Rylann O'Bannion, researched by Matlock himself.

Following his excellent overview of the whole field of research and the strength of the evidence, Matlock presents his own unique theory. He mentions five scholars who inspired him, namely Frederic W.H. Myers, C.D. Broad, Alfred North Whitehead, Henry Stapp and of course Ian Stevenson.

In addition to the publication of his books and numerous papers, for the online *Psi Encyclopedia* of the Society of Psychical Research as well as printed journals, Matlock has been interviewed repeatedly by psychologist Dr. Jeffrey Mishlove on his popular YouTube-channel *New Thinking Allowed*.

Additional types of evidence for reincarnation

Other sources provide evidence in favour of reincarnation, yet few are approached on a rigorous scholarly basis.

Mediums and psychics

One such source is rooted in the Spiritualist tradition. Entities claiming to be the spirits of past people have been reported occasionally to have supplied information about their former selves or others through their current selves that would be connected to previous lives.

The case best known in this context is that of the medium Hélène Smith, studied by Théodore Flournoy. Among other things, during séances Smith recalled that she had spent an incarnation in India, that she had been none other than Marie-Antoinette, and even that she had lived on the planet Mars. A bizarre detail of the case was that subconsciously she developed an infantile "Martian" fantasy language and writing system.

Remarkable claims have been offered by or about several psychics, such as Edgar Cayce, which, if authentic, would suggest that some of them really are able to tune in to another person's previous life by extra-sensory perception.

On one occasion, Cayce did a reading for a blind musician with a strong passion for railways and a great interest in the American Civil War. Cayce claimed that the man had been a Southern soldier, in his previous life, who worked for the railways. His name would have been Barnett Seay and Cayce claimed that this data could be found in archives in Virginia. The musician made some inquiries and was able to confirm Cayce's statements. One of us, Titus Rivas, checked the name on Ancestry.com and found that there really had been a Barnett W. Seay from Virginia who lived during the Civil War.

Ian Stevenson studied the case of a Dutch woman, Henriette Weisz-Roos, who had been married to a Hungarian pianist named Weisz and felt so strongly attached to this surname that she kept it after their divorce. From a young age, Henriette showed a talent for painting and music.

Around the age of 33 she repeatedly heard a voice that exhorted her to get up from her bed and start painting. She felt the urge to place her painter's easel in a dark corner of her room. She started to paint feverously without being able to see what she was doing. The next morning, she discovered that she had painted the portrait of a young woman. After a while, she showed this painting to a good friend who put her in touch with a local clairvoyant medium. During a reading, the medium had a vision of large golden letters that together formed the name Goya. The medium claimed that this Spanish painter knew Henriette from a previous life. Francisco de Goya would have fled from enemies and ended up in Southern France, where he would have been hospitably received at her home. As a discarnate spirit, Goya would want to guide her on her artistic path. Later on, Henriette stumbled upon a booklet about Goya's life. In it, she read that Goya had stayed in Bordeaux for some time with a person called Leocadia Weiss and her daughter Rosario Weiss.

Stevenson decided to investigate the case and established that Rosario Weiss had had strong artistic and musical gifts and that Goya had tried to stimulate her. It turned out that Goya was so fond of Rosario that he sometimes called her "my daughter".

During a therapeutic session for a depressed female patient, the Japanese parapsychologist and psychic Hiroshi Motoyama went into a deep trance. He saw images of a samurai who lived about 300 years ago. The man would have been called Hachirouemon Nakanose and he would have lived in Suwa, about 240 kilometers north of Tokyo. Motoyama claimed that this samurai had been the woman's father in his previous life. The patient herself would have fallen in love with someone who belonged to a lower class. When it turned out that the family could not accept this, she committed suicide.

The woman traveled to Suwa to look for information about Hachirouemen Nakanose. She found out that there really had been such a samurai in Suwa some 350 years ago.

Hypnotic and similar forms of induced regression

The best-known alternative source of empirical evidence for reincarnation is hypnosis and similar methods involving suggestion, with or without the induction of an altered state of consciousness (such as a trance). Judging by the recent popular literature about investigation into reincarnation, hypnosis seems to be more popular with the general public than the naturalistic study of spontaneous cases of the reincarnation type.

Some therapists claim that psychological problems in adults frequently derive from trauma in previous lives, which can be discovered and healed through the aid of hypnosis. Famous names in this context are Albert de Rochas, Arnall Bloxham, Morey Bernstein, Dr. John Björkhem and Dr. Helen Wambach. Of these, Dr. Wambach is famous for her study of patterns that have shown up in large groups of hypnotized subjects who were regressed to alleged previous lives, which seemed to correspond with historical patterns of specific eras. The evidence she found does seem remarkable. As Arya Bhushan states:

> Most striking are the sex and population distributions for different time periods between 2000 B.C. and the twentieth century. Her subjects recorded 49.4 % past lives lived as women, and 50.6% as men – which accords with biological fact. These lives were lived in different parts of the world and the distribution agrees with the known population densities of these areas at the appropriate historical times. Because each recall is individual, there would be no way that telepathy, fantasy, or chance alone could determine the way in which the cumulative statistics emerged when the data was evaluated.

However, in many hypnotic cases fantasy and other normal processes could have been excluded more thoroughly. This problem was partially addressed by the publication of *Reincarnation?* by historian Ian Wilson. Though Wilson's investigations of spontaneous cases play a minor role in the book, his discussions of hypnotic cases are valuable.

One case described in *Reincarnation?* is that of Blanche Poynings, which he explains through *cryptomnesia* – subconscious, hidden memories normally acquired in the subject's present life but without the subject's being aware of them. The subject of this case, "Miss C.," was hypnotized in 1906, and claimed a prior existence dating back nearly six hundred years! While being regressed, she claimed that she was talking with a lady by the name of Blanche Poynings, a good friend of Maud, Countess of Salisbury. The conversation was apparently taking place at the end of Richard the Second's reign, near the end of the fourteenth century. "Blanche" supplied a considerable amount of information about her own life and that of the Countess, which turned out to be correct after verification. In her debriefing, Miss C. could not recall that she had ever read anything about the countess of Salisbury. However, she later remembered that she had read *Countess Maud* by Emily Holt, a novel that contained all the details she had claimed to recall.

Similar cases that include probable cryptomnesia were studied by Dr. Reima Kampman of the University of Oulu, Finland, and by Melvin Harris who investigated the famous case of Jane Evans, a Welsh housewife who recalled six lifetimes with historically correct details.

It is known that in hypnotic experiments, subjects often tend to want to meet the expectations of the hypnotist. They seem to adapt their "previous lives" to their hypnotist's ideas about reincarnation. For instance, Joe Keeton, a well-known reincarnation hypnotherapist in the UK, believes that after death the soul immediately reincarnates in a recently fertilized womb. Surprisingly, his subjects usually recall being born nine months after their previous death and they do not remember any intermediate states or experiences, whereas subjects hypnotized by other hypnotists who do not believe in this concept may recall intermission periods of several years or even longer. Accounts from Edgar Cayce convey that in many cases there is a significant passage of time between incarnations often amounting to periods of a lifetime or longer.

Some subjects appear to think that if they experience strong feelings during a hypnotherapy session, or if they see images that seem authentic to them, this alone would conclude that the experience is evidence of a previous life. Unfortunately, this is a naive idea; if we dream about something and experience everything in it as very real, including the emotions involved, this does not prove that the dream is real.

Nonetheless, we should not ignore the exceptions among the many hypnosis cases, which point to evidence of previous lives. Two such exceptions are those of Jensen and Gretchen, which were studied by Dr. Ian Stevenson himself. Though they both remain unsolved they seem to have involved a degree of *xenoglossy*[6], a specifically parapsychological term that denotes the ability to understand or speak a foreign language without training. Xenoglossy in the parapsychological sense should not be confused with *glossolalia* or speaking in tongues. Glossolalia concerns non-existent or unverifiable languages, such as a language of angels. Glossolalia may often be related to a psychiatric condition or religious exaltation.

Another exception within the body of hypnosis research is the case of Bridey Murphy. This case centers on an American housewife Virginia

---

[6] Of Swedish and German respectively.

Tighe (known under the pseudonym Ruth Simmons), who was studied by hypnotist Morey Bernstein. In a hypnotic state Tighe seemed able to recall certain specific details of the life of an Irish woman, Bridey Murphy who lived in the nineteenth century.

As a child, Bridey supposedly lived in a house in Cork, Ireland. She was the daughter of Duncan Murphy, a barrister, and his wife Kathleen. At the age of 17 she married lawyer Sean Brian McCarthy and moved to Belfast. Bridey told of a fall that caused her death. Virginia Tighe herself had never been to Ireland and did not speak with even the slightest hint of an Irish accent.

Upon investigation, not all of the details mentioned were correct, and sceptics stressed that the correct details could be fully explained by normal factors such as cryptomnesia. Virginia Tighe did have Irish ancestry and, as a young child, she may have been exposed to information about life in Ireland. However, the late Morey Bernstein stressed that not all of Virginia's statements could be explained away so easily. For instance, she correctly mentioned the name of two grocers in nineteenth century Belfast, Farr's and John Carrigan. Ian Stevenson regarded this case as one that deserved closer scrutiny.

One of the more recent cases of memories of a previous life being accessed through hypnosis is the case of Laurel Dilmen ("L.D".) studied by psychotherapist Linda Tarazi. Ms. Dilmen had already undergone hypnotic sessions in which she had been regressed through several previous lives. During one of them she was repeatedly attracted to the life of a lady called Antonia Ruiz Prado, born on the island of Hispaniola during the sixteenth century. Among other things, Dilmen recounted that Antonia had been a prisoner of the Spanish Inquisition and that she had drowned.

Dilmen did not speak Spanish during the regression sessions, but mentioned many correct details, which she could not have learned by normal means. Some of the facts mentioned could only be found later in a book written in Spanish, which had been published in 1881. Dilmen had never been to Spain and did not speak Spanish.

Tarazi investigated all possible normal sources and concluded that although this case may contain elements that are based on fantasy, its foundation appears to derive from real memories of a previous life. On the other hand, according to Stephen Braude (Braude, 2003), British psychic researcher Alan Gauld established that there appeared to be no traces of a historical Antonia Ruiz Prado in Hispaniola.

In hypnotic regression experiments to a possible past life, one might be inclined to explain paranormal knowledge by some form of extra-sensory perception (ESP) such as clairvoyance or remote viewing, but Tarazi's subject was not prompted to view images of her possible previous incarnations, which suggests that ESP may be less plausible in this particular case.

More recently Jesper Bood, a 29-year-old Swedish literature student, claimed to recall a life as a Scotsman named John Smith from Dunbar, Scotland. Roy Pugh, a local historian, helped a Swedish television crew to trace a John Smith in the church records – a name that was, oddly, uncommon in this part of Scotland. Bood had also mentioned that his father was a blacksmith, also called John Smith, and his mother's name was Mary Craig, which matched historic records (Puhle, 2004).

Researcher Annekatrin Puhle also mentions that John Smith had a friend with the surname Wilson and that there were several families of local fishermen with that name. Bood said that, as Smith, he lived in a brown wooden house on the Public Road, Gateside, and it was found that there used to be such houses there. It was even established that there used to be a blacksmith there.

He also recalled that it took half an hour to reach his school and described the parish church, the first building he saw on his way to school, close to the sea. He could also see it through the window of his classroom. The school as described had a U-shape and three floors. According to Roy Pugh, Bood also gave a correct description of the old church windows and of the former Woodbush School, which had been demolished in 1950. He described a pub, the Fisherman's Tavern in Lamer Street, which had a green shield and had been run by a woman. This turned out to be correct. In the modern Creel Restaurant Bood recognized the town tavern, which had been called the *Jersey Arms*, a well-known pub for fishermen.

Finally, Bood drew a sketch of five places after the hypnotic session: the church, school, high street, Methodist church and harbour. The spatial relations between these places corresponded exactly with the geographical location of all five places. Just one of his statements was found to be incorrect, namely a description of the shape of the contemporary church tower. Bood also recalled that Smith drowned although this could not be verified. One of us (Rivas), had e-mail contact with Jesper Bood and concluded that we have no specific reason to dismiss this case.

In Australia, Peter Ramster, a rather controversial hypnotherapist, produced a controversial television documentary on cases of hypnosis in which he hypnotised four women who seem to have been selected on the sole basis of their suggestibility. The documentary (*Reincarnation?*) claimed that the cases presented were very strong and involved verified statements. The documentary was shown on the BBC and in other countries.

When Titus Rivas and his brother Esteban Rivas tried to reach Peter Ramster to get more details on his investigations, Ramster claimed that most of his original material had been lost. This made them suspicious and, in 2000, Titus Rivas published his doubts in a Dutch book about reincarnation research.

After the publication of this book, Rivas was approached by a reader of his work, Rudolf H. Smit, who kindly sent him a copy of a book by Peter Ramster dating from the early eighties. According to this book, the Australian hypnotist had been successful in uncovering past life memories even before the experiment shown on television. In the book, Ramster discussed several cases with varying degrees of evidence ranging from largely unverifiable memories to apparent instances of xenoglossy.

The strongest case in Ramster's book is that of a woman who claimed to have memories of living in seventeenth and eighteenth century in England. She correctly named streets and buildings, many of which no longer existed. Ramster also discussed the case of Judy Atkinson. Judy was a woman of about 18 who described a life as a woman called Jane, born in 1919 in Lancashire, England. About this case he stated:

> Judy was able to give the address of the home she lived in as Jane, even down to the postcode. Judy had never been to England, but the address she gave proved to be correct. She also correctly identified streets and townships, and named her family and relatives".

He added:

> The village concerned was a very small place in the country, exactly as she had described it. After speaking with a person from that district, I concluded that Judy knew a great deal more about the area than she could possibly have gained merely from noting details on a map.

In both his book and the documentary, Ramster claimed to have demonstrated evidence for memories of previous incarnations.

Having read the book, Rivas now concludes that thus far we have no specific reason to doubt the claims mentioned above. Perhaps Ramster's work deserves more serious attention from reincarnation researchers. That said, caution is still warranted. In 2008 Dutch sceptic Rob Nanninga showed that in one of the cases in the documentary, that of Cynthia Henderson, major errors were made concerning its historical corroboration. Ramster claimed that Henderson recognized a French castle near Flers in which she had lived as Amélie de Cheville during the eighteenth century. Later Nanninga discovered that the castle was built for an Englishman, Lord Burkingyoung, in 1870. Rivas checked Nanninga's claim using Internet sources which turned out to be correct.

We should mention the American case of Robert Snow, a Captain in the Indianapolis Police Department, in charge of the Homicide Division. Based on a dare made by a fellow police officer, Captain Snow visited a regression therapist to undergo a past life regression. Snow did not expect to have a meaningful experience because he did not believe in reincarnation. During the regression, he experienced himself as an artist painting a portrait of a hunchback woman. Snow remembered 28 specific details of this lifetime that could in principle be verified.

Though sceptical, Snow treated the past-life regression experience as he would a detective case. He methodically examined art books, visited art galleries and contacted art dealers. For a year he researched the art world trying to find the portrait of the hunchback woman. When he had given up, his wife suggested they take a wedding anniversary trip to New Orleans. When Snow wandered into a small art gallery in the French Quarter, he was shocked to find the portrait of the hunchback woman, exactly as he had seen it during the past life regression. The portrait was painted by an artist named James Carroll Beckwith who was commonly known as Carroll Beckwith.

Snow found that the largely unknown painter Beckwith had kept a diary, which was now at the New York Academy of Design. Upon reading it, Snow was able to validate 26 specific memories from his past life regression. These included his dislike of painting (which he did for financial reasons); he and his wife not having any children; he had been in France; he had received prizes for his work and a woman close to him had died from a blood clot.

One detail remained unverified: the twenty-eighth, which Snow got wrong, was his past-life wife's name, but during the hypnotic regression he had already said that he did not recall her name correctly.

The irony about this case is that Snow had intended to falsify his claimed memories, since he did not believe in the "supernatural". He had a very difficult time once he discovered that almost all of his memories applied to the life of a historical person.

He wrote about his surprising discoveries in a book entitled *Looking for Carroll Beckwith*. In this book, Snow remarks that if his reincarnation case were presented in court, he would win "without plea bargaining". He concluded that his memories could not have been based on hidden memories from his present life, consisting of what he would have read about the artist years before. There simply were no ordinary sources, which he could have had access to before his journey began[7].

More recently, Dr. Masayuki Ohkado published a Japanese case of xenoglossy under the state of hypnosis. It concerns a Japanese housewife who, in 2005, recalled two impressive past lives. In one of these she would have been Tae, a young Japanese girl who sacrificed her life for villagers in the Yedo period[8] and in the other Rataraju, a village chief in Nepal. She told researchers that she had been a man who lived in the village of Nallu, whose wife's name had been Rameli. She had two sons, Adish and Kailash and the king's name was Gorkha. According to three Nepalis researchers consulted, the unknown language spoken by the subject under hypnosis was indeed the Nepali language.

Staying in Japan; Masayuki Ohkado (2013) published a report on a Japanese boy, Tomo, who recalled having lived in Scotland in his past life. When Tomo was not yet three, he heard the Carpenters song, "Top of the World" for the first time; he surprised his mother by singing along to it.

Finally, retired German engineer and psychical researcher Dieter Hassler wrote extensive and informative books on reincarnation research, including a book on regression to past lives, published in 2015. These include very thorough and interesting analyses of well-known and lesser known cases of hypnotic regression. We hope that his books will be translated into English to open up his research to a wider readership. Hassler shows that the scholarly debate about reincarnation regression hypnosis is far from over.

---

[7] Some of these details can now be found on Wikipedia and other websites, but not at the time Snow first published his book.

[8] Also known as Edo (the former name for Tokyo) period, the era from 1603 to 1868, in which Japan was ruled by the Tokugawa shogunate.

Reincarnation research is still in its infancy and a lot of work needs to be done to make sure that this field of research flourishes internationally. For that reason, in 1998, we decided to establish an *International Centre for Reincarnation and Survival Research* to allow researchers in the field to co-operate and exchange views and case reports. We hope that it will play an important role in the study of reincarnation cases.

3

CLASSICAL CASES OF SPONTANEOUS
RECALL BY CHILDREN

~

In this chapter and the next we will discuss some of the strongest
cases supporting the idea of reincarnation. These cases are considered
"solved," meaning that in each case, a specific deceased person was
found whose life corresponded strongly to the statements made by the child
regarding his or her former life. These cases give a good impression of the
strength of the best cases of reincarnation. For reasons of convenience, we
will sometimes use the term previous personality, to refer to the subject's
previous life. This does not imply we believe there is no true identity or
continuance between the soul of the previous and the present life.

Please note that in our original e-book *Reincarnation* we included
several maps to show where the cases we discuss were located.

The Case of Prabhu

The case of Prabhu is one of four studied by Dr. R.B. Sunder Lal and
published in *Revue Métapsychique*, July / August 1924, the bulletin of
the French Institute Métapsychique International in Paris. Prabhu is
important because his is one of the rare cases in which the statements
made by the subject were written down *before* anyone tried to verify
them. Sunder Lal states:

The case of this child was drawn to my attention by his Highness of Maharajah of Bharatpur in August 1922. The child is called 'Prabhu' Brahmin and is the son of Khairati Brahmin of Salimpur (State of Bharatpur) and at the time of our inquiries he was 4 years, 7 months and 18 days old.

As soon as he was able to talk, Prabhu began to tell his father alleged memories of an earlier life. Dr. Lal's inquiry into the matter had two phases; in the first phase, the Naib Tehsildar[9] questioned the child at his father's home in March 1923. In the second phase, the child was taken at Dr. Lal's request to Hatyori, the village where he claimed to have lived in his previous life. The Tehsildar of Weir took the child and on arrival immediately assembled the four chief people of Hatyori.

These were Dharam Singh Faujdar, aged 60 years, Foujdar Azmat Singh, Lambardar of the village, aged 50 years, Foujdar Sam Singh, aged 73 years, and Harknath Brahmin, aged 40 years; and in the presence of these men the child was questioned.

Prabhu claimed a recollection of his past-life name, caste, and village. He spoke of two sons and two daughters and gave their names. He also gave the names his sons-in-law and named the home village of one of his sons-in-law. He said that he had accepted dowry money for the marriage of his first daughter. Prabhu described his house and the name of the person whose house was next to his own. This neighbour, Prabhu said, had a son and a daughter.

He also gave some other details of the location of his house like saying that "there was a raised path paved with stones" and "there was a tank in the middle of which there was a house and above the tank there was a chhatri (domed cenotaph); there were two houses, one on top of the other in the tank".

Prabhu said, "In the year of famine (...) I lived at Hatyori and had a pair of buffaloes with which I ploughed my fields". He also gave the names of his father, and the places of his maternal uncle and father-in-law. He said that he was the Purohit (priest) of a village.

All these statements were found to be completely correct in every detail. He gave the name of his wife as Ganjo, which means bald. Actually, her name was Gauro, but she was given the nickname of Ganjo, because she was slightly bald.

---

[9] The term "Tehsildar" is roughly equivalent to "magistrate". Native titles and other terminology are explained in the glossary at the end of this book.

Other statements made by Prabhu were found to be only partially correct, such as the descriptions of the three water wells for drinking along with their names; only two wells were found. Similarly, he described a fortress at Hatyori in which there was an inscription and also recollected a snake. Although there was indeed a fortress at Hatyori, there was no inscription or snake known to have been connected with it.

It was found, though, that there was a legend involving the fortress, an inscription, and a snake in the village. Harbux (the previous personality) could have believed this legend to be true. Prabhu talked of his three brothers and gave the names of two of them. One of them, he said, had died before he (Harbux) did. This, too, is only partially correct. Harbux had only one brother, whose name did not resemble either of the two given by Prabhu. Again, though, the statement might be taken as true: the two names given by Prabhu were those of Harbux's first cousins, and in India cousins are often called "brothers".

There were few statements that could not be verified at all, such as Prabhu's claim that he had a Gujar (caste) of the village of Bhore as Jajman. He also claimed, "Moola Jat fell into my well and I saved his life" and "One day I met a snake in the jungle, hypnotized it and then killed it with a tree (stick)". Another few claims were unverifiable by their very nature, such as: "after my death, I lived in the spiritual world," and "God told me to go to Salimpur where I was born".

Only one, out of 24 statements made by Prabhu before verification, was found totally incorrect: "I died during my father's lifetime in a bungalow outside the village". In fact Harbux died after his father's death and in his home in the village.

Shyam Sunderlal reports:

> When this inquiry had been concluded, Prabhu was asked to find his previous home in the village. He set off, walked a few steps, then stopped, hesitating. The Tehsildar (magistrate) then took him by the hand. After a moment, the child again started walking. After some hesitation he went by himself right to the previous home and there took 'his' son Ghure by the hand.

It turned out that the way to the house was long and curvy, but Prabhu nevertheless reached the end. The houses along the way were in ruins. When Prabhu reached the place where the porch of his previous house used to be, he stopped. It appeared that he felt uncertain and could not exactly place his house in the middle of the ruins piled around there.

Unfortunately, Prabhu did not recognize anyone he met in Hatyori who were from the previous life he recalled, nor did he recall the names of anyone else.

The Naib Tehsildar concluded that Prabhu had not been given any information about these matters by anyone and that it therefore involved real memories of a past life.

As suggested by honourable C.C. Wilson, special agent to the Governor-General of Rajputana, the team tried to gather more testimony and confirm that he had no prior normal knowledge of Hatyori. This involved interviewing Prabhu's father about the circumstances in which the boy had first remembered his previous life and also whether anyone from the village of Salimpur had ever been to Hatyori.

Prabhu's father told the investigators that he was the first person to whom Prabhu talked about his past life:

> One day he suddenly cried out that his little sons were in very bad condition and that he would carry them on his shoulders. He said this several times and when I asked him who his sons were and where they were and why he said such foolish things, he became silent. Later, sitting by his mother, who was churning butter, he said that she was extremely stingy with butter at our home, since his previous mother had him sit beside the churn and gave him large pieces of butter from it.

His father also told them that his mother had asked Prabhu where his previous mother was and that the boy had replied that she was at Hatyori, that his real name was Harbux and that he should now be called by that name and not "Prabhu".

He added that on another occasion, while sleeping with his mother around midnight, Prabhu had been trembling and crying out: "O Rama, my children are in a terrible condition!" So his parents had asked Prabhu to tell them about his previous life and he repeated the facts that he had already repeated to the Naib Tehsildar.

The case of Prabhu was investigated by Dr. Lal who was then the Diwan (Chief Minister) of the Maharajah of Bharatpur State and some other officials of that state. Along with the Maharajah, the agent for the Governor-General of Rajputana, the Honourable C.C. Wilson had also taken interest in the investigation of the case. The case was later also investigated by H.N. Banerjee, Director of the Department of Parapsychology, University of Rajasthan, Jaipur. He published a complete monograph on the case.

The Case of Jagdish Chandra

In 1927 a lawyer called K.K.N. Sahay of Bareilly described seven cases of children who remembered their previous lives in a monograph entitled *Reincarnation: Verified Cases of Rebirth After Death*. One of these children was his son, Jagdish Chandra. Sahay's account on Jagdish starts on June 6, 1926, when he had to take care of his wife and son, owing to illness:

> My wife had a very high fever, which took many days to lower down. It was on the 6th day that Jagdish asked me to get a motor car. I replied that I would get one soon. The child grew impatient and asked me to get one soon. I asked him 'Where should I get it from?' He said that I should get his car. I asked him where his car was. He replied that it was at the house of Babuaji. I again asked him and in reply he said that [Babuaji] lived at Benares (Varanasi), and was his (Jagdish's) father.

After a few weeks, when he had ascertained some of his son's statements, Sahay sent a letter to the Editor of a regional English called the *Leader* on June 27, 1926, entitled "Strange story of former life Enquiry about Babuaji[10] Pande of Benares":

> My son, Jagdish aged three years and a half, gives the story of his previous life in a very connected form. He gives his father's name as Babuaji Pande, place of residence Benares, describes the house of Babuaji in Benares and makes particular mention of a big gate, a sitting room, and an underground room with an iron safe fixed in one of the walls. He also describes the courtyard in which Babuaji sits in the evening. He describes that Babuaji and the people who collect there, drink Bhang [a tea made of cannabis].

[10] *Babu(a)* is a honorific title, as is the suffix -ji often encountered in Indian cases.

Sahay also states that his son had told him Babuaji had Malish [an Ayurvedic type of massage] on his body and painted his face with powder or earth before bathing or washing his face in the morning. Jagdish described two motor cars and one phaeton and pair [a carriage with horses]. The boy claimed that Babuaji had two sons and one wife and that all had died, so that Babuaji was all-alone. Jagdish also described many private and family matters.

Sahay declares that he had no friends or relatives at Benares and that his wife had never been there either. He had never heard of Babuaji before.

[There follows a list of seven eminent people who had questioned the boy.]

Sahay invited all gentlemen [sic - no ladies] who may feel interested to ascertain the truth of the story given by his son in a scientific spirit.

K. K.N. Sahay received several inquiries regarding Jagdish Chandra's story and wrote another letter to the editor of the *Leader* on June 30, 1926 saying:

> The boy began to tell his story on the 6th June and completed it by the 11th replying to the questions I put him. I then asked the members of the Bareilly bar and other friends to examine this phenomenon and to advise me if the case is worth further inquiry. Friends and members of the bar continued to come and talk to the boy and it was decided on the 16th that no man should be sent to Benares, as it would afford a loophole for sceptics.
>
> They may argue that suggestions regarding the house and other details of Benares have been conveyed by the messenger to the boy.

For this reason a letter was sent to the Chairman, Municipal Board, Benares, and, on receipt of his reply, letters were sent to the press.

Sahay also requested some of the Leaders of India to send their representatives so that Jagdish might be taken with them to Benares to point out, on the spot, the things mentioned by him. Sahay was convinced that Jagdish would be able to point out many things on the spot, because the boy had already told him so many things, corroborated by respectable people whom he did not know.

He goes on to quote from two of the letters he had received. One of these is a letter by Munshi Mahadeva Prasad M.A., LL.B., a lawyer and Chairman of the Municipal Board of Benares, saying:

On receipt of your letter I made the necessary inquiries and found that most of the things told by your boy are quite true. In fact they all correctly related except that Babuaji Pandey's[11] son, Jai Gopal, died about two years and a half ago. The rest of the facts are all correct; about the phaeton, ekka, horse, malish, goondas, bhang and the rest. Babua Pandey – for that's the name of person referred to by your boy as Babuaji is well known to me, having been also my client for the last many years, and I could see on the mere first reading of your letter that he was the person meant by the boy. So I sent my man to Babua Pandey to make the necessary enquiries, when his men, learning of this, came and took away the letter from me. Now they may be going to Bareilly to enquire and corroborate the facts for themselves. Babua Pandey is otherwise known here as Pandit Mathura Prasad Pandey and lives at Pandey Ghat, Benares City.

The other letter K. K. N. Sahay quotes from is from Pandit Uma Kant Pande, Vakil, and Benares who writes:

I saw your letter in the *Leader* of today. Babua Pande is a friend of mine. I have seen this boy who is born in your family. The descriptions given by him are in the main correct. Pandeyji does not possess a car though he used one or two. I am informing him about the boy and we shall very soon go to see him at your [house].

After the *Leader* published Sahay's letters, he received in his home, for a full two months, a number of visitors who wanted to hear Jagdish talk about his previous life.

The baby became quite tired of this and began to refuse to see people or to talk in their presence. I, therefore, wrote to Mr. V. N. Mehta, I.C.S., District Magistrate, Benares for his help before I could make up my mind to visit Benares with the boy. I was afraid of the crowd as it confounded the child very much. He very kindly promised his help. I started on the 13th August in the afternoon for Benares and reached there the next morning ... B. Hanuman Prasad sub-judge, Dr. Ganesh Prasad, Mr Tandon,

---

[11] Both spellings are used, i.e. *Pande* and *Pandey*.

Income Tax officer, and several respectable people came to see us. Pt. Laxmi Kant Pande, Vakil, also came to see us. The baby recognized him at once. At first the baby said that he was Uma Kant. On his refusal he said that he was then Lakshmi Kant as both brothers were similar in features.

Jagdish also mentioned the relationship between Pt. Laxmi Kant and Babua Pande with some accuracy. In the evening Mr. V. N. Mehta the Collector reached Babua Pandey's house before the rest of the party. Babua's house turned out to be near the river and the road was about two furlongs (around 400m) away. One had to pass through a maze of lanes to reach his house. Jagdish pointed out the way through the labyrinth of lanes up to the house. On reaching there the number of the crowd had grown to over a thousand. In the room of Babua himself Jagdish found 35 men seated on the floor close together, which made him upset, so that he refused to reply.

Afterwards, Jagdish was taken to the other house where he pointed out the place where they prepared Bhang. Jagdish was taken inside the Zenana (the part of a house for the seclusion of women where he pointed out his "chachi" (aunt)) and said that he had come to her house.

As a footnote Sahay adds that Jagdish had a birthmark on each of his ears: "The mark is in the upper part of the ear and looks as if a hole has been closed. People say that in Benares it is customary to wear pierced earrings in the upper part of the ear". However, Dr. Ian Stevenson who studied the case later on could find no trace of these marks in 1961 or 1964. Also, neither Jai Gopal's mother nor his sister Kamla Pandey could tell him whether he had worn earrings or not.

As an adult Jagdish wrote (in 1960) an autobiographical account which is important for its description of the feelings and in particular his strong attraction to the family he claimed was his in the previous life.

Ian Stevenson first learned about the case in 1959 and started to study it in 1961 when he had interviews with Jagdish and his two older brothers. He continued his studies through to 1973 when he interviewed Babu Panday's oldest daughter. The main contribution of Stevenson's research into this case has been the addition of some details and verifications. However, he also highlighted the correspondences in behaviour between Jagdish and Jai Gopal, and the evolution of the emotional components in Jagdish's memories.

One of the observations that Stevenson made was that when Jagdish's father said in his report that he had "no friends or relatives at Benares", that was not entirely true. A cousin and her husband lived in Nuddesar, about four kilometres from Babu Pandey's home.

Also, Babu Pandey was a Brahmin and K. K. N. Sahay belonged to the Kayastha caste, which formed more of a barrier to social relations than would be the case nowadays. Then, K. K. N. Sahay had stated the following about the relationship between Jai Gopal and Babu Pandey:

> Pandit Laxmi Kant Pandey's view is that this boy was the grandson of Babu, the son of his daughter who lived at his house and died, leaving this boy to Babu to bring up. I also think that this explanation is quite in keeping with the account given by Jagdish Chandra except that he calls his grandfather his 'father'. It may be that, as his mother left her child to her father to bring up; the child did not know any other father except Babu Pandey.

Dr. Ian Stevenson thinks that Babu Pandey was indeed Jai Gopal's father. About Babu Pandey he also writes:

> A more important obstacle to Babu Pandey's cooperation was the 'disparaging facts' given out by Jagdish Chandra, which K. K. N. Sahay alluded to, but did not specify, in his report. Babu Pandey was upset by the interest taken in the case by the district magistrate. This is not at all surprising as Jagdish Chandra later told me what one of the 'disparaging facts' was; namely that Babu Pandey had killed a pilgrim for his money and that the body had been put down a well, which had then been covered over.

Stevenson has not independently verified this statement but if it was correct, it could have been trouble for Babu Pandey. Wells are often covered over in India when a better source of water becomes available. A covered well, by itself, attracts no attention. But such a well could easily be opened up to see whether it contained a corpse, and, as a result, Babu Pandey may have suddenly found himself in a very delicate situation.

If Babu Pandey endorsed Jagdish Chandra, he ran the risk that the boy would reveal the "disparaging facts". On the other hand, if Babu Pandey refused to accept the evidence of the boy's accuracy on many details, that might have led to further inquiries by the police and district magistrate. According to Stevenson, he therefore chose the somewhat risky third alternative of remaining silent. For Stevenson the uncooperative attitude of Babu Pandey could have explained at least part of the very few seemingly incorrect details stated by Jagdish Chandra:

> Babu Pandey was the real father of Jai Gopal, and not the grandfather, as was given out in Benares and accepted by K. K. N. Sahay. Both Kamla Pandey and Minto Pandey Tiwari, Jai Gopal's sisters, told me he was Jai Gopal's father.

The longing for the car that first triggered the expression of Jagdish Chandra's memories persisted into adulthood. In his own 1960 report Jagdish Chandra wrote that as a child he would sometimes roll on the floor dressed in a loin cloth, asserting to his family that he was loosening up before wrestling. This could have related to the wrestling that went on at the home of Babu Pandey, who had an akhara (wrestling arena) specially constructed in front of the house.

Jagdish Chandra made fifty-one statements concerning his previous life. Of these, a dozen were recorded in writing before verification was attempted. Another twenty-four were recorded in writing and verified before the two families met, with the other fifteen statements being made still later. Jagdish recalled among other things his own name, the name, occupation, habits of his father and the names of his father's employees. He gave the location of his home near the river Ganges, some details about the house and the goondas (meaning "bouncers" – the English word "goons" is derived from it) whom his father had employed.

He also gave details about his "Chachi". Literally, this means "aunt," but Stevenson thinks that in the typical extended families of India a child may hear older cousins calling its (the child's) mother Chachi and develops the habit of calling her Chachi too.

There were only a few statements that could not be verified. For example, Jagdish stated that his brother Jai Mangal had died of poisoning, whereas there was only a suspicion that Jai Mangal died of accidental poisoning. He claimed he had a car, but Babu Pandey actually used cars borrowed from friends to drive Jai Gopal around. Jagdish stated that he died of enteritis or cholera, whereas the correct diagnosis had been uncertain.

Jagdish Chandra told Stevenson in 1961 that when he first visited Benares in 1926 the site of the burial ghats, where bodies are cremated, this stimulated in him memories of the funeral of Jai Gopal.

> He then recalled seeing the body of Jai Gopal taken out for the funeral and mourners chanting around it. In his memories he

44

could not make out what they were saying. He did not recall the cremation or any other details of the interval between the death of Jai Gopal and his own birth.

Ian Stevenson made a list of behavioural traits of Jagdish Chandra that seemed to relate to the boy's previous life:

1. Insistence on eating ahead of other members of the family.
2. Refusal to eat with non-Hindus or to allow non-Hindus to touch his food.
3. Dislike for bearded people (Muslims).
4. Fondness for sweets, especially rabri.
5. Reluctance to eat salty foods.
6. Refusal to eat garlic, onions, meat and eggs.
7. Liking for bhang [cannabis tea].
8. Preference for wearing a loincloth.
9. Rolling on floor preliminary to wrestling.
10. Interest in cars.
11. Interest in swimming.
12. Interest in previous family.

Stevenson comments that even if Jagdish's knowledge could be explained by normal means, another hypothesis is required to explain its behavioural features.

Stevenson claims that fraud is out of the question in this case, because K. K. N. Sahay published details of it in a newspaper before verification. Also, he firmly excludes the possibility that the two families had had any prior interaction, which would have contaminated the child's original statements:

> The principal items of the statements made by Jagdish Chandra concerning the previous life were written down before verification was begun, and most of them were in fact verified before the two families had met. The great physical distance between the families, their separation through membership in different castes, and the close surveillance of Jagdish Chandra when he was a child makes it virtually impossible that he could have picked up all the detailed information he showed about Babu Pandey and his family without someone's being aware of the person who was passing such information.

The Case of Bishan Chand Kapoor

After K. K. N. Sahay published his letters in the Leader about Jagdish Chandra's memories, he was surprised to receive information regarding many similar cases of reincarnation. One of them concerned a boy known by the pet name of Vishwa Nath during his childhood, whose correct name was Bishan (or Bishen) Chand Kapoor. K. K. N. Sahay sent two letters to the Editor of the Leader describing the circumstances of the case.

On August 12, 1926, he wrote:

> Vishwa Nath was born on Feb. 7, 1921, in Mohalla Khannu, Bareilly. He began to ask about Pilibhit[12] when he was one and a half years old. He asked the distance between Pilibhit and Bareilly and wanted to know the time when his father would take him there. When he was three years old he began to give a detailed account of himself. The parents were afraid and tried to hide these strange facts. There is a superstition in India that children who recall a past life do not live long and the sooner they forget the better for them. [Parents may even use drastic methods, such as washing their children's mouths out with filth or soap.]

Around August of 1926 K. K. N. Sahay heard of this case from Thakur Moti Singh, Vakil, and an ex-member of the Legislative Council. Sahay decided to visit B. Ram Ghulam and go to Pilibhit to verify the facts. So the two of them went to Pilibhit, on Sunday, August 1.

They went directly to the Govt. High School, Pilibhit, which Bishan Chand did not recognize as his school of the previous life.

At the time, the school building was new; it had been erected recently. Sahay requested the Headmaster, Rai Sahib Babu Asharfi Lal, to help him in his investigations, which he kindly did, accompanying Sahay to various places.

> I had taken down the story of Vishwa Nath [Bishan Chand] on my first visit to him and had to verify only the following facts about him. He had given his uncle's name as Har Narain, Caste

---

[12] Also spelled as Pilibheet.

Kayastha, Mohalla Ganj, City, Pilibhit and his age 20 years. He said he was unmarried. He said his neighbour was Lala Sunder Lal, who had a green gate, a sword and a gun and had nautch parties [parties with learned courtesans, comparable to the Japanese geishas] in the courtyard of his house.

Bishan Chand described his own house as a double storey building, with separate apartments for ladies and gentlemen. He described how singing parties and feasts were frequently held at this house. He also described how luxurious their way of life had been. Bishan Chand said his father was a so-called Zamindar. He added that his father had loved him very much and had always given him silk clothes, and pocket money.

The boy also confessed how fond he had been of wine, rohu fish, and nautch girls.

Regarding other aspects of his previous life, Bishan Chand told Sahay that he had studied up to the sixth class at the Government School, which was situated near the river and that he had known Urdu, Hindi and English. He described a Thakurdwara at his house.

When we reached the gate of the late Sahu Shyam Sunder Lal, the boy got down from the tonga [carriage drawn by a horse] and recognized it as the green gate of Sunder Lal. He also pointed to the courtyard where nautch parties were held. This was corroborated by the neighbouring shopkeepers.

I saw the gate myself. It had a green varnish, which had grown faint by lapse of time. Then when we went to the house of the late Lala Debi Pershad rais [an honorific title], the boy recognized it as his house. He shouted that that was the house of Har Narain.

Sahay explains that Har Narain was the son of Lala Debi Pershad. Portions of this big old house had fallen and the family had abandoned the building. Har Narain's neighbours told the party that the place had undergone a great change. Bishan Chand recognized the building by the gate and the place where they used to drink wine, eat Rohu fish and hear the songs of the nautch girls.

Sahay asked Bishan Chand where the staircase was situated and the boy correctly showed him where it was, among a heap of bricks and mud. He then recognized the so-called Zenana apartments and specially mentioned a room on the upper storey, which was occupied by the ladies of the family.

The sole surviving member of the family, Babu Brij Mohan Lal, who lived in a separate house, showed them an old, faint photograph of Lala Har Narain and his son.

In the presence of a big crowd Bishan Chand immediately put his finger on that photo and said, 'Here is Har Narain and here I' pointing to the photograph of a boy seated on a chair.

This was most remarkable and immediately established his identity as Laxmi Narain, son of Babu Har Narain. The party next took Bishan Chand to the old Government High School, which he recognized immediately as his School, and they went around it.

Bishan Chand then swiftly began to ascend the staircase, situated in the right hand corner of the house. Sahay and three other men followed him up. When they reached the upper part of the roof, the boy pointed out his house, which was visible and the river Deuha, which flowed behind it.

The party then questioned Bishan Chand about the place where his class six was held in this time. He pointed out a room. Two old class-fellows of class six admitted that this was the correct room.

These two class-fellows included Babu Bishambar Nath whose old photograph was recognized by Bishan Chand, and Babu Ram Ghulam of Pilibhit. They asked the boy about the name of their teacher.

Bishan Chand then proceeded to describe the teacher as a fat, bearded man and, before he could mention the name, it was given by the crowd as M. Moinuddin of Shahjehanpur.

In his house he had correctly pointed out the old Thaku Dwara that we had mentioned before. The boy was given a pair of Tablas on which he played with ease. His father, Babu Ram Ghulam, informed me that the boy never had seen the Tablas in his present lifetime.

The name of the prostitute with whom the boy associated in his previous life was repeatedly asked by the people. He reluctantly mentioned the name of 'Padma,' which the people certified as correct.

Sahay adds that the information about this case was given to the District Superintendent of Police and the Civil Surgeon. The superintendent visited them and took Bishan Chand for a trip in his car. A large crowd had gathered at the railway platform when the party left, including several prominent people.

In his second letter to the editor about this case, published in the *Leader* on 30, August 1926, he adds:

> Babu Laxmi Narain, son of Babu Har Narain died at Shahjehanpur on Dec. 15, 1918 at 6:00 a.m. of fever and lung trouble. His age at the time of death was 32 years and 11 days. He died after a protracted illness of five months. I am indebted to B. Upendra Narain, the maternal uncle of B. Laxmi Narain for the above information. He also writes that the boy, Vishwa Nath has narrated several incidents, which were forgotten by the members of the family.

Sahay also mentions that this uncle wrote to him that it was very remarkable that Laxmi Narain had also remembered his previous life at Pilibhit, up to the age of six years. Laxmi Narain had said that he came from Jehanabad. However, it was kept a secret because Laxmi's parents thought that publicity would be harmful for his life and welfare, which meant that no attempt at verification was made.

> So now we know that Vishwa Nath [Bishan Chand's pet name] of Bareilly, was Laxmi Narain of Pilibhit who was somebody of Jehanabad. Research scholars can now frame their theories. The character of Laxmi Narain was very gay [cheerful]. He loved wine, flesh and women.
>
> Laxmi Narain's mother was staying with his brother Upendra Narayan in Bareilly. When the child was taken there, the mother asked many questions. Based on his responses she firmly believed that her dead son Laxmi Narain had been reborn in the form of Bishan Chand.

Sahay wrote down a conversation between Bishan Chand and Laxmi Narain's mother:

Q. Did you fly kites?
A. *Yes.*
Q. With whom did you contest?
A. *I contested with every kite that came in my range but particularly I contested with Sunder Lal* (neighbour).
Q. Did you throw my pickle? [chutney relish]
A. *I did not throw it, but was it possible to eat that rotten pickle? You wanted me to eat that rotten pickle hence I threw it.*

Q. Did you ever enter into service?
A. *Yes; I served for some time in Avadh Railways.*
Q. Who was your servant?
A. *My servant was Maikua, a dark, short statured person – a Kahar (Kahar is a caste). He was my favourite Khansama* (Cook).

Pilibheet was a town just about fifty kilometres away from Bareilly, and Bishan Chand's family had no relations there. Of the fifty-six statements Bishan Chand Kapoor made over the years about his previous life, forty-four were found correct, nine could not be verified and only three were incorrect. One of the unverified statements concerned a treatment given by an Ayurvedic doctor called Hanuwant Vadya in Shahjhanpur. Babu Ram Gulam went to Shahjahanpur to confirm the statement and managed to trace out the name of the doctor but found that he had died.

Some revelations that Chand gave were totally wrong. He claimed to have lived in Mohalla Ganj in Pilibheet while Laxmi Narain's relatives told that Har Narain's (Laxmi Narain's father) house was situated in Mohalla Saray. The child also said that Har Narain was his uncle while he was his father. This might be because, as mentioned in the case of Jagdish Chandra, Indian children may often imitate their elders and address their parents in a manner different from "mother" and "father". A more mundane explanation is that there was another person living in Bareilly whose name was also Har Narain, who was called Har Narain Uncle (Tau). This word it seems somehow was unconsciously related in the child's memory.

Finally, the child said that he was 20 years of age at the time of his death (in his previous life) while Laxmi Narain's maternal uncle stated that he was 32.

When asked the name of the dancing girl with whom he had sex, the boy replied rather reluctantly "Padma". People present there confirmed it. Bishan Chand also said that once while he was drunk, he saw another man visiting Padma and he shot him dead out of anger. He himself used to drink with Padma from the same cup. These statements could not be verified.

A well-known lawyer of Bareilly, Babu Jwala Prasad told that in 1918 he had defended Laxmi Narain of Pilibheet in a criminal case relating to events, which took place at the house of Padma, a prostitute. Laxmi Narain took part and gave evidence after Har Narain's death.

The people of the village were sure that Har Narain had buried his money somewhere but no one was aware of the place. When Laxmi

Narain's mother asked Bishan Chand about the money, he took her into a room where the hidden money was found. To Dr. Rawat, similar information was given when he interviewed Kamini Kapoor, the wife of Bishan Chand Kapoor.

The child's emotional expressions were also important, particularly his affectionate behaviour towards Laxmi Narain's mother. Before meeting her, he used to plead with his father that he must invite her to live with them. He used to say, "Papa, she will not increase your expenditure. She just wears a simple sari and petticoat and spends most of her time in prayer". Similar things were noted when Laxmi Narain's mother came to see the child.

Bishan Chand visited Laxmi Narain's mother often and many times he stayed the night there. Once, the mother came to Bareilly from Lucknow and stayed with Ram Gulam. Bishan Chand opposed her going back.

Ultimately, when she was leaving, the child told the riksha driver that if he returned with news of her safe journey, he would be rewarded. (The boy was unaware of the fact that the riksha driver would just leave her at the station). According to Bishan Chand himself, he was more attached to Laxmi Narain's mother than to his own.

After K. K. N. Sahay's investigation of this case, it was studied by Dr. Jamuna Prasad, Dr. L. P. Mehrotra, Dr. Kamal Singh Rawat, Prof. P. Pal, Dr. Ian Stevenson and Dr. K. S. Rawat (along with his wife Vidya Rawat).

Dr. Ian Stevenson studied the case first in 1964 and then in 1974. On 26, June 1985, about two and a half years after Bishan Chand's death, Dr. K. S.Rawat, and Mrs Vidya Rawat contacted a few important people related to the case in order to study and compare the most outstanding personality traits of Laxmi Narain and Bishan Chand Kapoor.

The most outstanding six personality traits of Laxmi Narain were:

1. Laxmi Narain was very fond of meat, especially "Rohu fish".
2. Particularly after his father's death, Laxmi Narain freely indulged in his fondness for alcohol.
3. He was much interested in beautiful women and also indulged in this liking after his father died. Till the end of his life, he was interested in women singers and dancers. He was so much attached to a prostitute – Padma – that he shot down a person coming out of Padma's house out of sheer jealousy.

4. Another notable feature of his personality was his short temper. This irrational behaviour was revealed in his willingness to shoot dead a total stranger.

5. Despite his anger and instabilities, he could be very generous. He once gave a poor Muslim man, who was otherwise destitute, 500 rupees – an enormous amount in those days – to open a watchmaker's shop.

6. Laxmi Narain was a worshipper of Lord Shiva. He had a temple erected and dedicated to the Lord Shiva in his own garden. After the murder that he had committed, he hid himself in that place for six months. Dr. Stevenson writes: "Laxmi Narian had strong religious inclinations. [...] Laxmi Narain would worship austerely for ten to fifteen days, keeping himself secluded in the thakerwada (shrine room) of the house during this period and even having his meals there". (Ibid., Pp.181)

Taking note of these traits of Laxmi Narain's personality, Dr. K. S. Rawat and Vidya Rawat tried to conduct a sort of focused interview on all these points with three people most intimately related to Bishan Chand. These were – Mrs Kamini Kapoor (his wife), Sudhir Kapoor (his son) and Lala Shriniwas Agarwal (an intimate friend), at Bareilly.

The findings were:

1. *Meat-eating*: Not only close relatives, but several people who were not very familiar with him said that Bishan Chand as a child was very fond of meat and Rohu fish. Although his present family were vegetarians, he became a self-invitee to places where it was cooked. Later on, he gave up meat but continued eating eggs.

2. *Drinking*: When he was about four or five years old, Chand was caught red-handed drinking brandy from a bottle. Once, noticing a bottle placed at somewhat a higher place, he at once climbed on a table and tried to get it, while his father and elder brother were present. When they pulled Bishan Chand down he cried for a long time, staring at the bottle. Later, also, he was found very fond of drinks. He always used to carry a bottle of liquor while visiting Padma in his present life also. A few days before his death he was burnt in an accident and the doctors were surprised to note that tranquilizers hardly worked on him. The

doctor said that he must be used to some intoxicants and that was why even strong pills had no effect.

3. *Violent temperament*: As a child, Bishan Chand boasted about the murder that he committed in his previous life. Bishan Chand was a person of very short temperament. His son Sudhir Kapoor told us: "He was very hot tempered. When in anger, he knew no limits. I have not seen such anger in anyone. His anger was limitless". Bishan Chand's wife Mrs Kamini Kapoor and his son also told Dr. K. S. Rawat about some incidents.

Once, in violent disagreement, Bishan Chand jumped from the balcony of his house out of anger.

On another occasion, as his wife recalls:

> It so happened that once he did not go on his duty for more than a week's time. I asked him why don't you go on your duty? How could we afford your sitting idle? What for after all, have you taken leave? Any reason? At that very instant, a friend of his came in. He asked: 'How come, Kapoor Sahib, you did not go on your duty today?' On this, he said: 'He also says this thing and you also say the same thing. I will not go – I will leave the job'. He became very angry. Then he said: 'I am not feeling well'. He sat down, took out a number of sleeping pills and gulped them down.
>
> His wife asked him: 'Why have you taken these pills?' He replied: 'I have pain in my stomach. Now, I will be off.' She called for a doctor, because he had started losing consciousness. The doctor advised them that he should be transferred to a hospital. So his wife and others took care of this. There he was given something to help him to vomit and he remained unconscious for 48 hours.
>
> His great anger was also a cause of his death. In his old age, Bishan Chand was lying unconscious and it became necessary to give him a dose of medicine. No one in the house had the courage to wake him up to give him the medicine and without it he died.

4. *Generosity*: There are also many substantiated tales of his generous nature. A close friend of Bishan Chand, Lala Shrinivas, told that Bishan arranged a job for a poor boy, making tireless efforts. His wife Kamini

Kapoor declares: "He was very generous by nature. For example, if you came and said I am hungry; I have to marry my daughter; and I am very perturbed, then he would not think about his own condition and would give away the money in his pockets."

Once he gave away his uniform. He was on tour along with a guardsman when they saw an old man shivering with cold. Bishan Chand said to the guardsman: "Look, this man is shivering with cold, he will die!" "What can I do, sir?" The guardsman asked. Disgusted with this tepid response to the suffering of a fellow human being, Chand took off his uniform and sweater and gave it to the old man. On seeing him without uniform and sweater, his wife asked him for the reason. He said: "It's quite hot today". When she pursued her enquiries he said a monkey took it away. Chand's wife later stated that: "I know if somebody is hungry he would give ten rupees to him and would remain hungry himself".

5. *Religious practices*: Bishan Chand, as was Laxmi Narain, was a devotee of Lord Shiva. Lalaji told that he used to go regularly to "Mopa" (about eight kilometres from Bareilly) in the month of "Sawan" to visit the temple of Lord Shiva. He never missed the chance, come what may. If somebody advised him to sit in meditation, he would keep sitting for hours at a stretch, meditating together with him or her.

6. *Relationships with women*: His wife confided to us that Bishan Chand had sexual relations with a number of women. His wife used to leave him and go to her parents for periods from six months to a year!

Lalaji also confirmed that Bishan Chand had several affairs. Mrs. Kamini Kapoor gave Dr. Rawat and his wife details of an incident that took place when Bishan Chand got transferred to Janakpur. On the occasion of Holi (a festival), he was working late at night when he heard a band of singers and dancers outside his house. Bishan Chand listened carefully and said: "Oh, it's Padma's voice". He called for her and asked, "Are you Padma?"

"Yes," Padma replied, surprised at hearing her name from a stranger. "Haven't you recognized me? I am Laxmi". After he reminded her of all the sweet moments that they had shared together, Padma could not help accepting the truth of the situation.

It is important to remember, too, that Padma was considerably older than Bishan Chand. In spite of this, he started going to meet Padma with a liquor bottle at a place quite far off from his office in an isolated hilly area. One day Padma gathered all her courage and, fearing his terrible temper, asked Bishan Chand: "Why are you wasting your life with me?" But Bishan Chand refused to agree with her. "Now I am of your mother's age – forget me," she said, and threw the liquor out.

The above details strongly indicate that the main six traits of Laxmi Narain's personality were found in Bishan Chand's personality also. Concerning other traits that link the two personalities, Dr. Stevenson had already mentioned a desire for expensive clothes that faded in adulthood, an interest in music, the ability to read Urdu, and an interest in kites, also faded in childhood.

Of all the paranormal phenomena involved in the case of Bishan Chand Kapoor, Dr. Stevenson writes that the case is unusually strong with regard to authenticity. This is based on the fact that K. K. N. Sahay, who himself had no connection with the subject's family, recorded many statements before he tried to verify them. It is extremely unlikely that Bishan Chand could have acquired by normal means all the information about his previous life.

Also, he stresses that in this case, as with many others, a full interpretation of all the facts requires a broader understanding of the child's behaviour apart from the information that he exhibited about the past life. As a small boy Bishan Chand, so Stevenson argues, showed the habits and attitudes of a spoiled, rich young man and, additionally, of one belonging to a caste different from that of his family.

This is of enormous importance within the culture of India several generations ago, where caste determined nearly everything about one's life, including such things as the work one could do, the places one might frequent, and the person one might be allowed to marry.

> His father tolerated this alien behavior and gradually guided his son toward important modifications. His parents could have had no reason for promoting the sort of attitudes that Bishan Chand showed as a child. Or can someone seriously suppose that B. Ram Ghulam wanted to hear his son boast of a murder he had committed and scoff at his family for their poverty? (Stevenson, *Cases of the Reincarnation Type, Vol. I*, Pp. 201-202).

Stephen E. Braude (2003) comments on the case of Bishan Chand as follows:

Assuming the accuracy of the reports, this case does pose a substantial challenge to anti-survivalists. Bishen Chand evidently produced a long string of verified statements; along with various behaviours appropriate to the previous personality but unusual (if not unprecedented) for a young child. (Pg. 187)

The Case of Shanti Devi

Shanti Devi was born in Delhi on December 11, 1926. From the age of four, when she started speaking (this in itself is unusual and as far as we know, it remains unexplained), she talked about her husband and children. She said that her husband was in Mathura – a town 145 km from her birthplace in Delhi – where he owned a shop in front of Dwarkadheesh's Temple. She also said that she was a 'Chauban' (Chaubey's wife) and her name was Lugdi Bai.

Her parents ignored her claims but she persisted. They thought it was a child's fantasy, but she insisted on a visit to Mathura. The parents became concerned, because she talked repeatedly about her past life and, over time, narrated a number of incidents connected with her life in Mathura, and with her husband. By the time she was six years old, she had given a detailed account of her death following birthing a child.

The parents consulted a family physician, who was amazed at how a little girl narrated so many details of the complicated surgical procedures involved in a caesarean section. Shanti, however, never mentioned her husband's name up to the age of eight or nine. It is customary in India that wives do not utter the name of their husband. Even when specifically asked, she would blush and say that she would recognize him, if taken there, but would not say his name.

One day, a distant relative, Babu Bishan Chand, told Shanti Devi that if she told him her husband's name he would take her to Mathura. Allured by the offer, she whispered into his ear the name Pandit Kedar Nath Chaubey[13]. Babu Chand then wrote a letter to this man detailing all the statements by Shanti, and asked him to visit Delhi. Kedar Nath replied, confirming most of her statements, suggesting that one of his relatives, Pt. Kanji Mal, who lived in Delhi, be allowed to meet this girl.

A meeting with Kanji Mal was arranged during which Shanti recognized him as her husband's cousin. She gave him some more details

---

[13] Also commonly spelled as Choube.

about her house in Mathura and informed him about the location where she had hidden some money. Kanjimal was so impressed that instead of writing back he himself went to Mathura to report about the girl.

Consequently, in November 1935, Kedar Nath came to Delhi along with Lugdi's son, Navneet Lal and his present wife. On seeing Kedar Nath, Shanti told her mother: "Did not I tell you that he is fair and he has a wart on the left side cheek near his ear?" Shanti requested her mother to prepare a stuffed potato paranthas (a type of fried pancakes) and pumpkin curry for dinner. Kedar Nath was dumbfounded, as these were his favourite dishes.

After dinner, Shanti asked Kedar Nath "Why did you marry her?" referring to his present wife, "Have you not decided you will not remarry?" Kedar Nath had no reply. Before retiring for the night he asked to be allowed to talk with her alone. The next morning declared he was fully convinced that Shanti was his wife Lugdi Bai, reborn.

Shanti's story spread all over the country through the media. When Mahatma Gandhi heard about it, he called Shanti and talked to her. He requested her to stay in his ashram (spiritual centre). This meeting profoundly touched Shanti; when Dr. Rawat interviewed her in 1986 she still recalled that she felt the bones of the Mahatma's body while she was on his lap.) On Gandhi's advice a committee of 15 prominent people were constituted to verify the claims made by the girl.

The committee persuaded her parents to allow her to accompany them to Mathura. On November 24, 1935 they left by train with Shanti for Mathura. The committee's report describes some details of what happened. The first incident that drew their attention on reaching Mathura happened at the platform. Shanti was in Deshbandhu's arms. Very soon, an older man, wearing a typical Mathura dress, whom she had never met before, came in front of her, mixed in the small crowd, and paused for a while.

Shanti was asked whether she could recognize him. His presence reacted so quickly on her that she at once came down from Mr Gupta's lap and touched the stranger's feet with deep veneration and stood aside; on inquiring she whispered in L. Deshbandhu's ear that the person was her 'jeth' (older brother of her husband). All this was so spontaneous and natural that it left everybody with surprise. The man was Babu Ram Choubey, who was really the elder brother of Kedar Nath Choubey.

Shanti was asked to guide the tonga (a carriage drawn by a horse) from the station to her house. Shanti correctly described changes that had taken place since her life as Lugdi and she reached the house unaided.

There she recognized Lugdi's in-laws and her parents and other family members from among the crowd. Somebody from the crowd, who wanted to test Shanti, asked where the jajaroo was. Jajaroo was a word unknown to the Delhiites. Shanti immediately and correctly pointed towards the toilet.

Someone else asked the meaning of the word 'katora'. Shanti correctly responded by saying that it meant "parantha" (a type of fried pancake). It is significant to note that barring the Chaubey community of Mathura, everywhere else in India the word means a 'bowl'.

When asked about the money she had hidden, Shanti took the party to the second floor and showed them a spot where they found a flowerpot, but no money. The committee wrote:

> She cast her eyes around and put her foot in a corner, saying that the money lay hidden underneath the spot. The spot was dug up and about a foot deep under the spot an old-fashioned 'galla' – an arrangement for keeping valuables under ground – was found but there was no money.
>
> The girl would not believe; somewhat later on we learned that the money [about 150 Rupees] was taken out by Lugdi's husband Pandit Kedar Nath Choubey after her death.

When Shanti was taken to Lugdi's parents' home, at first she identified her aunt as her mother, but soon corrected her mistake. She also recognized her father. The mother and the daughter wept openly at their meeting. It was a scene that moved everybody there. Shanti Devi was then taken to Dwarkadhish temple and to other places she had talked of earlier and almost all of her statements were verified.

The publication of the committee's report attracted worldwide attention. Many learned personalities, including scholars, writers, psychologists, saints, parapsychologists, and philosophers came to study the case – some in support and some as critics trying to prove a hoax.

A prominent writer of that time, Saint Nihal Singh, expressed a desire to examine Shanti personally, and Shanti Devi was taken to Mathura once more; this time with no publicity. The party reached Mathura on April 2nd, 1936. She was taken to a small garden of which she had talked earlier, but which had not been covered on the first trip. Again, most of Shanti's statements were found to be correct.

Shanti was keen to go to her house. Afterwards, she was taken to Vrindaban, a religious place nearby, where she confidently identified different places and described some of the details. These were found to tally, with few exceptions. For example, she said that the floor was covered with red and white tiles, while they were actually black and white.

An effort was made to confuse her, but she did not fall into the trap. When she recognized a particular temple there, someone said that it was not; for some time she was puzzled and doubtful but later, as they neared it, she was insistent and was proven correct.

In February 1936 a rationalist and a hard-core disbeliever of reincarnation, Mr. B.C. Nahata met Shanti Devi and wrote a small booklet expressing his doubts and pleaded against the case.

On April 13, 1936 she was hypnotically regressed by Prof. Jagdish Mitra in the presence of some other prominent people. As a result of this, some incidents between the death of Lugdi and the birth of Shanti came to light and are available in a report of the hypnotic session presented by Dr. Begg. This report has some interesting features such as how Lugdi is taken to God and how she is brought back as Shanti.

Dr. K.S. Rawat met Shanti first in 1986. He interviewed her in detail about her past life memories and her recollections of Mathura. He also interviewed her younger brother Virash Narain Mathur who had accompanied her on her first visit. Then he went to Mathura and asked her various relatives to describe when Shanti Devi first visited them at the age of nine. He also interviewed a close friend of Kedar Nath, Pt. Ramnath Choube, who gave him some explicit information about the way Kedar Nath became convinced that Shanti was actually his wife in her past life.

Some of the strong features of this case are:

1. At least 15 statements made by Shanti *before* she was taken to Mathura or met any member of Lugdi's family were found to be correct on verification by the committee. For example her putting about 150 rupees in the corner of her room, the place of a well in the courtyard of the house, etc.

2. Shanti's behaviour towards the husband and other relatives of her alleged past life was in complete harmony with the tradition of her culture. Not only that, she did not utter the name of her husband (a Hindu wife traditionally is not supposed to utter the name of her husband) until she was almost forced to do so when her grand uncle insisted that

unless she let him know the name he would not take her to Mathura.

When she saw Kedar Nath for the first time "she evinced great fondness for 'her son' ... showing motherly affection" (Committee report, Pp. 6). On reaching Mathura station she not only recognized Kedar Nath's elder brother correctly but also touched his feet in reverence as is customary among Hindus in India. She did the same on meeting her father-in-law.

3. As very commonly found in many other cases and quite in accordance to the law of memory, Shanti recalled many incidents when she found herself in the familiar surroundings of her past life. Dr. Indra Sen, a prominent philosopher and a scholar deeply interested in psychology who was perhaps the first one to study the case scientifically, wrote in an article: "I have observed that when she finds herself in the circumstance of memory associated with her previous life she assumes such a seriousness which is usually not found in children". (*Kumari Shanti Devi and reincarnation*; Chitrapat (a Hindi magazine), July 4, 1936, translation by Dr. Rawat.)

4. When someone, trying to test her, asked the meaning of the words 'jajaroo' and 'katora', she could give correct answers even though the usage of those words was unique to an area she had never visited before.

5. At least some of Shanti's personality features corresponded with that of Lugdi: both of them were highly religious and strictly vegetarian. Shanti's being vegetarian was of special importance because it was unusual for the Kayasthas, the community to which she belonged, who are in general non-vegetarians.

6. At the age of six she described the complicated caesarean section performed on Lugdi and, as a girl of only nine, could describe the exact position of the intercourse which she had with Kedar Nath in order to conceive a child.

Dr. Rawat's last interview with Shanti Devi was four days before her death, on December 27th, 1987 (this last interview with Shanti Devi was recorded on videocassette).

As is true for all alleged cases of reincarnation, Shanti's case is not foolproof. It is important that people who investigate such episodes are fully conversant with the scientific methods of research. Fortunately, Dr. Indra Sen was such a person. In his paper presented to the Indian Philosophical Congress in 1938, he mentioned that he could not continuously observe the girl and had to depend on others for information. Further, Shanti's case had received so much publicity from the very beginning that it was difficult to determine which statements were her own and which of them were based on the information supplied by others directly or indirectly. Lastly, as has been mentioned earlier, there are some discrepancies in her statements.

At the same time we have also to keep in mind that Shanti had never been to Mathura before the committee took her there. After reaching there, she independently recognized numerous people from her past life, a fact that cannot be overlooked. Some memories of hers were revived when she visited the familiar places during her visit. For example, during Dr. Rawat's visit to Mathura, Lugdi's brother told him that Shanti, after seeing certain women there, remembered old friends and enquired about them.

Similarly, Lugdi's sister informed him that Shanti told a number of womenfolk about Lugdi having lent them some money, which they confirmed. Shanti's emotional reactions on meeting relatives from her previous life were very significant. The manner in which she burst into tears on meeting the parents of her past life moved everyone present there.

The committee mentioned in their report that it was a blessing that past lives are forgotten: "We confess we had taken a grave responsibility on our shoulder in bringing the girl to Muttra (sic). We had to snatch her away from her parents and without waiting for further inquiries we had to leave the place". (Pp. 14-15).

During Dr. Rawat's investigations a friend of Kedar Nath, 72-year-old Pt. Ramnath Choubey told him of a very significant event which he could confirm from other sources. When Kedar Nath was in Delhi to meet Shanti he stayed at Pt. Ramnath Choubey's place for one night.

Everyone had gone to bed and only Kedar Nath, his wife, his son Navneet and Shanti were in the room. Navneet was asleep. Kedar Nath asked Shanti how she became pregnant if she was suffering from arthritis and could not even walk and get up. Shanti, hardly nine years old, described the whole process of sexual intercourse with him, which left Kedar Nath in no doubt that Shanti was his wife Lugdi in her previous life. When Dr. Rawat mentioned this incident during his interview with Shanti Devi she immediately said "Yes, that is what fully convinced him".

Shanti Devi's case is also significant for the fact that it is one of the most thoroughly investigated cases, studied by hundreds of researchers, critics, scholars, saints and eminent public figures from all parts of India and abroad from the mid-1930s on.

One critic, Sture Lönnerstrand, when he heard of this case, came all the way from Sweden to expose the 'fake' as he thought it to be, but after investigation wrote: "This is the only fully explained and proven case of reincarnation there has been". We may not completely agree with Lönnerstrand on that point, however we would like to finish this account with Dr. Ian Stevenson's words:

> I also interviewed Shanti Devi, her father, and other pertinent witnesses, including Kedar Nath, the husband claimed in her previous life. The accounts available to me indicate that Shanti Devi made at least 24 statements of her memories, which matched the verified facts.

The Case of Swarnlata Mishra

Swarnlata or Swarn Lata Mishra was born on March 2, 1948, in Shahpur, District Tikamgarh, Madhya Pradesh, of India. When she was about three and a half years old, her family lived in Panna, also in Madhya Pradesh. Her father took her with him on a trip to Jabalpur, one of the leading cities of the state and almost three hundred kilometres away. On their return journey she unexpectedly asked the driver of the truck they were in to turn down a road toward "my house" in the city of Katni, where they would stop for tea.

Katni is about 160 kms from their home city of Panna. Swarnlata said they could obtain much better tea at "her" house nearby. Later on, she related more details to her siblings, which her father noted down on Dr. Rawat and Pandit Ramnath Choubey's (Chaubey) piece of paper. The following statements made by Swarnlata were recorded in Chhattarpur prior to any contact between her family (Mishra) and the family of her alleged past life (Pathak):

1. She belonged to a family named Pathak in Katni.
2. She had two sons.
3. The names of her sons were Krishna Datta and Shiva Datta.
4. Her own name was Bindiya (or, *Binda*) (though Ian Stevenson mentions the name as *Biya*).
5. The head of the family was Hira Lal Pathak.
6. Their house was white.
7. Their house had four stuccoed rooms.
8. Other parts of the house were less finished.
9. The doors were black.
10. They were fitted with iron bars.
11. The front door of the house was of stone slabs.
12. They had a motor car (not common).
13. There was a girls' school behind the house.
14. A railway line could be seen from the house.
15. There were lime furnaces visible from the house.
16. Her family lived in Zhurkutia Mohalla.
17. She had pain in her throat.
18. She died of a throat disease.
19. Dr. S.C. Bhabrat of Napiertown, Jabalpur had treated her.
20. She had once gone to a wedding at a village called Tilora.
21. She had gone there with Srimati Agnihotri.
22. They had had difficulty in finding a latrine.

Of these statements some were actually found to be incorrect at verification, such as her own name (close but not exactly the same), the name of Bindiya's father, which actually was Sri Chhikori Lal Pathak. Also, although Bindiya had indeed had some trouble in her throat, she actually died of heart disease, which she may not have been aware of. After meeting the previous family, Swarnlata uttered some additional statements, such as that her husband had taken 1200 rupees from a box in which she had kept money, and that she had had gold fillings in her front teeth.

In 1958, Swarnlata, whose family had by this time moved to Chhattarpur, met the wife of Prof. R. Agnihotri, who came from the area of Katni and whom Swarnlata claimed to recognize from having known her during the previous life in that city. The following year, when Swarnlata was 10 years old, news of the case reached Mr. H.N. Banerjee. Banerjee based his research on the notes her father had made (of some nine statements made by Swarnlata) and journeyed to Katni to determine if Swarnlata's memories could be verified.

Using nothing more than the description that Swarnlata had given, Banerjee found the house, despite the fact that the house had been enlarged and improved since 1939 when Bindiya died. It belonged to the Pathaks, a wealthy and prominent family with extensive business interests.

The lime furnaces were on land adjoining the property; the girls' school was behind the Pathak's property, but not visible from in front.

Mr. Banerjee interviewed the family and verified everything Swarnlata had said. Bindiya Pathak had died in 1939 leaving behind a grieving husband, two young sons, and many younger brothers.

The Pathaks had never heard of the Mishra family (who lived over a hundred kilometres away) and the Mishra's also had no knowledge of the Pathaks, despite their prominence.

In the summer of 1959, Bindiya's husband, son and eldest brother journeyed to the town of Chhatarpur, the town where Swarnlata now lived, to test Swarnlata's memory. They did not reveal their identities or purpose to others in the town, but enlisted some townsmen to accompany them to the Mishra home, where they arrived unannounced.

Swarnlata immediately recognized "her" brother and called him "Babu," Bindiya's pet name for him. She went round the room looking at each man in turn; some she identified as men she knew from her town, some were strangers to her. Then she came to Sri Chintamini Pandey, Bindiya's husband. Swarnlata lowered her eyes, as Hindu wives learn to do in the presence of their husbands, and spoke his name. She also correctly identified her son from her past life, Murli, who was only 13 years old when Bindiya died.

Murli was naturally reluctant to accept that this girl, so much younger than himself, could be his late mother, and he schemed to mislead her. For over a day insisted against her objections that he was not Murli, but someone else. Murli had also brought along a friend and tried to fool Swarnlata once again by insisting that he was Naresh, Bindiya's other son. Swarnlata insisted just as strongly that he was a stranger. Finally, Swarnlata reminded Sri Pandey that he had purloined 1200 rupees Bindiya kept in a box. Sri Pandey admitted to the truth of this private fact that only he and his wife had known.

A few weeks later, Swarnlata's father took her to Katni to visit the home and town where Bindiya lived and died. Upon arriving she noticed immediately and remarked on the changes to the house. She asked about the parapet at the back of the house, a verandah, and the neem tree that used to grow in the compound; all had been removed since Bindiya's death. She identified Bindiya's room and the room in which she had died.

She recognized one of Bindiya's brothers and identified him correctly as her second brother. She did the same for her third and fourth brother, the wife of the younger brother, and the son of the second brother, calling him by his pet name "Baboo". She identified accurately a close friend of the family – correctly commenting that he was now wearing new spectacles, and his wife, calling her by her pet name "Bhoujai". Swarnlata pointed out Bindiya's sister-in-law, a former servant, and an old betel nut seller, all with appropriate emotions, such as weeping and nervous laughter, as well as other emotions. She also identified correctly the family cowherd despite her youngest brother's testing Swarnlata by insisting that the cowherd had died.

Swarnlata was presented to a room full of strangers and asked whom else she recognized. She correctly picked out her husband's cousin, the wife of Bindiya's brother-in-law, and a midwife, whom she identified, not by her current name, but by a name Bindiya had used.

She also recalled that she had gold fillings in her front teeth – a fact that Bindiya's brothers had forgotten and were forced to confirm by consulting with their wives, who reminded them that what Swarnlata said was true.

In Maihar, the place where Bindiya had lived for much of her married life and where she died, Swarnlata recognized additional people and places and commented on various changes that had occurred after Bindiya's death. It is noteworthy that Swarnlata knew nothing about the Pathak's family history.

Swarnlata's behaviour was in accordance with that of Bindiya on several points. She behaved appropriately towards Bindiya's elders, but when alone with Bindiya's sons, she was relaxed and playful as a mother would be. This constitutes behaviour that would otherwise be totally inappropriate for a ten-year-old girl in the company of men in their mid-thirties who were unrelated to her. Obviously she was able to relate to these people as family even though they were not family of her present life. This substantiates that indeed she believed that she was among family.

The Pathak family came to accept Swarnlata as Bindiya reborn: so much so that the Pathak brothers and Swarnlata ritually observed the Hindu custom of Rakhi, in which brothers and sisters annually renew their devotion to each other, together. In fact the Pathak brothers were distressed and angry one year when Swarnlata missed the ceremony;

they felt that because she had lived with them for 40 years and with the Mishras for only 10 years that they had a greater claim on her.

The Pathaks admitted that they had changed their views of reincarnation upon meeting Swarnlata and accepting her as Bindiya reborn. Like many Hindu families of status and wealth, the Pathaks had emulated Western ideas and had not believed in reincarnation before this happened. Swarnlata's father, Sri Mishra, also accepted the truth of Swarnlata's past identity; years later, when it came time for Swarnlata to marry he consulted with the Pathaks about the choice of a husband for her.

Dr. Ian Stevenson visited Swarnlata in 1961 and corresponded with her for ten years after this case was investigated. He reports that she grew up normally, received an advanced degree in botany, and got married. She said that sometimes, when she reminisced about her happy life in Katni, her eyes brimmed with tears and, for a moment, she wished she could return to the wealth and life of Bindiya. But her loyalty to the Mishra family was undivided and, except for regular visits to Katni, she went about the business of growing into a beautiful young woman, accepting fully her station in this life.

A number of eminent reincarnation scholars around the world have studied the case of Swarnlata, including Dr Rawat.

When Dr. Rawat met Swarnlata in 1983, she was working as a lecturer and married to a local municipal commissioner named D.P. Tiwari in Indore (Madhya Pradesh, India). Dr. Rawat wrote at the time:

> Generally memories of past lives fade, as one grows older. To find out whether it was true with her, I inquired if she still remembered the previous lives. Srimati Tewari (Swarnlata's married name) is a lady with dignified and sober personality. She spoke softly and sweetly: 'I have very faint memories. I have remained in contact with those people and so the memories have survived.' Srimati Tewari has maintained the same relationship with her brothers of the past life. She joins them on different occasions of happiness and sorrows. [...]
>
> She ties the rakhi (a sacred thread of trust between brother and sisters) on Raksha Bandhan day (celebrated in India as Brother's Day). On being asked about her past life memories she informed me that these happened up to the time of her marriage in 1973 when she was 25 years old.
>
> About the reactions of her family on her relating the memories of her past life, Srimati Tewari said that nobody

believed them; and her brothers and sisters even made fun of her. Later her father's attitude changed, but the mother continued to oppose the idea, being afraid that she might lose her daughter because of the prevailing superstition that those who speak of past lives will die young.

It is natural that the recollections of memories of previous lives should have an impact on the personality of the people in their present life. Several instances have been seen in Western countries where people have not been able to adjust to their present personality.

Srimati Tewari is a mature and well-educated person and should, therefore, be able to judge such an effect on her personality. She informed me that she feels she belongs to the family of the past life when she is among them, while when she is with those of the present life; she thinks that the latter are her family. She is able to live a well-adjusted life at both places.

Dr. Rawat wanted to find out if Swarnlata had any extraordinary powers of perception. In response to his question, Swarnlata told him that she had had such faculties from the very beginning. Quite often, even in waking state, she would get hunches, and sometimes she gained knowledge in dreams. Dr. Rawat asked her specifically if she got such inklings in the past to which she replied in the affirmative. On being asked to narrate some examples, Srimati Tewari told him that one night she dreamt that her brother had lost his bicycle at Satna. Later, she learned through a letter that it was so. About a week later, she dreamt that her brother recovered the bicycle from near a pond. This was also confirmed to have happened. Srimati Tewari, narrating another incident of precognition, said that eight years before her marriage, she repeatedly saw a particular house in her dreams. After her marriage, she came to the same house.

What is quite remarkable about this case, apart from the affectionate and cooperative relationships between the two families, is that Swarnlata's memories have persisted into her adulthood and that Bindiya's life, as Swarnlata had not ended in a traumatic death. While some would say this case has the hallmarks of a person suffering from multiple personality, the fact that both families are involved makes this possibility much reduced. We might imagine that her memories are strengthened and her personality stabilized by their interest and acceptance of the situation.

The Mishra and Pathak families firmly denied any acquaintance with each other prior to their meeting in connection with the verification of Swarnlata's statements. Although the Mishra family did journey from Panna or Chhattarpur to Jabalpur from time to time, the two groups had no contact, and it is not conceivable that Swarnlata picked up intimate details about the Pathak family such as those of the interior of their house.

Swarnlata also made statements of a much more fragmentary nature about another life, which she believed she had lived *subsequent* to the life as Bindiya in Katni. She stated that after she died (as Bindiya), she was reborn as one Kamlesh in Sylhet, Assam (now in Bangladesh) and that in that life she died as a child of about nine and was then reborn in the Mishra family. Some of the statements concerning this life do, indeed, accord with the geography and other facts of Sylhet. It has not yet been possible, however, to identify a particular child of this area whose life corresponds with the sparse details given by Swarnlata.

When her family lived in Nowgong, the five or six-year-old Swarnlata performed for her mother, and then in front of others as well, unusual dances and songs, which she had no opportunity to learn in her current life. These songs and dances seemed to belong to the aforementioned life in Sylhet. The language of the songs was identified as Bengali by Prof. Pal, who transcribed some of them for further study. Sylhet is in a Bengali-speaking area whereas Madhya Pradesh, where Swarnlata was born and has lived, is a Hindi-speaking area.

Swarnlata always performed the songs and dances together, never one without the other. It was as if she had learned them together and could not separate them from each other.

Professor Pal managed to trace two of the songs and dances to poems by Rabindranath Tagore. The third song, also definitely Bengali, was by an unidentified poet. The poems by Tagore were *Poush Toder Daik Diyecche* (a harvest song) and *Ore Grihabasi, Khol Duar Khol* (a spring song). Professor Pal once attended a performance of the second song in Visva-Bharati, an institution founded by Tagore, and he noted that the tune was "very much the same" as that of the song performed by Swarnlata. He also observed that the Swarnlata's dances accompanying the spring song were of the Shantiniketan style, which he had himself observed during his visit to the Visva-Bharati.

Swarnlata claimed that she had learned the songs and dances from a friend, Madhu, during her previous life as Kamlesh. Professor Pal learned that, before the partition of India, some of the children of well-to-do families in Sylhet had studied at the Visva-Bharati in Santiniketan, West Bengal (India).

The fact that Swarnlata performed in Bengali is difficult to explain without reincarnation: The Mishras owned no phonograph or radio until Swarnlata was about eight years old – that is, until about three years after her first performance of the songs and dances. She had also never been to a moving picture theatre before that, as far as her father knew. Even if she had been, it is unlikely that she would have seen a Bengali movie. Bengali movies are only rarely shown in Hindi-speaking areas of India. And a five-year-old would be unlikely to completely memorize and mimic complex foreign songs and dances perfectly at a single showing.

Dr. Ian Stevenson concludes about these songs and dances that they are "skills and skills can only be acquired by practice. My own conclusion is that Swarnlata's songs and dances belong to the paranormal components of the case and are among its strongest features".

This is the transcription made by Professor Pal of one of the songs written by Tagore together with the original version of the poems and an English translation in prose furnished by Professor Pal:

Original Poem by Tagore	**As sung by Swarnlata**
Poush Toder Dak Diyechhe, Ay Re Chale	Posheta Dak Diyechhe Ayre Chute
Ay Ay Ay	Ay Ay Ay
Dala Je Tar Bharechhe Aj Paka Fasale,	Dala Ji Aj Bharachhi Tay Paka Fasale
Mari Hay Hay Hay	Ki Mari Hay Hay Hay
Haowar Nesay Uthla Mete Dik Badhura Dhaner Khete	Haoyer Nishay Uth Na Mithel Dekhbo Mora Dhaner Shishe
Roder Sona Chhariye Pare Matir Anchale,	Roda Sona Chhariya Pare Ajio Chhale
Mari Hay Hay Hay	Ki Mari Hay Hay Hay
	Note: Swarnlata sang this verse out of sequence, at the end of the song.

Mather Bansi Shune Shune Akas	Mathe Bansi Shune Shune Akas
Khusi Holo	Kesi Holo
Gharete Aj Ke Rabe Go, Kholo	Gharethe Ma Ke Elo Balo Kholo
	Kholo
Duar Kholo	Duar Kholo Kholo Duar Kholo
Alor Hansi Uthlo Jege Dhaner	
Sishe Sisir Lege	
Dharar Khusi Dhare Na Go, Ai Je	
Uthale	
Mari Hay Hay Hay	

English translation of the song based on a poem by Tagore[14]:

Poush (the tenth month of the Hindu calendar) calls you.
Come away,
Come, Come, Come.

Her basket is overflowing with ripe grains. Oh, Oh, Oh.
The fairies are revelling in the paddy fields, intoxicated with the
wintry breeze. The golden sunbeams have spread over the skirt
of the earth Look how beautiful it is.
The sky is delighted hearing the notes of the field flutes.

Who would stay indoors today? Unbolt your door.
The smile of the sunbeams is kindled in the dewdrops on the
sheaves of the paddy.
The earth is overflowing with joy. Oh, Oh, Oh.

Stevenson quotes Professor Pal about Swarnlata's deviations from Tagore's poems:

Some of the words are blurred, modified or changed by Swarnlata, though the sound, meter, and tune are maintained fairly intact, just as would happen to someone who does not understand English, but learns an English song sung by an English singer from his singing (*Twenty Cases Suggestive of Reincarnation*, p. 85).

---

[14] Ian Stevenson does not consider the possibility that Tagore's poem was based on another popular song.

If we compare the words of the poem with the song sung by Swarnlata we note that many of them seem to appear in both, for example Fasale or Kholo Duar Kolo, though sometimes pronounced wrongly (Kesi in stead of Khusi, Haoyer instead of Haowar). The order of the sentences seems to have been changed by Swarnlata, but it seems that the song is derived from the Tagore poem.

Dr. Rawat also recorded one of the songs. Swarnlata told him that she did not distinctly remember the Bengali life in detail, but she still remembered the Bengali songs. He writes: "At my request she sang one of them. Its pleasant melody is still ringing in my ears".

Photo copy of historial case.
Recorded in the time of
Emperor Aurangzeb. Written in
Persian language.

Report in Persian about a case, which occurred during the
reign of Mughal emperor Aurangzeb.

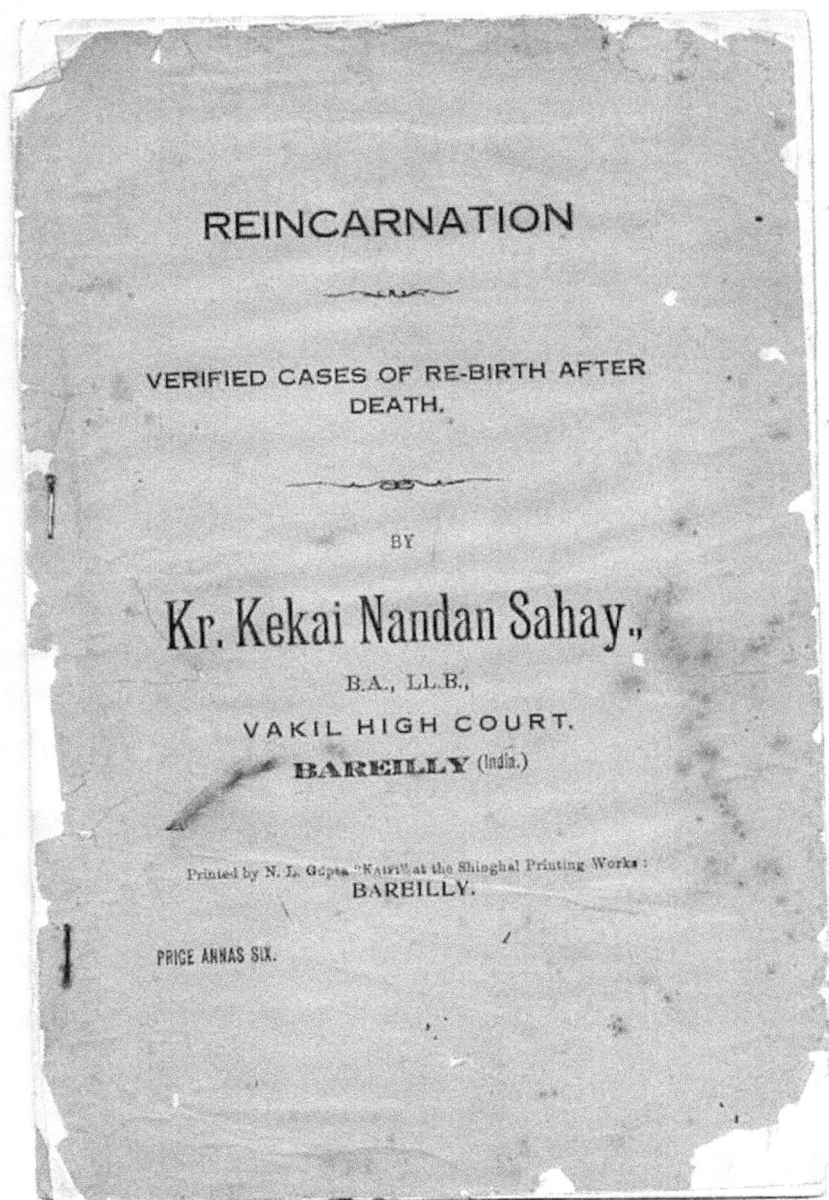

Booklet by K.K.N. Sahay of 1927, entitled
Reincarnation: Verified Cases of Re-birth after Death.

Titus Rivas with his dog Moortje

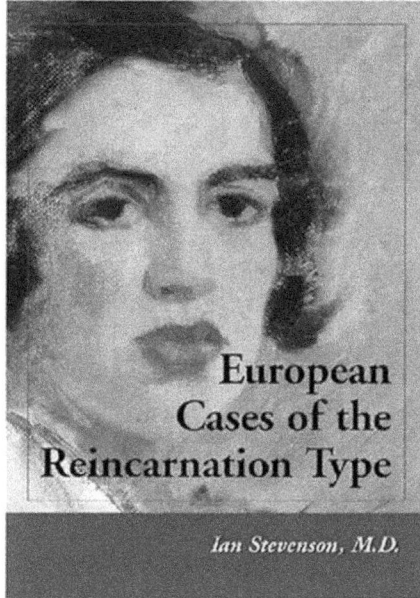

European
Cases of the
Reincarnation Type

Ian Stevenson, M.D.

Painting by Henriette Weisz-Roos

Shanti Devi with the Committee
of Inquiry,Mathura 1935

Kamini Kapoor with Dr. Rawat

Dr. Rawat with Jagdish Chandra

Dr. Rawat with Pandith Ramnath Choube

Swarn Lata Mishra

The house in which Henny tragically died during a fire

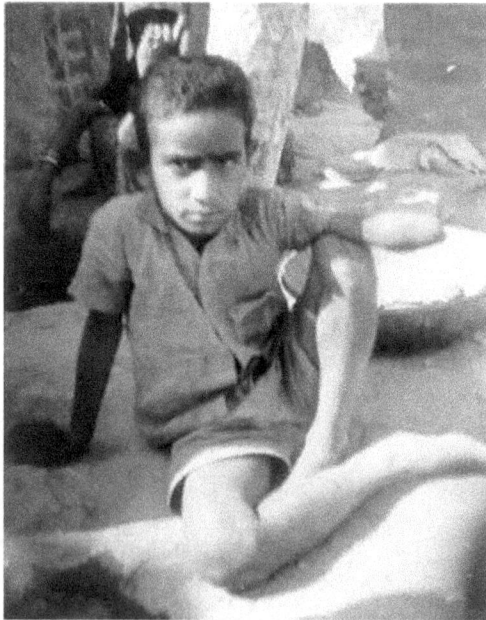

Neera

Dr. Rawat with Roda

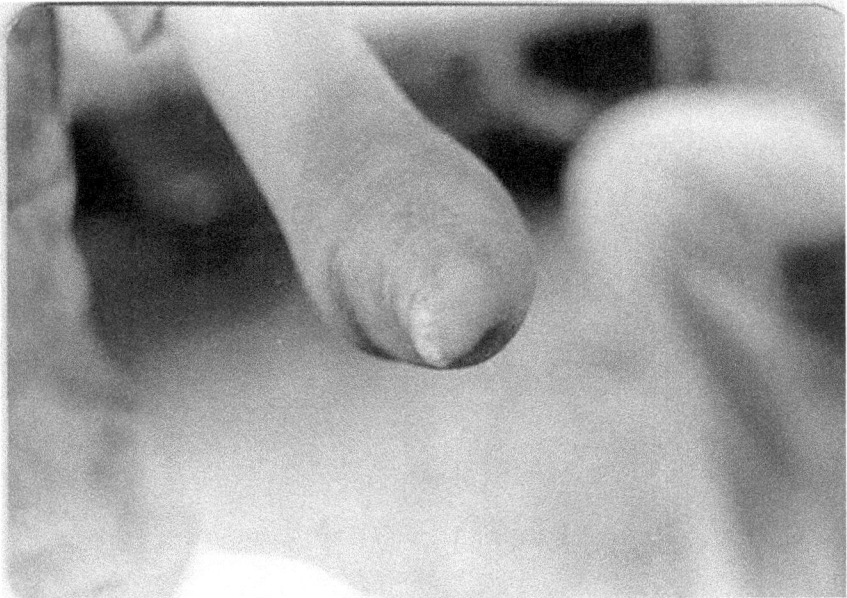

Closeup of Neera's arm

Titanic

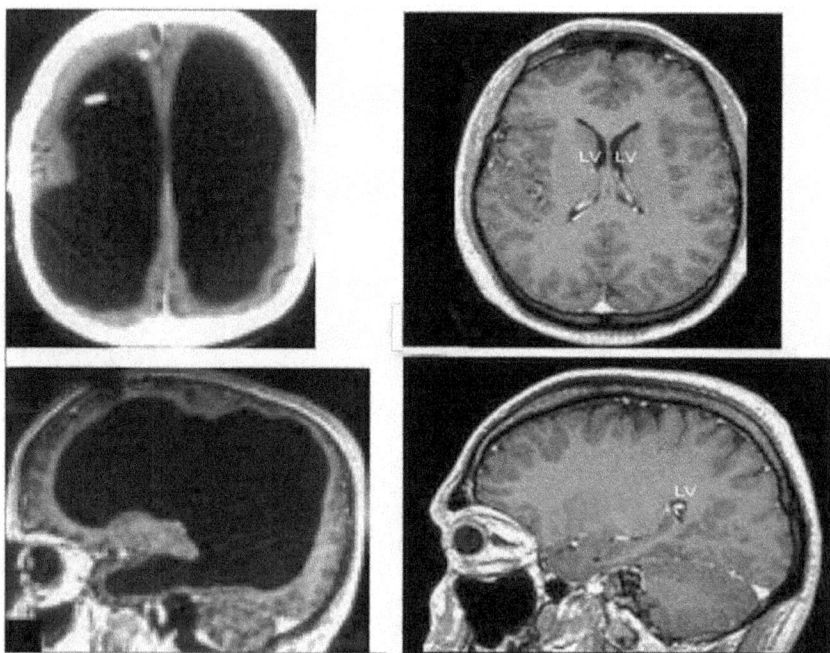

The brain of a French patient (left) with a condition similar to that of the patients studied by John Lorber.

Laxmi recalled six lifetimes

Dr. Rawat and Radha

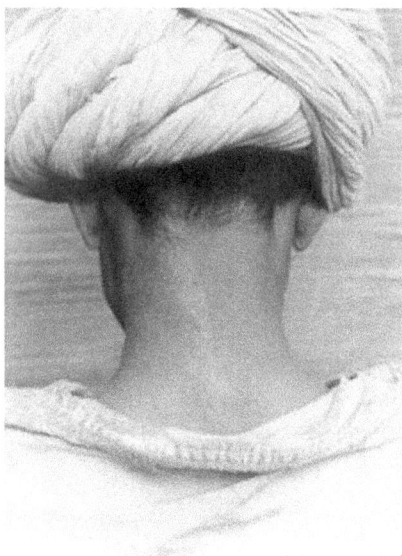

Suwa's birthmark

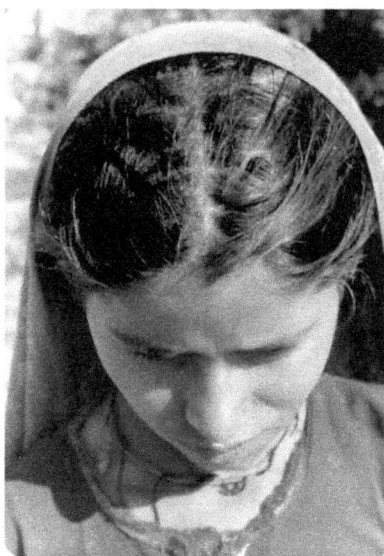

Radha's birthmark (forehead)

Experimental birthmark

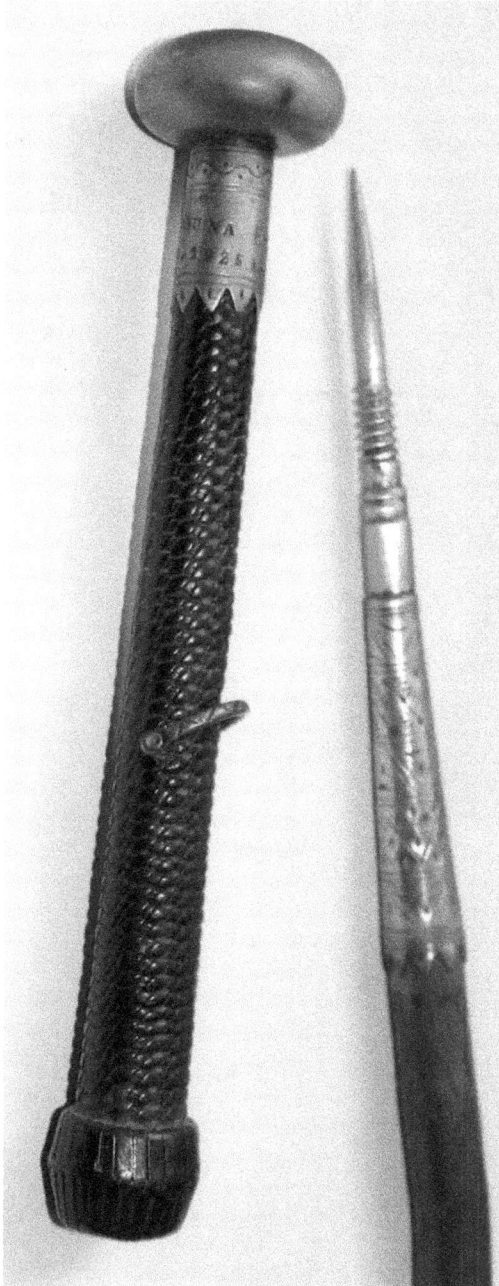

Makila

Anny Dirven

4

MORE RECENT CASES OF SPONTANEOUS RECALL BY CHILDREN

~

The Case of Kumkum Verma

Kumkum Verma was born on March 14, 1955 in Bahera about 40 kms from the city of Darbhanga (Bihar, India). Her father was Dr. B.K. Verma, a farmer and homeopathic physician.

At the age of three and a half, she began speaking of a previous life in Urdu Bazar, Darbhanga. She described in great detail her life at Urdu Bazar, and especially mentioned "her son" Misri Lal and grandson Gouri Shankar. Kumkum seemed almost in a trance when she talked of this previous life.

She would sometimes say: "Call me Sunnari". Because the word "sunnary" means "beautiful," her family at first thought she wanted to be called beautiful. However, as they learned later, she was instead referring to the name of her claimed past life.

She found willing listeners in her grandmother and in her uncle's wife, Swarna Probha Verma. Swarna Probha Verma lived with the family for a time, while Kumkum was still three years old and made written notes of details Kumkum mentioned about the previous life.

Kumkum's family resisted taking Kumkum to Urdu Bazar. She had already shown strong emotions at times in talking about the previous life, and some family members were afraid she might become ill, and perhaps even die if she met her previous personality's relations.

Eventually, in 1959, Dr. B.K. Verma, Kumkum's father, told a friend who lived in Darbhanga and was a senior official of the Darbhanga Raj Estate about Kumkum's statements. Their friend Harish Chandra Mishra decided to look into the matter. After some enquiries one of his employees found and brought Gouri Shankar's father, the blacksmith Misri Lal Mistry, to him. Misri Lal verified that everything Kumkum had said about her life in Urdu Bazar was correct.

Both of her statements and her behaviour corresponded closely with facts in the life of his mother, Sundari, who had died in Darbhanga about 1950, some five years prior to Kumkum's birth.

Dr.Verma never allowed Kumkum to go to Urdu Bazar to meet her previous family. However, he himself went there in 1961. He met members of the family and photographed objects and people whom Kumkum might recognize.

An account of this case appeared in the newspaper *Indian Nation*, of Patna, Bihar, on March 5, 1961. In October 1963, Professor P. Pal studied the case and he wrote a long report of his interviews. Thereafter, Drs. Ian Stevenson, Jamuna Prasad and L.P. Mehrotra also investigated the case. Kumkum made at least eighteen statements that were recorded in a notebook by her aunt. Dr. Stevenson obtained an English translation of only parts of her notes and he was unable to borrow the original notebook, since it had been loaned to someone and not returned.

These 18 statements were recorded before verification and being translated into English:

1. She ("Sunnari" – Kumkum's previous incarnation) lived in Urdu Bazar.
2. There was a pond at the house.
3. She paid the workers, who dug out the pond with spades and carried the earth in bamboo baskets.
4. There was an iron safe at her home.
5. The safe was at the northern side of the house.
6. She had a sword hanging near her bed.
7. A snake with a hood lived near the iron safe.
8. She fed the snake milk and "zalli" [an unknown word].
9. Her father lived at Bajitpur.

10. To reach her father's place, it was necessary to cross water.
11. There were mango orchards near her father's place.
12. Her son was called Misri Lal.
13. Her son Misri Lal worked with a hammer.
14. She had two daughters-in-law.
15. Her grandson was called Gouri Shankar.
16. She gave the red coloured bed to her older son when he married.
17. Her daughters-in-law cooked parval and tilkar (Indian vegetables) for her.
18. She observed Ekadasis (Hindu days of fasting) and Sundays.

In total, she made 56 statements about circumstances, belongings, relatives and events that corresponded to the life of Sundari. Of these only nine were unverifiable; the other 47 statements were found to be correct, although some of them were not specific and could apply to many places, especially in the Darbhanga area.

Dr. Stevenson comments on the distribution of Kumkum's statements over different themes:

> She was never reported to have mentioned Sundari's second son, Shiv Nandan, or his two sons. She talked only of Misri Lal and his son, Gouri Shankar. Sundari is known to have preferred Misri Lal and his wife to her other son and daughter-in-law and also to have preferred Gouri Shankar to her other grandsons. In addition, Kumkum mentioned Sundari's second husband only once, in connection with an allegation that he had poisoned her. These omissions of Sundari's husbands from Kumkum's preoccupations accord with what we might have expected from inferences concerning their place in Sundari's life.

Along with these statements, and her possible recognition of Gouri Shankar when he visited her in Bahera, Kumkum used dialect expressions typical of Urdu-speaking Muslims from Darbhanga. She also had a different accent from that of her family.

Dr. Stevenson draws attention to some similarities between the personality-traits of Kumkum Verma and Sundari. During her pregnancy with Kumkum, her mother Subhadra Verma dreamed of a girl child surrounded by snakes. Sundari had a rapport with snakes that enabled her to enjoy a cobra as pet, and Kumkum also had a special interest in snakes. Both of them were unusually religious, generous to others and interested in young children. Both also were very interested in snakes and showed a tendency to dominate others.

Commenting on the evidence of paranormal processes in this case, Dr. Stevenson writes:

> I feel confident that the two families in this case had no contact of which they were aware before Kumkum began talking of the previous life in Urdu Bazar ... Sundari led a relatively obscure life and her death was not even recorded, so far as I know, in the Municipal Register of Darbhanga. It is difficult to understand how events of her life could have become known normally to a small girl in a village 40 kilometres away. The difference in social class between the two families would have separated them as much as geographical distance or more.

The case of Kumkum Verma is important. First, because a written record of Kumkum's statements had been made six months before any attempt was made at verification. Secondly, a person who was not connected with either of the two families, Harish Chandra Mishra, made the first verifications. Third, Prof. Pal and Dr. Jamuna Prasad, independently of Dr. Stevenson, studied the case yet the information obtained by all the three investigators was substantially the same. We can safely conclude that the case is authentic and that there is no convincing normal explanation for it.

The Case of "Christina"

"Christina" K. (a pseudonym corresponding to her second Christian name) was born on February 24, 1979 in the village of Malden (Gelderland), the Netherlands. She died when she was seventeen years old after being struck by a car. Her death occurred before her memories could be fully investigated. Nonetheless, her case deserves serious consideration.

When Christina was about three years old she was afraid to go into the attic alone. She could not explain her fear. One Friday morning in 1982, when she was about three and a half, she was crying and told her mother she had had a nightmare. It was a dream about a different, big, white house with high windows, somewhere in a town. She knew she had a father and mother. She told her mother that they were very different from her. She also had more brothers and sisters than she had in the present life.

What she told her mother Hannie about her dream amounts to the following:

It was Easter. They were sitting at the table and her brother and sisters were quarrelling. Their parents had sent them to their rooms. Her younger brother had been playing with matches and his mattress appears to have caught fire. She ran to the balcony of her room and saw her mother and a fireman who shouted at her that she should jump. She simply was too frightened to do so, although one or two of her sisters did. The smoke overcame her.

A lady in white told her she had died and took her through the burning house. She was shown several possible mothers and asked to pick one of them. She chose a woman with blond hair who was typing at an office.

After this dream, Christina sometimes spoke about her recollections of the dream. Titus Rivas, investigating elements of the case after her early death, tried to find as many witnesses as possible, i.e. people she had told the dream to. He succeeded in tracing a cousin who remembered Christina's telling her about it when Christina was between eight and ten years old. Christina's sister also confirmed the main story line of the dream and the phobia she had felt for the attic. The position of the attic might be related to the position of her room seen in the dream.

Christina's mother Hannie K. told Rivas she had heard of and read about a story of a terrible fire in which several children had died, some years before Christina had been born, when she herself was still a teenager. Hannie is very certain however that she never shared her knowledge of the fire with her daughter.

The fire had taken place in Arnhem, so Hannie determined to test Christina by taking her to that town when she was 15. After having arrived at the central station, Christina led her mother straight to a white house and claimed to recognize it.

Rivas visited the municipal archives of Arnhem and found that on Easter 1973 there had been a fire as described by Christina. There were minor discrepancies between the archived version and her recollections but the dream generally accorded well with the historical events of this fire. One of the casualties of the family, which was afflicted by the catastrophe, was a girl of nine called Hendrika who died as a consequence of the smoke caused by the fire.

For several years, Rivas could not find any living relatives of this family. However, he soon established that Christina's mother had not made up the dream.

Various independent people, including Christina's best friend, Laura, testified to the fact that she really did have this dream long before her death. Finally, the age at which she had the dream is classic, as is her phobia.

The case became even stronger in 2007 when Anny Dirven, the main Dutch collaborator of Titus Rivas for Athanasia Foundation, was approached by living relatives of Hendrika who turned out to be known as Henny Brugman. They had read the first report of the case on the Internet.

Accompanied by Christina's mother, Rivas and Dirven finally met Henny's oldest brother, Joopie Brugman, at his home in Arnhem. They were also shown the house where the tragic fire of 1973 had taken place. Understandably, the family turned out to be very traumatized by the events and Joopie was the only family member who wanted to speak about his sister.

Although Joopie had not been present during the fire, he naturally had heard all about it and had attended the funeral. More importantly, Joopie did not believe in reincarnation when Hannie K., Rivas and Dirven met him. He really found it difficult to lend any credence to Christina's story.

Nevertheless, he did confirm several of Christina's statements about the tragedy, which were not included in newspaper articles. He also found it striking that Christina had talked almost exclusively about the mother of the previous life and not about her father. It turned out that his mother had remarried to Henny's stepfather who, according to Joopie, had brought a lot of hardship on the family. When asked to compare Hannie's description of her daughter's personality with that of his sister's, Joopie confessed that these traits were also characteristic of Henny:

Witty
Cheerful
Lively
Musically gifted
Spontaneous
Thoughtful
Intelligent

Compassionate
She was always willing to help others
She had many friends
She always took a lot of friends home

Perhaps one of the most interesting aspects of this case is Christina's vision of her mother. She saw her as a lady with blond hair who was typing at an office. It is remarkable that Christina's mother told Rivas that she remembered the fire at Arnhem as occurring somewhere during the late sixties. She thought that she might have been around 13 or 14 when it happened. The fire in the records actually took place in 1973, when Hannie was working at an office, and dyed her naturally darker hair blonde.

This level of detail excludes the possibility of conscious fraud and, together with the other features, suggests that Christina's is a classical case that falls within the standard pattern of reincarnation cases.

The Case of Sunita Khandelwal

Sunita Khandelwal was born on September 19, 1969 in Laxmangarh, District Alwar (Rajasthan, India). Her family belonged to the caste of Banias (businessmen). When Sunita was about two she first began to speak of a previous life. She asked her family to take her to Kota, at some 475 km and 17 hours by bus from Laxmangarh.

She told them that she had two brothers and no sister, and that her family owned a silver shop and a safe. Her family also owned a car and a scooter, and her mother had many saris. She had a *tau* (paternal uncle older than her father) but no *chacha* (paternal uncle younger than her father). She said that the river Chambal is at Kota. She added that she had fallen down "from a small height".

She also pointed to the birthmark on her head saying: "Look here. I have fallen". Her parents continued to ignore Sunita's pleas to be taken to Kota, but by the time she was three she was refusing to eat unless she was taken there and she became so malnourished that they took her to a hospital.

Dr. Behari Lal, the family's physician recalled a time when Sunita became ill with grief over not being taken to Kota. "I found the girl extremely agitated and disturbed when she was brought to me by her father," he said. "I advised (her father) to make the journey to Kota to pacify her. He refused my advice, but brought Sunita to me several times for treatment".

Sunita told Banerjee that her father used to take her out on a scooter, and that he would often go to his big iron safe in his store where he kept the silver coins. She used to drink a lot of milk in her previous life, and her parents took her every year to a fair near their home in Kota. When she lived in Kota her mother made "narangi ka sag" by crushing tangerines into juice, then throwing pieces of tangerine into a pot of melted sugar and adding some spices. Banerjee knew that, "narangi ka prasad" was made only by the Hindu devotional sect called Vaishnev who use the preparation for offerings during religious ceremonies. In Laxmangarh "narangi ka prasad" is virtually unknown.

Sunita added: "We also ate 'bijou ki barfi'. It was very sweet and my mother made it from milk and sugar. She would put in peeled cantaloupe seeds". Banerjee knew that this food is also typical for the Vaishnev sect and not usually eaten in Laxmangarh.

To end her stubbornness, her family pretended to take her to Kota. They took her to Jaipur and told her it was Kota. Sunita replied: "This is not Kota. This is Jaipur. You are telling lies and will be punished". Later she added that the shop in Kota was in Chauth Mata Bazaar and the house was in Brijrajpura.

She did not mention any personal names but stated that she was a Bania, just as she was in the present life. Her paternal grandfather was living, but her paternal grandmother had died. Upon being questioned further, she said: "My cousin pushed me down the stairs because I had asked for water. I have come here to drink water". She also said that she had been a girl and died at the age of eight.

Only when Sunita was already about five years old, did Kranti Modi, a lawyer and friend of the family, send a summary of Sunita's statements to H. N. Banerjee in Jaipur. He came to Laxmangarh and established a comfortable rapport with Sunita.

According to Banerjee she told him that she had died at the age of seven as a result of an injury to the right side of her head. She also described vividly how she had fallen from a great height. Her mother told Banerjee: "Sunita is always telling me that I am not her real mother and continually pleads with her father and me to take her to Kota and threatens that if we don't take her soon she will fall from the roof and die as she did in her former life".

The family was finally persuaded they should all go to Kota. Sunita became exuberant. When they almost reached Kota, Sunita was visibly excited when looking out of the window of the bus.

In Kota a relative of Banerjee's, Pratap Singh, took Banerjee and his research associate, Margit Fedoruk, to a clock tower at a main crossroads of the town. From that tower there are roads that lead in different directions, one of which leads to Chauth Mata ka Bazar. Banerjee then decided to test Sunita to see if she could choose the correct road. Sunita started without hesitation to walk the road that led towards Chauth Mata ka Bazar. She paused before a store full of silver ornaments. Pratap Singh introduced Banerjee to the shop owner, whose name was Prabhu Dayal Maheshwari and Banerjee told him the details of Sunita's claims to a previous life in Kota.

It turned out that Prabhu Dayal had a daughter, Shakuntala, who died at the age of seven years and ten months after falling from an iron balcony at his house. He also confirmed that he had two older sons, and that Shakuntala had been extremely fond of milk and on many occasions she had watched her mother prepare "narangi ka prasad" for religious ceremonies and "bijou ki barfi," made from solidified milk mixed with cantaloupe seeds.

He further confirmed that his wife had many saris and that he kept many silver coins in a big iron safe in his silver shop. He also used to take Shankuntala for rides on his scooter, and every year he took her to a fair called Dol Geras held near his home. After some confusion on Sunita's path to her former home she led the party to an iron rod gate and said: "This is the door of my house," which Shankuntala's father confirmed.

Inside the house she could not identify her brothers or even her mother from the previous life. She did, however, point towards a photograph of Shakuntala and said: "This is my photograph". She also stated that there was one more house next door also belonging to the family, which was correct. In order to give Sunita an opportunity to recognize things from her previous life, Banerjee took her around the house. When they reached a balcony, she clutched him tightly in fear and said:

"I'm afraid I might fall down".

Shankuntala's mother told Banerjee: "It is from this balcony that my late daughter Shakuntala fell head-first. She died eight days later of a brain haemorrhage". Banerjee also discovered a large birthmark on the right side of her head that looks like the mark of a healed wound. It is located exactly where Shankuntala received her injury when she fell from the balcony of her parents' home.

All in all, Sunita made 34 statements about her previous life, of which only two were incorrect and three remained unverified. The first incorrect statement was that the family owned a car, which they did not. The second was that her father applied "mehandi" (henna) to her, a red dye sometimes used in a healing ritual. Not her father but her mother applied "mehandi" to both of Shakuntala's hands, a fairly common practice in India.

Banerjee consulted Professor Rajneesh Kumar Chaudhury, Professor of Statistics at Jawaharlal Nehru University in New Delhi, who established beyond a doubt that she could not have made her claims by chance guessing. He stated that the probability of the number of correct statements accurately being made by chance was less than one in a billion billion. More recently, Prof. Jim Deardorff proposed a similar assessment for all paranormal cases of the reincarnation type or CORTs.

Sunita was entirely comfortable and relaxed at Shakuntala's home in Kota. Her Hindi seemed to have more English words than that of other members of the family. This corresponds to the fact that Shakuntala's family was more well to do and therefore used more English loan words used mostly for objects invented and developed in the nineteenth and twentieth century. She also referred to vegetables with the word "sabzi," whereas her family used the word "bhaji". Shakuntala's family did indeed use the word "sabzi".

In 1975 Dr. Satwant Pasricha also studied the case. Dr. Ian Stevenson first studied the case in March 1979. They particularly wanted to find out if Sunita's statements could also refer to another person. The hospital records in Kota did not give a conclusive answer to that question, but they did increase Dr. Stevenson's confidence that no other child in Kota could have fitted Sunita's statements as well as Shakuntala did.

Dr. K.S. Rawat studied the case in 1986 and again in 1997. He was informed that some of the personality traits in Sunita resemble those of Shakuntala. Her brother Ram Babu Khandelwal told him that the members of Shakuntala's family still treat Sunita as one of them and invite her to all the functions and celebrations of the family. Interestingly, he also told him that the parents of Shakuntala had once offered lakhs of rupees (quite a huge sum) in exchange for Sunita. Sunita's parents politely declined the offer.

The two families in this case had never met before the case had developed. Although Shakuntalal's father Prabhu Dayal had previously known Sunita's maternal uncle Radhey Shyam, a jeweller, he had never been to his house. The records of the M.B.S. Hospital in Kota showed that after Shakuntala fell from the balcony she was unconscious, vomiting and bleeding from her right ear.

The birthmark on Sunita's head is located to the right parietal area (parietal = pertaining to the "wall" of the skull). The mark is approximately round in shape with irregular edges and about 2.5 cms in diameter. Oddly, it was bleeding when she was born, and only stopped after 3 days.

The Case of Gnanatilleka Baddewithana

Gnanatilleka was born on February 14, 1956 near Hedunawewa in central Sri Lanka (or Ceylon as it was known then). When she was one year old she began to speak, talking about another mother and father. She was two when she uttered her first specific statements about her previous life, such as her claim that she had two brothers and many sisters.

After hearing about villagers there, who had been to the nearby town of Talawakele, she said she wanted to visit her former parents, and gave further details of the location of her former home and names of members of her family. Two investigators from the town of Kandy heard about the case, the Venerable Piyadassi Thera and Mr. H.S.S. Nissanka. They were able to identify a family in Talawakele that corresponded with the statements Gnanatilleka had made. The family had lost a 14-year-old son called Tillekeratne.

Shortly afterwards Gnanatilleka was taken to Talawakele by her family. She correctly recognized a number of buildings there. She also directed her family to a place where there had used to be a house in which Tillekeratne had lived, but which had been torn down after his death. Later, three of Tillekeratne's schoolteachers visited Gnanatilleka. She recognized them appropriately and described in detail certain aspects of and events occurring at the school.

Early in 1960, Gnanatilleka was once more brought to Talawakele where she accurately identified seven members of Tillekeratne's family and two other people of the community. From 1961 onward Dr. Stevenson also investigated the case.

Gnanatilleka made 34 statements and recognitions related to her previous life, 15 of which were made before the families had met. She gave very specific details such as mentioning that her father was a postman, and also recounted a Jataka (Buddhist) story which Tillekeratne's schoolteacher Mr D.V. Sumithapala had told him. All of the statements were correct and verified. Dr. Stevenson also found the recognitions important as they occurred spontaneously or after someone had asked her an open question about the person she recognized.

In 1966, Dr. Stevenson learned that while Gnanatilleka had been talking most actively about her past life, she had mentioned a sister Dora or Lora. The person was identified as Lora Almeda who had been a schoolmate of Tillekeratne. Lora was invited to accompany Dr. Stevenson's team on an unannounced visit to Hedunawewa in 1970. By then Gnanatilleka was 15-years old and had identified her sister as "Dora".

Gnanatilleka also showed child-like behaviour that was appropriate for Tillekeratne. For example, when she was angry with her parents, she threatened to return to her "Talawakele mother". When Gnanatilleka recognized Tillekeratne's mother, she showed great affection for her and also for Tillekeratne's father. She showed a markedly greater affection for Tillekeratne's older sister Salinawathie than for his three other sisters and a distinct coolness toward his brother, Buddhadasa. These responses were entirely appropriate to the relationships of Tillekeratne because Salinawathie had been his favourite sister and Buddhadasa had been an unfriendly and sometimes hostile brother to him.

Gnanatilleka's behaviour toward the schoolteacher of her past life seemed strikingly appropriate as well. Mr Sumithapala appears to have taken a special interest in Tillekeratne. Sometimes Gnanatilleka's affection for him even surpassed that for her parents. Tillekeratne had developed a definite tendency toward feminine behaviour by the time he died and once he asked his schoolteacher if it was possible to change sex from one life to another. Gnanatilleka had shown a tendency toward masculine behaviour. Concerning the sex change, she said to her parents: "I was a boy. Now I am a girl". When Dr. Stevenson asked her about this, she told him that when she had been a boy, she had wished to be a girl.

Gnanatilleka preferred blue dresses and had said that she preferred blue in her previous life. Tillekeratne always liked blue and wore blue shirts. Tillekeratne was more religious than the average Singhalese boy in his past life and Gnanatilleka also showed a strong interest in religious beliefs and practices.

Tillekeratne seems to have had some visceral disease when he died. He suffered these injuries when he fell off a chair. They appear to have contributed to the terminal illness from which he died in a hospital one or two weeks later. Gnanatilleka had a noticeable fear of doctors and hospitals and did not like to climb on anything from which she might fall down.

About the paranormal processes in this case, Dr. Stevenson writes the following:

Gnanatilleka's home lay in the jungle, reached only by a tortuous footpath some half-mile (about 800m) distant from the village of Hedunawewa, which, as I have mentioned, was itself rather difficult to reach from the main road between Talawakele and Kotmale. Nobody would reach the house of Gnanatilleka's family unless they were intent on visiting them.

For inaccessibility, it would be difficult to plan or achieve a better location. I am confident therefore that no one from outside the village of Hedunawewa itself (and probably no one in the village) could have reached the home and talked with Gnanatilleka without her family knowing of the visit. (Ian Stevenson, *Twenty Cases*, Pp. 133.)

Thus, Stevenson concludes that if we accept her parent's statement that they were not visited by anyone from Talawakele prior to the verification process, Gnanatilleka must have acquired the detailed information she had about Tillekeratne and his family and life in a paranormal way.

The Case of Imad Elawar

Imad Elawar was a Druze boy, born on December 21, 1958 in Kornayel, Lebanon. When he was between one and a half and two years old he started to speak about a previous life. He recalled names of people, some events and some belongings. He sometimes talked to himself about the people of his previous life and asked himself about their well-being.

Sometimes he was stimulated to mention details related to his past life by external events, and he also appeared to talk about his memories in his sleep. He mentioned the name of the village as Khriby, and that of the family as Bouhamzy. He also mentioned the names "Jamileh" and "Mahmoud".

He mentioned an accident with a truck that had driven over a man and broken both his legs as well as inflicting other wounds from which the man died a short time later. Imad seemed very happy that he was able to walk and repeated time and again that he could walk "now".

Imad asked his present family to take him to Khriby, however his father did not respond positively to his story about a previous life at all, so he told his mother and paternal grandparents about it. One day somewhat later someone from Khriby visited Kornayel and Imad recognized him. Soon after Imad's father attended a funeral in Khriby and he met some people there who pointed out to him two men whose names corresponded to those given by Imad.

Imad's family had tried to deduce a pattern of family relationships from the names he had mentioned about his past life. They thought Imad was referring to the life of one Mahmoud Bouhamzy of Khriby who had a wife called Jamileh and who had been fatally injured by a truck after a quarrel with its driver. Imad had never stated that he himself had been the victim of this accident, nor that Jamileh had been his wife either. In this way, his parents made a lot of inferences that were unwarranted. Dr. Stevenson comments on these errors on the part of the parents:

> The errors of inference made by Imad's family add considerably to the evidence of their honesty and also the improbability that they themselves could have provided a source or a channel for the information given by Imad. (*Twenty Cases*, Pp. 277).

Dr. Stevenson investigated the case of Imad Elawar from 1964. He made written records of the statements that Imad had made before any verification. On the way to Khriby, Imad made more statements and his father also mentioned additional details. On investigation Dr. Stevenson soon found that Mohamed Bouhamzy had not been killed in a truck accident like the one mentioned by Imad. There had been such an accident involving one Said Bouhamzy, but Said had no connection with a woman called Jamileh. Furthermore, to add to the confusion and uncertainty there was already another boy (Sleimann Bouhamzy) claiming to be Said Bouhamzy reborn.

However, during his investigations, Dr. Stevenson discovered that the house and events Imad had described matched with those of one Ibrahim Bouhamzy, a cousin of Said Bouhamzy. Ibrahim did not have a wife but he had a beautiful mistress called Jamileh. Imad's joy about being able to walk again corresponded to the fact that Ibrahim had suffered from tuberculosis of the spine – a terrible disease which made it painful for him to walk, especially in his last few weeks of life.

Imad made 57 statements before he went to Khriby, 39 of which were recorded before verification. These included:

1.   His name was Bouhamzy and he lived in the village of Khriby.

2. Mahmoud (name mentioned).
3. He had a mistress called Jamileh.
4. Jamileh was beautiful.
5. Jamileh dressed well and wore high heels.
6. He had a "brother" called Amin.
7. Amin lived at Tripoli.
8. Amin worked in the courthouse building in Tripoli.
9. There was someone called Mehibeh.
10. Adil (name mentioned).
11. Tallil or Talal (names mentioned).
12. He had a "brother" called Said.
13. He had a "brother" called Toufie.
14. He had a "son" called Salim.
15. He had a "son" called Kemal.
16. He had a friend called Yousef el Halibi.
17. He had a friend called Ahmed el Halibi.
18. A truck ran over a man, broke both his legs and crushed his trunk.
19. He went to the "doctor's place" where he had an operation.
20. The accident happened after a quarrel and the chauffeur meant to kill him. (This connection between the two may actually have been added by his parents.)
21. The quarrel began as a result of the driver insulting his sister. He had struck the driver and knocked him down. The police and his friend Ahmed el Halibi arrived soon after.
22. The driver was a Christian.
23. He (Imad's former personality) was a friend of Mr Kemal Joumblatt, a well known Druze philosopher and politician.
24. He was very fond of hunting.
25. He had a brown "hunting" dog.
26. His house was in the village of Khriby.
27. They were building a new garden at the time of his death.
28. There were cherry and apple trees in the new garden.
29. The truck that killed his cousin was full of stones, which they were using in the construction work on the garden.
30. He had money and land, but no other regular business.
31. He had a small yellow automobile.
32. He had a truck.
33. He himself did not drive the truck.

34. There was an oil stove at this house.
35. He had five children altogether.
36. He was "well to do".
37. He had a farm.
38. You have to go to Khriby via Hammana.
39. When he was two years old, he recognized a native of Khriby, running to him and threw his arms around him. Imad said he was his neighbour.

Of his full total of 57 statements only three were incorrect and three unverifiable.

In Khriby he recognized places and people related to Ibrahim Bouhamzy's life. He failed to identify his house specifically but he pointed in the correct general direction. Imad also recognized some changes and accurately pointed out the former position of his bed during his illness and a window through which he could see and talk with his friends, and he recalled his last words before he died.

In Khriby Imad recognized a former soldier he had known. He and the man had a long talk and the man declared he was satisfied with what Imad had told him. Ibrahim and the soldier had been close companions during their army service.

There were also behavioural traits in Imad that related to the personality of Ibrahim Bouhamzy:

1. He recognized the portraits of his sister Huda and his brother Fuad and these recognitions accorded with the preferences of Ibrahim.
2. When someone trying to mislead him said that the Druze statesmen Kemal Joumblatt had died, Imad became extremely angry.
3. Imad clearly longed for Jamileh: her name was the first word he uttered clearly when he began to speak. This desire drove him to such an extent that when he was three to three and a half years old he was lying on a bed one day with his mother and suddenly asked her to behave as his woman Jamileh would, in a manner certainly not expected of a child of that age.
4. In general Imad showed signs of happiness when in Khriby which may be due to the memories of his previous life.
5. When he was only an infant, he already showed a notable phobia of large trucks and buses, which corresponded to

the fact that Ibrahim was bothered by the recollections of the truck accident and death of his cousin and friend Said Bouhamzy.

6. Ibrahim had been very fond of hunting, and so was Imad.
7. Ibrahim used to quarrel a lot with other men, usually about women. Imad also showed a very quarrelsome character.
8. Ibrahim could speak French well and Imad was precocious in school and especially advanced in French.

Dr. Stevenson said that Imad was aware of various events spread out over some period of time during the previous life. He indicates that this information could not have been acquired through normal means by lengthy questioning the Bouhamzy family or their close friends and neighbours.

Both families insisted they had never previously met or even known of each other's existence prior to my bringing them together in Khriby ... I have already explained why I think it virtually impossible for the Elawar family to have acquired such detailed and intimate information about the life of Ibrahim Bouhamzy as Imad showed unless they had made deliberate inquiries.

This line of thought, [when] pursued, returns us from cryptomnesia to fraud, which I have already rejected as an unreasonable hypothesis... If we can then reject both fraud and cryptomnesia as hypotheses for the case, we have left, as serious contenders to explain it, either some kind of extrasensory perception plus personation [identification], possession or reincarnation (*Twenty Cases*, P. 315).

Brazilian author Júlio Siqueira has given an overview of some sceptical attacks on the case of Imad Elawar by Leonard Angel. In his article, *Another Look at The Imad Elawar Case – A Review of Leonard Angel's Critique of This 'Past Life Memory Case Study'* published in 2004 on the website *Criticando Kardec*, he concludes that it remains, in principle, possible to account for the case on "naturalistic grounds," but that it seems very difficult to do so. By "naturalistic" he obviously means an explanation in terms of mainstream psychology or sociology.

The Case of Nazih Al-Danaff

A more recent Lebanese case was studied by Erlendur Haraldsson (Haraldsson & Abu-Izzeddin, 2002, Haraldsson & Matlock, 2017). It concerns a Druze boy by the name of Nazih Al-Danaff. He was born in 1992, 24 km away from Beirut.

When he was only a year and a half, he would tell his mother: "I am not small, I am big, I carry two pistols. I carry four hand-grenades. I am 'qabadai' (a fearless strong person). Don't be scared by the hand-grenades. I know how to handle them. I have a lot of weapons. My children are young, and I want to go and see them". He also described the way he had died. "Armed people came and shot at us. I also shot at them and killed one. We were shot and later taken by ambulance". Nazih also compared the beauty of his wife of the previous life with that of his mother and older sisters. When he was four he saw a woman who reminded him of his wife and even wanted to marry her.

He also showed a desire for cigarettes and alcohol.

Nazih wanted to visit his previous home in Qaberchamoun, a small town about 17 km away. He wanted to fetch some papers for money that he had lent to people so that he could get the money back, but also to show his father the weapons from the past life, and to see his children. He asked his parents to take him there and threatened them that otherwise he would walk there alone.

The boy also mentioned other details of his previous life, such as that he had a mute friend who also had something wrong with his hand, and that he had a red car.

Finally his parents agreed to take him to Qaberchamoun where he led the way. There, the family found the son of someone who matched Nazih's memories, a man named Fuad Khaddage who had died many years before. Nazih seemed to recognize him and answered specific, sharp questions from the previous family correctly. He recalled numerous specific incidents in Fuad Khaddage's life.

Later on, Nazih also visited Fuad's brother and made further correct statements and recognitions there. All this convinced the previous family that he was Fuad Khaddage reborn.

Haraldsson considers this case to be one of the strongest CORTs, because of an unusually high number of witnesses and statements, including the one about the mute friend. Almost all of Nazih's specific verifiable statements fitted Fuad's life. In addition, he gave correct and specific answers to questions from the previous family.

The Case of Neera

Dr. K.S. Rawat first met Neera, Neera's father, and a neighbour in the village of Chang, in the district Pali, (Rajasthan, India) on July 2, 1976. Following that, during 1979, 1980, 1984 and 1985 he interviewed a number of others connected with the case.

Neera, who was probably born during the first months of 1972, told Dr. Rawat that his name in the past life had been Kajja. In that life he lived in a village called Shyamgarh and had two sons and three daughters. His wife's name was Kalli. He and one of his sons, named Babu, were killed in a family dispute over a piece of land. They were assaulted with axes and lathis (sticks).

At Shyamgarh, Dr. Rawat found that there really had been a family dispute over a piece of land in which Kajja and his son Babu were killed. He went to the police station and after a long search traced the record of the crime in which Kajja and his son Babu were reported murdered in an attack by seven people. Five of these people were sentenced to life-imprisonment. The date of the murder was June 20, 1970.

The perpetrators spent twelve to thirteen years in prison for the murders and, after they were released, Dr. Rawat searched out two of them. After much persuading they told him that Kajja was indeed assaulted with axes and lathis. Roda, one of the murderers told Dr. Rawat: "We broke both of his hands and legs. He did not die immediately but remained lying unconscious under a tree for some time". Dr. Rawat got a copy of Kajja's post-mortem report from the hospital dated June 21, 1970.

The report mentions a number of wounds and fractures. Neera was born with a foreshortened left arm. It appears to be chopped off at the point of his mid forearm. With the background of many details matching correctly, we would expect the post-mortem report mentioning a chopped off left hand. But, it is not exactly so. The report mentions "a contused wound one inch by half an inch, bone deep, back, left-hand mid forearm".

As mentioned above, Kajja was indeed assaulted by axes and lathis on both of his hands and legs but had not died instantaneously. Perhaps, after being dealt a very severe blow at the mid of his left forearm, Kajja felt as if his hand had really been chopped off. He might have died with this impression in his mind and that might have caused the birth defect that Neera bears.

In any case, the details of the location of the wound on the left arm of the deceased person, Kajja, and Neera's stunted left hand should not be ignored. Neera recollected correctly the names of most of the relatives of Kajja but in a few cases he was definitely incorrect. He recalled many events from Kajja's life, which were mostly correct. He was reported to have correctly recognized the wife, son and some other relatives of Kajja. However, during Dr. Rawat's investigations, Neera failed to recognize some important, related people.

The Case of Sujith Lakmal Jayaratne

Sujith Lakmal Jayaratne was born on August 7, 1969 in Homagama, Sri Lanka. At the age of eight months Sujith was visibly terrified of lorries (trucks) and even of the English word "lorry" (adopted by the Sinhalese). His mother would even mention this word to force him to eat.

When Sujith was between one and a half and two, he started talking about a previous life, also using nonverbal sounds such as that of a railway engine and gestures such as that of a man walking with a cane. Eventually he insisted that his parents take him to Gorakana.

One day he announced in anger that he would go to his wife's and not return. He said he was called "Gorakana Sammy". His father was called Jamis and had one bad eye. Someone had fallen off a train and become lame. He also claimed that he had worked with trains and sold arrack (a hard liquor). He was married to a woman named Maggie with whom he used to quarrel. After one such quarrel, he had gone to a boutique to purchase cigarettes, had been struck by a lorry, and died.

He also mentioned many other details about members of his previous family and about the town of Gorakana.

A relative of Sujith's, the Ven. G. Gnanaratana, who was a monk in a nearby temple, listened to what he was saying. He informed another monk, the Ven. Wattarappola Nandaratana, who took written notes of 16 of Sujith's statements before verification in March 1972. He investigated some of the boy's claims, and managed to find the family of one Sammy Fernando. Sujith recognized relatives of this man.

Dr. Stevenson learned about the case through newspaper articles and investigated it himself. The following statements were recorded before verification:

1. He was from Gorakana.
2. He lived in the "Gorakawatte" section of Gorakana.
3. Jamis was his father.

4. Jamis was missing one eye.
5. He travelled by bus and by train.
6. He or someone else had fallen down and become lame.
7. He had attended the "dilapidated school".
8. Francis was his teacher.
9. He gave money to Kusuma.
10. Kusuma prepared string hoppers for him. (String hoppers are made from hot-water dough of rice-meal pressed out in circlets from a string mould.)
11. He gave money to the Kale Pansala.
12. There were two monks at the Kale Pansala.
13. One of the monks there was called Amitha.
14. He bathed in cool water.
15. The lavatory was beside the property line of his house.
16. His house was whitewashed.

In total his statements and recognitions numbered 59, only one of which was found to be incorrect, namely that he had died immediately, whereas Sammy died one or two hours after his admission to a hospital in Panadura. He did, however, adopt the correct position in which he was lying. He also knew at least two names that were no longer current in Gorakana, but that had formerly been used. He thus provided examples of a wide timespan of the events that he remembered.

He recalled Sammy Fernando's wife by intimate names such as Maggie and Maggio. Dr. Stevenson quotes directly from the translation of the Ven. Wattarappola's statement furnished in August 1972 (when Sujith was about three years old), a few months after the event:

On April 3, 1972, Maggilin Alwis called at the child's house, accompanied by a couple of other ladies of the same age group. For about twenty minutes the child did not speak. Thereafter he suddenly called out 'Maggie' to one lady and said: 'Maggie is going down the road.'

After this the child ran inside the house. During his absence I got all the visitors into a room unseen by the child and I myself remained on the veranda. The child came out after a few minutes and very excitedly started calling out: 'Where is Maggilin? Where is Maggilin? Went to Gorakana. Went to Gorakana.'

The Ven. Wattarappola adds that Sujith started running about in the house and dashed into the room where the ladies were. The boy told Maggilin that he loved her and she started crying and embraced Sujith lovingly. He said: 'Look what you did to me. Look what you did to me.'

When asked what he meant by this, he explained that on the day Sammy Fernando met his death, he came home roaring drunk and started to quarrel with her. She fled down the road. He started chasing her and was knocked by a lorry.

After the meeting when the party, along with Maggilin, were leaving to return to Gorakana, Sujith became agitated and wanted to go along with them.

Sujith did fail some tests to which he was put: he was unable to recognize in Gorakana the road to the house of Jamis Fernando, Sammy Fernando's father, but he satisfied many of the informants by the quality of his recognitions. Sujith also had some behavioural traits that may be related to his previous life as Sammy Fernando.

He often asked for arrack (liquor) and cigarettes. When drinking water or soft drinks he would habitually sit with his legs crossed or drawn up and drink from the bottle, just as Sammy used to drink arrack. After drinking, Sujith would make a sound in his throat similar to that of arrack drinkers and wipe his mouth in the same way. Sometimes he would also behave as if he were drunk and say "Bila" which means, "having drunk". He could act as a drunken man, even without taking any carbonated drink or "pseudo-arrack". Once, Sujith startled a drinking companion of Sammy Fernando by asking him "Sunil, shall we have a drink?"

Similarly, Sujith invited Martin Alwis, Sammy Fernando's brother-in-law, and another drinking companion for a drink. He was also sensitive about the consumption of arrack by other people. As his present life family abstained from drinking arrack, he had to go to neighbours to purchase it. Sujith had some unusual dietary preferences that accorded with his desire for arrack, like wade (fried patty made of ground dhal [split lentil] and spices), manioc and hot curries. Sujith sometimes also tried to smoke cigarettes.

He also showed habits regarding the way he dressed that related to those of the past life. For example, he would ask for a sarong to wear and then he would tie its knot below the navel as Sammy Fernando used to.

Sujith also suffered from some phobias, one of which was that of lorries (trucks). This, as we have already seen, corresponded to Sammy's cause of death. This is significant, since in general Sujith was free of all timidity and inhibitions and seemed quite bold. He even showed a tendency to aggression, as had also been the case for Sammy Fernando.

He used obscene words sometimes, which Sammy did. His use of some obscene words bordered on xenoglossy, because his family did not use these words. Dr. Stevenson admitted there was a possibility that neighbours influenced Sujith. By xenoglossy we mean here the active, meaningful use of parts of a foreign language, which the subject has never learned through normal means.

So, we see a number of similarities between the personalities of the boy Sujith and Sammy Fernando: a fondness for arrack, enjoyment of foods such as wade, manioc and hot curries, desire for cigarettes, dressing in sarong, tendency to violence, abusive language, lack of inhibitions and fear of lorries.

Commenting on the strength of the case, Dr. Stevenson says:

> I found no trace among the informants of any personal investment in it that could have biased their testimony ... (Sujith) has shown ... the behavior that characterizes the conduct of alcoholics. That he could have learned such behavior from the people immediately around him seems unthinkable. That he exhibited it so fully seems to me to add both to the authenticity of the case and to its evidence of paranormal processes ... this case is certainly one of the strongest ... because of the recording in writing of sixteen items stated by Sujith before they were verified. (*Cases of the Reincarnation Type, Vol. II.* Sri Lanka, Pp. 277)

Dr. Stevenson found that there was no evidence that members of the two immediate families in the case had known each other prior to this case's subsequent development.

The Case of Purnima

A SriLankan girl from Bakamuna, Purnima Ekanayake, was around three years old when, in 1990, she started talking about a previous life. Several years passed before her parents tried to verify her statements. Dr. Erlendur Haraldsson investigated the case during five visits to Sri Lanka, from September 1996 to March 1999. At the time she was still speaking of a previous life, which is unusual for most children who remember previous lives. Apparently, Purnima had made 20 statements about a past incarnation, although unfortunately they had not been recorded before verification.

In Haraldsson's report, he writes about Purnima's statements:

> The first unusual statement that Purnima repeatedly made as a small child was: "People who drive over people in the street are bad people". Sometimes she would ask her mother: "Do you not also think that people who cause accidents are bad people?" [...] Purnima also made statements about a fatal accident with a big vehicle. [...] Her mother thinks that this statement first came about (or she started to pay attention to it) after a traffic accident occurred near their home.

Purnima's mother was upset about the aforementioned accident. The girl tried to soothe her mother by saying: "Do not think about this accident. I came to you after such an accident". She told her how she closed her eyes after the accident and then came "here".

Her mother asked Purnima if she had been taken to a hospital". No," she replied, adding: "A heap of iron was on my body".

Purnima related that after the accident she floated in the air in semi-darkness for a few days. She saw people mourning for her and crying, and saw her body up to and including the funeral. There were many people like her floating around. Then she saw some light, went there and came "here" (to Bakamuna).

Purnima also told her mother that her family was making incense (Ambiga and Geta Pichcha) and had no other job. She later gave a detailed and correct account to Dr. Haraldsson of the ways to produce incense. Her parents knew very little about this subject.

Haraldsson checked the shops in Bakamuna and found only two brands of incense made in Kandy and one from India, no Ambiga or Geta Pichcha incense.

Shortly afterwards, her father, the principal of a secondary school, and her mother, also a teacher, took a group of schoolchildren to Kelaniya temple. Purnima was allowed to join this group. After arriving she said that she had lived on the other side of the Kelaniya river, which flows beside the temple compound.

Sumanasiri spent his working days in Bakamuna and the weekends in Kelaniya, where he had married. They decided that Sumanasiri would make inquiries across the Kelaniya river. Sumanasiri did not meet Purnima until after his inquiries. According to Sumanasiri the principal gave him four or five items to check:

1. She had lived on the other side of the river from Kelaniya temple.
2. She had been making Ambiga and Gita Pichcha incense sticks.
3. She was selling incense sticks on a bicycle.
4. She had a fatal accident with a big vehicle.

Sumanasiri and his brother-in-law tried to find out if there were incense-makers in the area. They found three small family incense-making businesses. One of the incense-makers, L.A. Wijisiri, had named his brands Ambiga and Geta Pichcha. His brother-in-law and associate, Jinadasa Perera, had indeed died in an accident with a bus while he was bringing incense to the market on a bicycle. This had happened in September 1985, about two years prior to Purnima's birth.

W.G. Sumanasiri informed Purnima's father about his findings. A week or two later Purnima, her parents, Sumanasiri and his brother-in-law made an unannounced visit to the Wijisiri family in Angoda.

> Before going to Angoda they spent a night at Sumanasiri's home in Kelaniya. There, according to her mother, Purnima whispered in her ear: "This incense dealer [she] had two wives. This is a secret. Don't give them my address. They might trouble me."

This turned out to be correct, although, officially, Jinadasa was married to neither woman.

Purnima's first meeting with the previous family was remarkable. She recognized Mr. Wijisiri as her brother-in-law from the previous life. When Purnima said that she had come to see her brother-in-law and sister, he did not realize that she was talking about a past incarnation.

However, when Purnima started to ask about various kinds of packets of incense and related matters, he was inclined to believe her story.

> Purnima said to Wijisiri that she used to sell these incense sticks. She asked: "Have you changed the outer cover of the packets?" Wijisiri used to change the colour and design every two years or so. She seemed to realize that the packets looked different from the time Jinadasa was working with Wijisiri. Then she talked

about the various packets, and about an accident Wijisiri had many years ago. (Since that time he has been unable to bend his knee).

Haraldsson mentions that Purnima added that Jinadasa [i.e. she in her previous life] had applied medicine to his knee after the accident. She asked about Jinadasa's friends, such as Somasiri and Padmasiri. Padmasiri was Wijisiri's brother who accompanied him on his business trip on the day Jinadasa had his accident. They had left home together, after which each of them had gone his own way. Purnima mentioned their names. Such things managed to convince Wijisiri.

Purnima also asked about what she considered to be her mother, and the previous sister from her previous life, who was also Wijisiri's wife. The sister was abroad working in Saudi Arabia, and the mother was not at her ancestral home. Purnima expressed concern when she learnt that the mother had gone to a distant place without company. Wijisiri's family still seemed quite confused by her memories.

Then Purnima showed them her birthmark and told them: "This is the mark I received when I was hit by a bus". She also told them where Jinadasa's accident had taken place, namely Nugegoda, which is near Angoda, and said that they had moved their home and factory to a different location within Angoda since she had been with them as Jinadasa, which was correct.

She also recognized an old co-worker, Somasiri. When Purnima's father asked who that man was, she answered: "This is Somasiri, my friend".

Purnima possessed several birthmarks that seem to be related to the cause of death at the end of her previous life. There was a large cluster of hypopigmented birthmarks to the left of the midline of her chest.

Prior to the contact with that family, Purnima never spoke about details of her injuries; nor do her parents remember her associating her birthmarks with her accident. It was not until Purnima's visit to Angoda that she said that the bus's tyres had run over her chest, and she pointed across the left side of her chest where she has her birthmarks. Someone in Wijisiri's family then mentioned that Jinadasa had been injured on the left side of his trunk. Purnima's birthmarks were at the same location. Then the case was considered confirmed by both families.

Haraldsson managed to obtain the post-mortem report, which gives a detailed description and a sketch of Jinadasa's injuries. These turned out to have been massive, particularly on the left side of the chest, where several ribs had been broken.

Although a few statements made by Purnima were incorrect, Haraldsson summarizes the evidence in this case as follows:

> This is a good example of a case with different characteristics that fall into a pattern and must be viewed as a whole: memories, birthmarks and, perhaps, how-to-do knowledge. Overall, one can state that the case of Purnima Ekanayake is of unusual quality.

And:

> The locations of the two families were far apart, and the two families were complete strangers.
>
> A third party succeeded in finding the person who matched Purnima's statements. Fourteen of seventeen statements that could be checked were found to match the life of Jinadasa, who had died two years before Purnima was born. Purnima's cluster of birthmarks was found to fall within an area of fatal injuries suffered by Jinadasa. Her birthmarks are on the left side of the chest, where most of the ribs broke, and where he is likely to have felt most pain.
>
> Also, there is some evidence of knowledge of incense making that is highly unusual for a child, which Purnima explains as stemming from her previous life.

The Case of James Leininger

Many (although by no means all) reincarnation-type cases involve memories of a violent death. If these cases amount to real memories of previous lives, we would expect many children to recall a violent death on a battlefield. In fact, this is exactly what we find.

For instance, there are unsolved cases of this type in Myanmar (formerly known as Burma) of children with memories of a previous life as a Japanese soldier who also identify with Japanese culture and military life. Another example of such an unsolved case is the Dutch case of Kees who recalled how he was shot dead as a foot soldier with the

French name Armand, after all of his comrades had fallen before him.

Investigators have also discovered several cases that could be solved because the personality, which the child claimed to have been, has been traced historically. Well-known examples are the British case of Carl Edon who remembered a life as a German pilot who crashed in the UK during the Second World War, and the case of Martin Heald who claimed he was a RAF-pilot shot down above the Netherlands.

An even more recent case in this category concerns an American boy, James Leininger, born in 1998.

From a very early age, James showed a remarkable interest in old aeroplanes.

Wes Milligan writes:

Andrea [James's mother] says planes had always been his fixation: He spent hours playing with toy planes and he would yell when he saw a real plane in the air.

Bruce [James's father] recalls his son's being mesmerized with the planes at the museum; the boy kept wandering back to the World War II section of the museum. When he tried to take James away from the exhibit, after being there for nearly three hours, James put up a fuss and started to cry. To satisfy his curiosity and to calm him, Bruce bought him a Navy Blue Angels flight demonstration videotape at the museum. James played it so much that he practically wore it out. ("The Past Life Memories of James Leininger". Milligan, *Acadiana Profile Magazine*, 2004.)

Some time later, it became apparent that this predilection was linked to recurring nightmares in which James was stuck in a burning, crashing aeroplane. He tried to free himself while kicking and screaming. His mother tried to reassure him, but he told her: "Aeroplane crash on fire, little man can't get out". These nightmares could not be traced to anything the boy had been exposed to, because his parents did not allow him to watch adult television programs.

Meanwhile, the furniture suffered from James' toy plane collection. James would crash his toy planes into tables and chairs, Andrea recalls with laughter as she points to the numerous nicks on the living room table. The table served as a landing strip for his planes. Crashing became such an obsession to James that whenever someone mentioned flying, James would blurt out, "Plane crash on fire," which, Andrea says, unnerved her.

After a while, James started to tell his parents that he had been shot down "by the Japanese". He told them he had been a pilot and his first name had been James, too. He mentioned the name of a ship from which his plane had departed, "Natoma". He also mentioned the name of a friend, Jack Larsen, and named his GI-Joe dolls after other friends: Billy, Leon and Walter. He claimed that these three friends had been waiting for him when he went to heaven.

Many other similarly specific details were also part of the boy's story.

His parents were practising Christians and did not believe in reincarnation. However, his mother accepted the possibility that James was indeed recalling a previous life and contacted researcher Carol Bowman.

His father, Bruce Leininger, resisted the boy's story and tried to prove that it did not make any sense historically.

In October of 2000, another piece of the puzzle came clear. After another nightmare, James gave his parents the name of Jack Larsen, and he said it was Larsen who flew with James.

During the following month, James added another piece of information to his story, which won over his sceptical father. Bruce was thumbing through a book, *The Battle For Iwo Jima*, by Derrick Wright, which he had recently received from a history book club. James jumped into his lap to watch cartoons. While waiting for the cartoons to come on, James and Bruce looked at the book together. Suddenly, James pointed to a map of Iwo Jima near Chichi Jima and said, "Daddy, that is where my plane was shot down". Bruce concluded that all of the statements clearly related to the life of Lt. James McCready Huston Jr. – who was shot down during the invasion of Iwo Jama on March 3' 1945. All of his scepticism disappeared. He admits he doesn't have a conventional explanation for all this.

Jack Larsen turned out to have survived the war while Billy Peeler, Leon Conner and Walter Devlin had all been killed before James Huston. They belonged to the same squadron as Huston and were among the 21 fatalities from the Natoma Bay. The colour of their hair matched that of the GI-dolls, which James had named after them. More generally, James showed a detailed, unlearned knowledge of aeroplanes.

He also met James Huston's sister Anne Baron and convinced her that he really was the reincarnation of her deceased brother. Among other things, he reminded her of a watercolour, which their mother had made of Anne during James Huston's life, and he knew that their father had had problems with alcohol.

The novel "Morgan" by Bas Steman

Journalist and writer Bas Steman published a curious novel in 2018, titled *Morgan: Een liefde*. It was loosely based on memories he claimed to have had of a previous life as a Welsh soldier Morgan Probert who died during Operation Marketgarden in the notorious Battle of Arnhem.

Although Probert was not a pilot himself, Steman did make realistic drawings, as a child, of soldiers jumping out of aeroplanes, which remind one of battle scenes from World War II.

The precise identity of Probert was identified to Steman under hypnosis and he finally managed to get in touch with Probert's relatives in Wales who were still alive.

Although Steman was more interested in writing a moving literary novel about reincarnation memories than in presenting serious evidence (which explains the fictional elements in the book), his case essentially seems to be authentic. Steman's wife, filmmaker Ariane Geep, confirmed certain elements of his story to Titus Rivas.

Other Recent Western Cases

More generally, it seems that the West seems to be slowly opening up more to possible memories of previous lives in young children. In recent years, various other American and European cases, studied by Jim Tucker and other local investigators, have surfaced. Examples of children who received attention in the media in recent years are Luke Ruehlmann and Christian Haupt. As a white boy from Cincinnati, Ruehlmann appeared to recall a verifiable past life as a black woman, Pamela Robinson who died in a fire in Chicago.

Christian Haupt is a baseball prodigy who, as a young boy, seemed to show paranormal memories of a life as baseball legend Lou Gehrig. His mother Cathy Byrd (2017) wrote a book about this case entitled *The Boy Who Knew Too Much*.

Dieter Hassler (2014) studied a contemporary German case, which includes a premonition experienced by the subject's mother; announcing dreams, behavioral features, special skills; and two incidents of a psychokinetic or poltergeist nature that were experienced by the previous personality's mother after his death. The case is rendered particularly unusual because it involves a chance encounter between the subject's mother and the previous personality at the moment of the latter's death, suggesting that the case could have evolved because this encounter offered an incentive to reincarnate with this particular mother.

A Contemporary Indian Case

Cases of the reincarnation type (CORTs) continue to be reported in Asian countries such as India.

The prominent Indian scholar Arya Bhushan[15] was personally involved in the study of a recent Indian CORT, which he and his son Abbay Bhushan briefly describe as follows:

> In Mainpuri, a District town in India, a girl born in a Brahmin family remembered her [previous] life as a sweeper woman. While the narration of her life had tallied in many respects and she had recognized her husband and children of previous life, she mentioned that she had been killed in a railroad accident. Dr. Stevenson asked Arya Bhushan, who was then Commissioner of Railway Safety dealing with railroad accidents, to obtain documentary evidence as a corroborative proof.
>
> As the approximate period when the accident had taken place was known, a railroad employee was instructed to go to the railroad station and look for old records. The person so deputized, was able to get the papers, which contained the accident telegram issued, as also the Police verification report and the documents through which the dead body of the deceased was handed over to the relatives.
>
> All this tallied with the statements, which the girl had made earlier about her past life.

---

[15] See his undated publication *Reincarnation: A Myth or Reality?*

5

ALTERNATIVE HYPOTHESES

~

And even supposing the evidence were too strong and unexceptionable to be got rid of by ... familiar devices they might yet be accepted as proof of rebirth; the mind can discover a hundred theoretical explanations for a single group of facts.

~ Sri Aurobindo

Now that we have presented some of the best cases of the reincarnation type or CORTs, let us see if they really provide evidence for reincarnation or if they can be explained by other hypotheses.

1. Normal Hypotheses

Fraud and/or Hoax

For a sceptic or more generally for an average layman the "obvious" hypothesis that can explain all reincarnation cases would be fraud and/or hoaxes. By this he would mean that due to one reason or another, all the cases are either deliberately perpetrated fraud or some mystification produced as a result of conscious or unconscious factors.

Titus Rivas has reviewed the unsolved cases of Dutch subjects (Rivas, 2020) and Dr. K.S. Rawat has reviewed the unsolved cases of Indian subjects for the possibility of deception at length. Their research concludes that conscious deception occurs only sporadically and then only in non-typical cases. In this respect, they confirm the conclusions drawn by Stevenson (1960; 1974; 1980; 1987) and his Brazilian colleague Andrade (1979; 1980).

An example of a real hoax is the case of Nimal Singh (pseudonym) in which Indian villagers had lied to a Singhalese Buddhist monk about statements this child would have made about a life as the monk's cousin. The villagers did so, because they wanted to take advantage of the Buddhist monk's generosity (Stevenson, Pasricha, & Samararatne, 1988).

Dr. Rawat has reported a number of cases in which the life of Mahatma Gandhi was allegedly recalled and in some half a dozen cases a child claimed to have been Jawaharlal Nehru[16] in his past life. These hoaxes did not require much effort to expose! In another case a "peon"[17] of a college was found to owe some money to the deceased principal whose life his son claimed to have had recalled. The hoax could easily be detected.

We should realize that in the vast majority of cases of children spontaneously recalling a past life, usually – contrary to what a lay person might think – they do not recall a life of a famous person. Fame and fortune (in this life) does not seem to be a motivation. On the contrary, the members of the subject's family often have to spend a lot of time and money in order to serve all the numerous, curious needs of the child.

Moreover, particularly in India, as we mentioned earlier, there is a widespread superstition that children who recall a past life die young. We see parents scolding and beating the child and resorting to odd practices such as putting a child on a potter's wheel and then moving it in an anticlockwise direction, or filling their mouth with soap or dirt just to make the child forget and not delve into the memories of a possible past life.

The way in which the child reacts in the presence of the alleged relatives (and others) needs to be explained. Could a child of two or three years be trained to play appropriate roles vis-à-vis wildly differently related people, friends and foes? As Dr. Stevenson writes:

---

[16] Leader of the socialist wing of the Indian National Congress during and after India's struggle for independence from the British Empire. He became the first Prime Minister of India at independence on August 15, 1947, holding the office until his death in 1964.

[17] Peon = usually an office messenger, an attendant, or an orderly.

"The complexity of the behavioural features of these cases alone seems to make fraud virtually out of the question". Children may be capable of occasionally acting with guile; however they are unlikely to perpetrate a hoax of this magnitude where so many details are involved.

Additionally, Dr Stevenson has mentioned six characteristics of cases of fraud or hoaxes:

1. The previous personality would have been famous or powerful.
2. The subject of such a case does not speak about the previous life until after the age of five.
3. The assumed status of the previous personality is exploited for selfish gain.
4. Such cases show unusual features not encountered in other cases, for example an extremely long time interval between the past life and this one.
5. Only the parents would know what the child has said about the previous life.
6. There is no mention of the child's having strong emotions about his previous life.

In the majority of cases, fraud is not a plausible or even a possible explanation; it would require a conspiracy by many people, with many opposing interests, to make it possible and there are rarely any times where real (financial etc.) gains could be made, so this makes it even less likely.

Self-Deception

In a relatively large number of cases of the reincarnation type (CORTs) of Dutch adults, studied by Titus Rivas, self-deception seems to be the origin of *paramnesia* (distorted memory) in the subject himself, i.e. the illusion of remembering something that the person has never really experienced him or herself. An illustration of this process can be found in an article written by Rivas about a Dutch retired technical engineer known as F. H.

F. H., a retired engineer, claimed he was Alfred Peacock, an infant who drowned on the *Titanic* in 1912. He claimed he had been able to verify certain elements of his memories. He claimed his case would be the best-proven reincarnation case ever to have been brought to light. The man claimed, among other things, that Alfred Peacock's second birthday was the same date as the day of the *Titanic's* departure, and that he had already verified this point in an English archive.

Apart from this, he knew that: his family had spent the night before at an aunt's in Hampstead; this aunt had a daughter, 14 or 15 years of age; the aunt was rich and possessed an old car from the beginning of the century; Alfred, his mother and his sister had been brought to the Underground (railway), and other verifiable and unverifiable details. However, with the assistance of survival researcher Dr. Alan Gauld and experts specialising in the *Titanic* catastrophe, Titus Rivas could establish with absolute certainty that the real Alfred Peacock who traveled on the *Titanic* – whose name F. H. had found in the passenger's list of a bestseller about the *Titanic* – had nothing to do with the engineer's statements about Alfred Peacock.

One by one, his statements were unambiguously falsified. In other words: however clear and vivid F. H.'s memories might have been according to his own declaration, they did not match with the facts on closer investigation.

One might still assume that the memories applied to another passenger of the *Titanic,* or to another ship disaster, but none of the other passengers matched his description, and F. H. himself said that it could only have been the *Titanic.* Thus, F. H. did not agree with the data, which Titus Rivas had found and claimed that they contained all kinds of inaccuracies. Finally, F. H. even went as far as to claim that he had become the victim of a conspiracy.

Historical information has, at times, been altered for political reasons; however there is no indication of records relating to disasters having been altered to suit anyone's interests. Insurance companies keep extensive records relating to disasters if and when they have to pay for the loss of life. Apparently, this case did not just involve self-deception, but a stubborn persistence in it even after it had been empirically proven that his memories as he presented them could not be real memories. This sincere man stuck to his "memories" in spite of the facts presented to him; he merely accused the researcher of being part of a conspiratory gang. One way or another, this self-deception must have had some meaning for the subject that made it impossible for him to face facts.

Dr. Stevenson writes about self-deception that in these cases, the previous personality is typically a famous person. He gives the example of Turkish children claiming to be the reincarnation of President John F. Kennedy:

> The father of one of these children, Mehmet Alkan, had dreamed of President Kennedy a few hours before the birth of a son ... and he named the son 'Kenedi.' ... In November 1967 Reşat Bayer and I met the two-year-old Kenedi, and his father told us that he was unaware of the likelihood that he was imposing another identity on his son ... . There is a sequel. In 1985 Can Polat learned of the case of Kenedi Alkan and met him. He was then a young man of about twenty.
>
> Kenedi Alkan firmly believed that he had been President Kennedy in his previous life. He even claimed to remember a few specific details relating to his life, such as that he had been rich, married, and had two children.

Dr. Stevenson holds that there must be some direct, specific reasons to assume that a specific case involves self-deception. However, perhaps a better criterion would be that if the subject might benefit emotionally or in some other psychological way from his or her self-deception and is, at the same time, capable of acquiring all the relevant information, then the case might, indeed, be explained by self-deception. Thus, our first impression is that a whole category of cases suddenly become dubious: namely cases in which the subject's parents have been relatives or close friends of the person whom the child claims to have been.

While mourning for a loved one, some people can be inclined to deceive themselves (unconsciously) in the sense of thinking that the deceased person still dwells somewhere in a physical object or has passed over to another person. For these reasons, parents might sometimes name their child after a deceased loved one's physical object. J. Bowlby speaks in this context of "mislocation of the lost person's presence in his *Attachment and Loss*.

Researchers Cain and Cain mention this in their paper "On Replacing a Child," stating "in a few stunning cases [of mislocation], parents even changed the living child's name to that of the dead child, while in other cases newly born children were given the dead child's exact name or his name slightly changed". The dead child's identity was further imposed upon the sibling by the parents' expectations and demands upon the replacement's being based on the idealized image of the dead child.

The children whom Cain and Cain themselves investigated, suffered from all kinds of disturbances, but they add that it is very well possible that such a child grows up without problems related to the replacement. Now, one might suppose that many CORTs could be the result of this.

However, Stevenson holds that such a mislocation hypothesis doesn't concur with the traditional view among Hindus and Buddhists that children who remember previous lives die young. The parents' subconscious desire to replace the dead relative or friend could, however, be stronger than the fear that results from this tradition.

On the other hand, if reincarnation is to be accepted as the best explanation for cases in which the previous life was not connected to the present one through family ties, it may eventually serve also as the most parsimonious hypothesis for some or even most same family cases. One of us, Titus Rivas, has followed this line of reasoning in the interpretation of a recent Dutch case (Rivas & Dirven, 2004) of a girl named Célina who showed memories and behaviour that seem to be related to a life as one of her own maternal great grandmothers. A similar approach has been followed by Carol Bowman (2001).

None of the cases that we have presented above could possibly be explained away by self-deception, since the present families never had any motive to impose (even subconsciously) a false identity on the child. Their child was never considered to be anyone else by them at the time of birth or at any time up to the point where the child indicated a past life.

Antonia Mills (1990) mentions cases of Muslim children recalling previous lives, pointing out that Muslims do not endorse the concept of reincarnation, so that the hypothesis of imposed identification becomes quite implausible.

Fantasy

In 1920, psychoanalyst Ernest Jones described a specific kind of childish fantasy he termed "reversal of generations". According to this fantasy, older people become smaller and smaller until they become babies again. (We may consider that not infrequently elderly people lose control over bodily functions and abilities to do things for themselves and in effect "become babies again," but this is clearly a different notion.) Jones writes:

"For example, a little boy whom I know, when about three and a half years old, often used to say to his mother with perfect seriousness of manner: 'When I am big, then you will be little; then I will carry you about and dress you and put you to sleep'

" (Ernest Jones. *Papers on Psychoanalysis*, London: Bailliere, Tindall & Coss, 1920.)

There are other, more recent authors who have confirmed the occurrence of such utterances among young children. Titus Rivas, found a case of this type that happened in the 1980s.

A Dutch girl of five said without being prompted: "When I will be dead, I want to be born again as your baby. But maybe you will be a baby yourself by then". When a lady living next door had passed away, this same girl wanted to know all about it. After they told her about the coffin in which the neighbour's body would be buried, she remarked: "How can she ever become a baby again with those clothes on?"

It is possible such utterances relate only to children's limited understanding of death and birth. It is also possible that they derive partially from real memories of previous lives, whether or not they were dreams or visions that have somehow become distorted. It is sometimes very difficult to draw the line between possible real memories of previous lives and possible false memories. Strange as this may seem, this fact actually adds strength to the hypothesis that in some cases we are dealing with real memories. This is because normal memory of events that occur within one and the same life can also be distorted. Gaps in one's memory are very common and they are subconsciously filled in with processes related to fantasy. We should not expect that this would be any different if people are, at times, really capable of remembering their previous lives.

In other words, if real memories of previous lives exist, we would predict from our knowledge of normal memory processes that they will contain deficiencies and distortions. Perfect memory of a previous life is as difficult or even more difficult to conceive of, as perfect memory of one's present life would be.

It is quite hard to assess what has caused an individual child's statements about reincarnation or rebirth if the child does not have any recollected images of a previous life. We can indeed imagine that sometimes they are caused by the childish fantasy that Ernest Jones calls "reversal of generations" or similar fantasies. How far can one extend a fantasy to explain cases of reincarnation? In most of the cases, the previous person was excruciatingly ordinary, and could, therefore, hardly be a fitting choice for a youngster's fantasies.

If the child shows non-trivial, specific knowledge that he or she cannot have acquired in any normal way, the plausibility of the fantasy hypothesis completely collapses. None of the cases we have presented in the foregoing chapters can be explained by fantasy.

Cryptomnesia

C.T.K. Chari holds that the subjects of these cases might have known a person or other source that had information about the previous family. Later on some have forgotten where they got their information, and they would start believing that the information derives from their own memories. This process is technically known as "cryptomnesia" or "source amnesia". (C.T.K. Chari. *Paramnesia and Reincarnation*, Proceedings of the Society for Psychical Research, 1962, 53, 264-286.)

In most cases, however, only a person could have provided the necessary information to the child, as, especially in Asian countries, written records about births and deaths are rare. In many cases the distance between the two families is so great that cryptomnesia can be ruled out or excluded. Very rarely do they even know each other. In addition, the way of life and contact base that characterizes the families in most cases excludes the possibility of contact between the child and a stranger who could provide a quantity of specific information about a life, which the present family knew nothing about.

The scope and intimate content of the child's memories is certainly too rich for their source to be casual contact with a stranger. Neither can spontaneous, unprompted recognitions, the behavioural aspects involved in these cases, or birthmarks be explained by cryptomnesia.

For these reasons, Ian Stevenson writes:

I feel entitled to ask critics who favour the hypothesis of cryptomnesia to discipline themselves by showing the evidence for this interpretation in particular cases. I am unmoved by an appeal to abstract principles. I would ask the critic to keep in mind what seem to me the essential criteria for attributing a case to cryptomnesia.

According to Stevenson, these essential criteria are:

a) A close correspondence between the information expressed by the subject and the information available to the transmitting person, or the information existing in another source from which the subject may have drawn it.

b) Evidence that the subject had, in fact, access to the supposed transmitting person or other source of the information.

It is, needless to say, a fact that in most or even all of the cases, which we have described in the foregoing chapters, neither of these criteria is fulfilled.

Paramnesia in others

The hypothesis of paramnesia in others does not concern the source of the child's memories but their very existence. The parents and other adults related to the cases would have had to misinterpret vague statements made by the child as memories of a previous life. They might have found a previous personality and falsely remember (as we know, paramnesia = distorted memory) that a child really gave a lot more details about the previous life than they actually did.

Stevenson comments that such a process may really take place among the Druze population, as a lot of parents would like to know who the previous personality of their child had been. We have already seen that something similar happened in the case of Imad Elawar, namely that his parents enthusiastically linked his words with the wrong previous personality and wrongly interpreted details accordingly. Their misperceptions coloured the research and the verification process.

However, in cases where written records had been prepared prior to any verification[18], this hypothesis is not sufficient to explain them.

Also, many adults, both from the present families and from the previous ones, show indifference or even negative attitudes toward the cases. This negativity could not easily be explained if these cases were nothing more than distorted memory on their own part.

---

[18] A recent article about cases in this category was published by Keil and Tucker (2005).

Genetic memory

Some critics propose an unconventional biological hypothesis for CORTs. They contend that if the present personality is born in the same family as that to which the previous personality belonged, he may have acquired the information about that previous personality through his genes.

This is an unconventional, Lamarckian[19] hypothesis. No orthodox biological theory would conclude that personal memory is somehow fixed in a person's chromosomes and then passed on to future generations.

Moreover, even if it were possible, genetic memory would not explain the high incidence of memories of the end of the past life shown among children. The postulated genetic memory would naturally reach only to the moment of conception, which (almost) never coincides with the death of the person involved in a sexual act. In other words, the mode of death could be recalled only if it occurred at the very same moment the present personality (or one of his ancestors) was conceived. Otherwise the information could not have been passed on via a supposed genetic connection.

More importantly, it is only in a small percentage of cases that the previous personality was an ancestor of the present personality. All the cases, extensively described in the foregoing chapters, concerned a previous personality completely unrelated to the present one.

Parapsychological Hypotheses

One category of CORTs concerns the "paranormal" cases, in which the subject seems to possess knowledge or skills related to the life of a deceased person and which the subject cannot have acquired through normal sensory channels.

All the CORTs we have presented thus far fall into this category, meaning that in none of them we can ignore the evidence for at least some kind of paranormal process involved.

This is vehemently denied by sceptics who claim that any concept of

---

[19] The term Larmarckian refers to Jean-Baptiste Lamarck (1744-1829) who is remembered today mainly in connection with a discredited theory of heredity, the "inheritance of acquired traits".

a mind, personality, spirit or soul that would survive death is *a priori* unscientific or even irrational. However, in many cases, sceptics' views are based on preconceived opinions rather than research and facts. We might even expect an increase in the number of scientists adhering to such a materialist worldview as more data is collected on the exact mechanisms of mind-brain interaction.

As Titus Rivas has repeatedly tried to show (Rivas & van Dongen, 2003; Rivas, 2003, 2004, 2006), this claim is based on a crude, naïve philosophy of mind, which overlooks the so-called *mind-body problem* and the related "hard problem" (a term coined by philosopher David Chalmers [1995]) of subjective, qualitative awareness or consciousness. The hard problem may be expressed in questions such as:

- Why does subjective awareness of sensory information exist at all?
- Why is there a subjective component to experience?
- Why do qualitative experiences (qualia) exist?

Most sceptics are materialists or epiphenomenalists and some of them even deny the very existence of subjective awareness. (For an analytical refutation of epiphenomenalism and the identity theory of mind and brain, see Appendix D. For a philosophical demonstration of the non-physical nature of at least part of our personal memory, see Appendix E.)

As Braude (2003) states:

> The physiological evidence doesn't show that selfhood or consciousness is exclusively linked to bodily processes, much less the processes of any particular physical body. Probably, physicalistic interpretations of the data seem initially compelling because physicalistic presuppositions are widespread and deeply rooted. And, if so, it may be a useful intellectual exercise to try to divest ourselves of those presuppositions and then take a fresh look at the data (Pp. 291).

Canadian neuroscientist Dr. Mario Beauregard has published extensively about experimental evidence for the impact of the mind on the brain. This includes evidence for the regulation of emotions by cognitive processes, the effect of psychotherapy, and the placebo effect, all of which are accompanied by an objectively measurable impact on brain physiology. He approaches such phenomena with his so-called Psychoneural Translation Hypothesis, according to which "conscious and unconscious mental processes are translated automatically into neural processes."

Even more shocking from a materialistic point of view are the findings of Dr. John Lorber in the 1980s. He discovered that there are so-called hydrocephalic patients who possessed only a tiny fraction of the neo-cortex yet functioned normally in terms of intelligence and social skills. One of his subjects was a young man with an IQ of 126 who had a first class honours degree in mathematics. He had "virtually no brain". A non-invasive measurement of radio density known as CAT scan showed the man's skull was lined with a thin layer of brain cells to a millimeter in thickness. The rest of his skull was filled with cerebrospinal fluid.

Materialists usually try to explain such cases using a theory that brain regions only become specialised during neurological development so that mental functions may be supported by areas different from normal if the deviant organisation of brain tissue occurs at an early stage. However, this still does not explain how a person could function with only a tiny fraction of the normal number of brain cells. Also, it suggests that mental functions may organise cerebral matter, which is inconceivable if the mind is nothing but the (functioning of the) brain (Lewin, 1980).

A more recent case of this type was published in 2007 in The *Lancet* by Lionel Feuillet, Henry Dufour and Jean Pelletier of the Faculty of Medicine of the Université de la Méditerranée at Marseille. It concerns a 44-year-old patient with a very thin layer of cortical cells. His cranium is almost completely filled with cerebrospinal fluid.

Unlike many of Lorber's subjects, this man had an IQ that was somewhat below average, but not to the extent that he might be called mentally handicapped. He leads a normal life, is married and has two children and is employed as a white-collar worker.

The monumental book *Irreducible Mind: Toward a Psychology for the 21st Century*, written by Edward F. Kelly, Emily Williams Kelly and others, contains a lengthy overview of a wide range of well-attested phenomena that are inherently irreconcilable with materialistic reductionism.

To mention just one example, the authors point to the everyday phenomenon of a unified consciousness:

Only one thing is certain: The unification of experience is not achieved anatomically. There are no privileged places or structures in the brain where everything comes together, either for the visual system by itself or by the sensory system altogether. McDougall [...] was already fully aware of this, and used it as a cornerstone of his argument against materialistic accounts of the mind. In his view, the evident disparity between the multiplicity of physiological processes in the brain and the felt unity of conscious experience could be resolved in physicalist terms only by anatomical convergence, and since there is no such convergence, physicalism must be false. (*Irreducible Mind*, Pp. 37).

Incidentally, reductionist philosopher Daniel C. Dennett acknowledges this point, but for him it is all the more reason to regard the experienced unity of consciousness as an illusion.

Still others even dismiss case studies as "unscientific," no matter how well documented they turn out to be. Some may claim explicitly that real science is, by definition, experimental or solely concerned with tangible, measurable, physical reality.

Scholars who do not agree with this dogmatic tunnel vision (sometimes termed "naturalism") are often attacked ad hominem and ridiculed in sceptical publications. Anything goes, if one wishes to keep the gates of science closed to "pseudo-science" at any cost.

We will leave aside sceptical dogma and focus on a more satisfactory, open-minded and rational interpretation of these cases.

Paranormal Cases

As regards skills, it is fairly easy to establish whether the subject could have acquired them in his or her (present) life or not. An example of a case involving paranormal skills is that of Swarnlata Mishra, in chapter 3, who performed dances and songs that she could not have learned by normal means.

Paranormal knowledge, on the other hand, may be present in many cases, but, after the subjects themselves have carried out verification, it is often a bit harder to establish. The safest procedure in this respect is therefore to focus, as we have done, on cases where investigators can show, on the basis of documents, or because they themselves took part in the verification of the past life, what paranormal items the subject knew with certainty.

In cases where statements have been written down or recorded before verification, "hits" prevail and those hits cannot, or only extremely improbably, be ascribed to mere coincidence; in these cases we believe it is safe to consider that it's the result of paranormal processes. The number of such cases seems to be increasing and, at present, there are at least 33 (Braude, 2003). This is because researchers have managed to get involved in a case before verification (Haraldsson & Abu-Izzeddin, 2002; Keil & Tucker, 2005). Also, Jim B. Tucker (2000) of the University of Virginia developed a strength-of-case scale. Ian Stevenson and Jürgen Keil (2000) looked at the stability of assessments of "paranormal connections" in CORTs.

Some scholars, such as Helen Joyce and Richard Wiseman, seem to hold that we ought not to accept the presence of paranormal information in CORTs unless we can establish in exact, statistical terms how great the odds are that matches between statements and historical facts are purely coincidental (the kind of assessment proposed by Jim Deardorff and others).

However, if in practice such a procedure turned out to be almost unfeasible, it would be quite strange to claim that first we need such an exact assessment before we can reach an overall rational evaluation of the fantasy hypothesis in a specific case. In many cases, the idea that the data can be reduced to fantasy and chance is simply too implausible to be taken seriously.

A few years ago, Richard Wiseman conducted an experiment for a television documentary produced by Channel 4 about reincarnation research.

Wiseman concluded from this experiment that if you ask children to make up a story about a previous life, they will sometimes construe a fantasy reminiscent of children's claimed memories of past lives. However, his unpublished experiment is only superficially related to spontaneous CORTs and ignores cases that have been verified. In genuine CORTs, children are usually not encouraged to fantasize about a previous life and in some of the strongest cases they are even discouraged from doing so.

Also, children in CORTs typically show strong emotions and an identification in relation to their memories, as well as behavioural characteristics and, in some cases, birthmarks or birth defects.

Moreover, the cases studied by Wiseman included much less specific information about names and locations than the stronger Stevensonian cases of the kind we've presented in this book. In other words, Wiseman's unpublished results fail to offer a satisfactory explanation for typical cases of reincarnation[20].

The rejection of CORTs as phenomena that are often inexplicable in conventional terms may, frequently, be based on an implicit dogma that reincarnation is an intrinsically exotic, outlandish or even irrational notion and simply does not or cannot occur. Probability assessments in exact mathematical terms could certainly be valuable but they should not be seen as the only valid method to evaluate matches between statements and historical facts.

Similarly, some sceptics claim that reincarnation researchers typically look exclusively for cases that might provide evidence for reincarnation, ignoring any evidence for the fictitious nature of claimed reincarnation memories.

Or as Prof. Archie Roy formulated it in a more general context:

> It seems to be a common assumption that any belief system, which a researcher brings to his field of study – whether it be merely a 'hunch' or a strong conviction that some hypothesis must necessarily be true – will cause him to concentrate on any material able to support his hypothesis and ignore or explain away anything in conflict with it ...
>
> Sadly, of course, examples have been found in most research disciplines (and in other occupations – even politics!) of people who have deliberately massaged or manufactured 'data' to promote their own theories and careers.

Roy points out that there also exists a powerful factor to prevent fraud in any research discipline, consisting of the very nature of research and peer-review: the publication of articles in professional journals, in which authors not only state the reasoning followed to arrive at their conclusions but also the available evidence, so that others may repeat their work and check its validity.

Roy complains that what he terms the "professional sceptic" holds that any researcher who believes in survival after death cannot be

---

[20] For a general critique of Wiseman's approach to parapsychology, see Carter (2010).

trusted to carry out valid research, because he or she would always favour data that supports the survival hypothesis.

Roy stresses that this amounts to equating such a psychical researcher with a fundamentalist who has a dogmatic belief system, and speaks of "the sceptic's arrogant contempt for the psychical researcher and disregard for their honesty and professional integrity".

According to Roy, such a dogmatic sceptic also ignores the fact that survival researchers usually work in a team, and discuss their findings with each other in a scholarly atmosphere.

He concludes:

> If, however, we were to adopt this point of view, would it not be logical to suppose it also true that the professional sceptic, likewise possessing a strong conviction amounting to certainty for whatever reason that paranormal phenomena do not exist, will never find any and will subconsciously influence the planning of his or her investigations into paranormal phenomena in such a way that they demonstrate that such phenomena do not exist?
> (Archie Roy, *The Eager Dead*, Pp. 184-186.)

In the context of reincarnation research, Robert Almeder stresses the following:

> If the opponents of reincarnation refuse to acknowledge any and all evidence for the thesis (because it is just too incredible for any reasonable person to believe), then their opposition to reincarnation is purely dogmatic. (Robert Almeder, *Death and Personal Survival*, Pp. 39.)

One of us, Titus Rivas, was mentioned in Stevenson's *European Cases of the Reincarnation Type* for having shown that the case of F. H. (who claimed to have memories of being one of the passengers on the *Titanic*) cannot be based on real memories of a previous life.

There is also no reason why all CORTs would always, a priori, be best explained in terms of a paranormal phenomenon. However, if it turns out that a considerable number of cases cannot be explained satisfactorily by any normal (non-parapsychological) hypothesis, this should be considered an important empirical finding and not simply an artifact of the methods of investigation. Sceptics who accuse reincarnation researchers of looking exclusively for positive evidence may be compared with critics of evolution theory who believe there is no serious evidence for evolution, because evolutionary scientists would concentrate on precisely such evidence.

There are cases that need a parapsychological hypothesis – this is a hypothesis focusing on a causal factor that does not derive from "orthodox," conventional psychology or physics. What should this parapsychological hypothesis include?

Extra-Sensory Perception (ESP)

The Dutch parapsychologist Peter van der Sijde has pointed out that in case paranormal knowledge seems to be present, we should first try to explain it by some kind of ESP hypothesis (Sijde, P. van der 1992). There is a group of writers challenging Stevenson, who do not have a problem with his data and no problem acknowledging that it is sufficient to support an extraordinary claim. Their argument is over what extraordinary claim it supports.

They prefer to say that the cases are best explained by a combination of a child's suggestibility and extrasensory perception. This is because (in their view) laboratory tests have provided at least consistent statistical evidence of ESP, whereas nobody has ever conclusively managed to measure the weight or dimensions of even the tiniest soul.

An ESP hypothesis is one that tries to explain any paranormal phenomena by citing as their cause one or more types of Extra-Sensory Perception (ESP) such as clairvoyance, telepathy or retrocognition. This is a matter of theoretical parsimony; if other parapsychologists have already concluded that these types of ESP do indeed exist, we should try to explain paranormal phenomena through such factors rather than postulating a new phenomenon such as reincarnation.

Van der Sijde was not the first person to try to explain paranormal CORTs type in terms of ESP. Another Dutch parapsychologist, W.H.C. Tenhaeff, had already tried to apply the ESP hypothesis to the case of Shanti Devi in 1954, and, after him, Indian critic C.T.K. Chari, British historian Ian Wilson and Czech investigator Milan Rýzl had done the same.

The main question in this context is not whether these authors were right in attempting to explain reincarnation cases with an ESP hypothesis. It is quite obvious that they were, as in science we should always try to look for the simplest hypothesis with the greatest explanatory power. The point is whether they are right in their claims that ESP can indeed satisfactorily explain paranormal CORTs.

First, let us consider cases with paranormal skills, such as those of Swarnlata Mishra. No one has yet formulated any plausible hypothesis about how a child could acquire such skills through ESP. ESP is generally seen as a form of paranormal perception or cognition and it is well known that perception or information processing are indeed necessary but not sufficient conditions for the acquisition of complex skills.

For such complex skills we often need instruction, and, in any case, *training* or *practice* is needed to acquire such skills. It is for this reason that Dr. Feldman says about gifted children that it can only be a myth that they have skills they have never acquired through learning. (See D.H. Feldman, *Beyond Universals in Cognitive Development*. Norwood: Alex Publishing Corporation, 1980.)

Stephen E. Braude (2003) has pointed out that we should distinguish between different types of skills, according to their complexity, but it is clear that Swarnlata's skill was not a simple one.

As far as we know, there has never been any well-documented case of the extrasensory acquisition of skills. General theories about skills indicate that we have no reason to believe that mere perception would ever be enough to acquire them. Thus, we have every reason to believe already that for CORTs with complex paranormal skills, such as that of Swarnlata Mishra, the ESP hypothesis will probably be insufficient.

This also holds for cognitive skills such as the understanding of religious rituals or other specific cultural customs. Young children aged two to four generally have little or no knowledge of rituals and habits practised by a group to which they do not belong themselves. And yet, there are many cases in which the children had precisely such knowledge.

In a case studied by Dr. Rawat, a Hindu boy named Mukul Bhavsar was born without foreskin. Not only did the boy know exactly how to perform the Muslim ritual of *Namaz*, but he also remembered the exact process of circumcision.

Dr. Rawat writes about this case:

In 1986, while we (Dr. Stevenson, Dr. S. Pasricha and myself) were in the Madhya Pradesh (India) area researching some cases, we got information with regard to a case in Soyat Kalan (a small city in Shajapur district of Madhya

Pradesh). We interviewed Mr. Satya Narayan Bhavsar and his wife about the recalls of their son, Mukul Bhavsar. When Mukul was of about three he used to ask the parents to give him keys of a shop he said he had to go and open. He gave out his name and also those of his two wives and his parents, all these of Muslim people. He said that he owned a cycle shop at the bank of a river. One fateful day the shop got swept away in flood. And he died in it. The boy use to sit in a "Namaaz" position in which Muslims sit for offering prayer at as early an age as two and a half years!

The astonishing fact was that the boy was born with a circumcised penis. He recalled the procedure of the circumcision done on him in his past life. (Hindus do not do circumcision).

This case of Mukul Bhavsar is reported by Dr. Stevenson in his book *Biology and Reincarnation.*

Recently, in February of 2004, I again visited Mukul at Soyat Kalan, alone this time and interviewed him and his wife there. I made him agree to photograph him and took some photographs. He is now about 30 years of age. Some of Dr. Stevenson's colleagues / members of his team tried to search out the previous personality but could not succeed. I am doing it again ...

Now how can we consider cases that seem to embrace only paranormal *information*? First of all, we should realize that such information does not appear to stand on its own, but is always part of the child's conviction that he or she has lived before; i.e. of the identification by the subject with the past life.

In most examples, as in all of the cases we have presented above, this identification is not just an unemotional, detached affair. It is usually accompanied by strong feelings, affections and longings, which fit into the life the subject claims to recall.

The only ESP-hypothesis we could regard as a serious candidate for the explanation of cases with paranormal information is one that would also explain the child's identification with the past life. As most paranormal cases of reincarnation involve young children, we should specifically be aware of developmental data on young children that may relate to this topic.

It has been found that children who are the primary subjects in reincarnation research usually start talking about their memories of it before their third year. Thus, it is relevant to note that infants and toddlers, according to various investigations, usually have a self-image that differs from that of older children or adults. While thinking about themselves, they put more emphasis on concrete dimensions, like physical appearance, possessions or play activities (Damon & Hart, 1982; Leahy & Shirk, 1985).

In general, this identification with someone else can lead to a shift in a person's self-image, so it corresponds more with the image one has of the object of identification. We should assume that the object of identification is somehow attractive to the child. This implies that it corresponds to his ideal self as a concept. An ideal self concept amounts to the way that a subject would like to be more than anything else or to the way he would like to lead his life (Milrod, 1982). Before we proceed we should realize it would in general be awkward, even embarrassing, for any child to choose an identity outside their direct social environment.

The question is: "What could possibly motivate a two or three-year-old child to prefer a recollection of being (like) a deceased, usually fairly remote, stranger as an object of identification, rather than a beloved relative or even a neighbour?"

Let us assume, therefore, that ESP is used by the child subconsciously to be able to choose a dead stranger as an object of identification.

This must mean that there is some kind of process through which the child tries to find a deceased person who would correspond as much as possible to his or her ideal self-concept and notions of an ideal life. We should, in that case, expect only CORTs with deceased objects of identification who would be attractive to young children, primarily because of their external characteristics. It seems highly improbable that they would choose characters of dubious backgrounds or scenarios that might test the limits of their family's tolerance.

Nor should the deceased personality suffer from unappealing inner conflicts that are linked to his or her life. Such inner conflicts would be unattractive for any young child. However, both dubious backgrounds and inner conflicts do in fact occur in paranormal cases of reincarnation.

Some readers may object that a motive to identify with someone does not always have to be inherently positive. For example, it is known that people may identify with an aggressor and adopt his or her ideas, attitudes or behaviour. However, this phenomenon occurs only under severe emotional or physical stress and when there is a direct link with an aggressor in the immediate environment of the subject. These conditions clearly do not apply to typical paranormal CORTs.

Another negative motive to identify with a less attractive personality roots in low self-esteem or outright self-hatred. Such a psychological condition would show in the general behaviour of the person in question, which is destructive, extremely insecure and pessimistic. All this bears no relation to the average (present) personality of children in paranormal cases either.

Therefore, we both think it is fair to say that the ESP-hypothesis turns out to be *insufficient* for most CORTs with paranormal features, when approached from a motivational, developmental psychological perspective.

Stephen Braude (2003) accepts this point, stressing:

> Subjects in typical reincarnation cases are children. So, at the age when they start speaking about a former life, it's unlikely that they're strongly motivated to simulate the behaviour of a previous personality. Therefore, super-psi explanations [explanations in terms of ESP] of those cases will usually have to posit relevant motives in people other than the subject – probably, one or the other set of parents or members of the immediate families, and, as I noted, if we can't plausibly attribute relevant unconscious motives for simulating survival of the child subject, then the next most likely culprits will be members of either the subject's or the previous personality's family.

Braude recognizes that it is hard to believe that these family members are psychic agents, even if plausible motives could be imagined for them.

For one thing, their presumed motives may not mesh neatly with other observed facts ... . And, for another, we may have to posit even more hopelessly convoluted and complex causal chains than we'd need if we treated the subject as the psychic agent. (Pp. 180-181).

Some proponents of the ESP-hypothesis deny that the child (or his parents) would subconsciously search (by ESP) for information about a personality, which attracts him (or his parents). They state that the identification is not something the child really wishes to achieve as a desirable goal. Instead, the child – at a subconscious level – randomly receives information about a completely *arbitrary* deceased personality and then, only after this strange process of gathering information about him or her has been largely completed, he identifies emotionally – at a conscious level – with the previous personality, with an increasing illusion that the personality and circumstances relating to it were his own.

These proponents claim that our knowledge of ESP is too limited and that we still have to learn how it works. For example, many precognitive dreams involve trivial events and it seems almost unthinkable that we have acquired the information about such trivial events because we were so interested in them.

Proponents do acknowledge that the range of ESP, which is needed to explain paranormal cases of reincarnation, surpasses that of everyday instances of telepathy or clairvoyance, but they believe that it is just a matter of degree. In other words, ESP would boil down to quite a random phenomenon, and, though it occurs mostly on a very small scale, sometimes it is manifested as so-called Super-ESP[21] or Super-PSI[22]. In both cases, we would need no *motive* whatsoever to explain its spontaneous occurrence in anyone.

This theory of ESP is misleading. Most recorded instances of spontaneous ESP point to a clear psychological motive in the person who experiences it. For example, most cases of spontaneous telepathy occur under emotional circumstances. Even if some precognitive dreams provide seemingly trivial events, those events are, at least to a certain extent, noteworthy to the person dreaming about them. This also means that he or she gets to *experience* them after the dream. In that sense, the experience relates, at the very least, to the person.

Does something similar apply to so-called "psychics," or people unusually gifted in ESP? Many critics doubt the very existence of such gifted "psychics". We shall give some attention to the talent because if it does exist[23], their paranormal gifts might

---

[21] However, Jürgen Keil even goes as far as claiming that most or possibly all paranormal CORTs could be explained through a more ordinary type of ESP. He holds that children may be influenced by "free-floating" thoughts of people from the past. His brand of the ESP-hypothesis clearly seems related to the *anatta* or bundle theory of Buddhism.

[22] An older term for this kind of theory derived from the context of psychical research into spiritualistic phenomena is "animism". An animistic theory explains any kind of paranormal phenomena in terms of the subconscious paranormal workings of the anima (soul) of the living rather than by the conscious intents of spirits of the dead. Scholars aware of this traditional terminology may use it as a synonym for Super-ESP or Super-PSI theories.

[23] Mary Rose Barrington, Ian Stevenson and Zofia Weaver (2005) make a strong case for this possibility in their book about the Polish clairvoyant Stefan Ossowiecki.

approach the Super-ESP postulated by the proponents of the random ESP– theory.

A leading investigator of psychics or "paragnosts" as he called them was the Dutch parapsychologist W. H. C. Tenhaeff. One of his main conclusions about the "paragnosts" he studied was that they all have their specializations: when they use ESP they focus on things that have a special personal meaning for them. For example, a psychic who was sexually abused as a young child might focus (through ESP) on revealing sex crimes. Tenhaeff therefore believed that separating a psychic's paranormal gifts from his or her psychological make-up was psychologically unfeasible.

Even if we ignore Tenhaeff's conclusions about the subjects he studied, there still would be an *a priori*, psychological reason to believe that he is right. Should ESP as a human faculty be severed completely from human motivation? There is no convincing evidence that it stands on its own, functioning completely *separately* from the rest of psychology.

It is sometimes claimed by survivalists that a strong Super-ESP hypothesis, based on (in principle) limitless and unmediated retrocognition of information about the past, is an unacceptable hypothesis because it could never be falsified. Any type of information could be explained by retrocognition and no case could ever show that the Super-ESP theory is wrong.

However, in our view this is misguided. The Super-ESP theory may be unfalsifiable if one looks at paranormal information exclusively without taking into account the context in which the information shows up. The falsification of Super-ESP is not primarily linked to its explanatory power of informational aspects of cases, but to its capability to explain cases as a whole.

Even if one went as far as to ignore the motivational, psychological argumentation against the theory of arbitrary, random Super-ESP (or Super-PSI), one would still find that there are only a few, really exceptional cases, in which a child recalling the past life also expressed the faculty of ESP. When reincarnation subjects do seem to be somewhat gifted in this respect, it is never to the extent of more notable psychics (claimed) abilities.

Moreover, as Dr. Stevenson stresses:

> The unusual behavior related to the memories that most subjects show (usually over several years) has no stimulus in contemporary events of the previous personality's family; events in the subjects

family may stimulate it, but it derives from past events in the previous family... and, the subjects sometimes show emotions that the previous personalities did not have, but that are appropriate from the point of view of a previous personality's perceiving himself in a different, and often disagreeable, situation.

Tom Shroder writes:

The argument against ESP is straightforward. The children weren't saying: 'The previous personality had three cows,' as they might if they were telepathically gleaning facts about a stranger. Instead they were saying, 'I had three cows,' and otherwise providing information as if they were that person. It was rare that any of these children exhibited any other evidence of psychic ability, which raised this question, why would a child exhibit intense psychic ability concerning just one specific dead guy? (Pp. 146-47).

Furthermore, as we have seen, some cases involve birthmarks and birth defects relating to a traumatic or fatal injury that ended the previous life. How could we explain such cases through even the far-fetched variant of the Super-ESP hypothesis?[24]

If we still wanted to explain those cases as resulting from ESP, we would first have to say that someone else, let's say the mother, created the birthmark and/or birth-defect through psychokinesis during pregnancy. There is some evidence for this possibility of so-called *maternal impression* (Stevenson, 1997), but it would not suffice to explain classical paranormal cases, because afterwards the child should subconsciously try to find a person whose mode of death seems to be related to the physical characteristics shown on his own body.

Therefore, birthmarks and birth defects show very clearly how far one must stretch the hypothesis of some sort of bizarre and random ESP-processes to explain certain paranormal CORTs.

---

[24] Jürgen Keil recently speculated that pregnant women would always be responsible for the birthmarks and birth defects in these cases. They would in turn be influenced by free-floating remnants of the thoughts of a deceased person from the past, as supposedly expressed in announcing dreams. In many CORTs, however, no such announcing dreams are even reported by the parents, so that Keil boldly suggests that the mothers must have had them anyway and simply forgotten about them after waking up!

We conclude that any Super-PSI hypothesis that leans on a general theory of PSI as a completely random and non-psychological phenomenon is based mainly on the desire (inspired by a dogmatic worldview) to explain away important evidence for reincarnation.

Morphogenetic Fields

Dr. Rupert Sheldrake has formulated a revolutionary and controversial theory of several types of biological "fields" which would contain information necessary for the morphogenesis (formation) of an organism. Sheldrake terms these "morphogenetic fields". His theory differs from that of orthodox biologists in that it postulates something that would be quite superfluous according to reductionist biology. For Sheldrake, the phenomenon of morphogenesis during pregnancy is so mysterious that biochemical processes alone cannot explain it.

(See: Rupert Sheldrake, 1985. *A New Science of Life: The Hypothesis of Formative Causation*. Blond and Briggs, London.)

The morphogenetic fields postulated by Dr. Sheldrake would not only contain information about the formation of an organism's various organs, but also about the instincts and behavioural patterns of a particular species. All the morphogenetic fields of a species would be connected and exchange information. The relation between Sheldrake's theory to the concept of telepathy or Jung's collective subconscious may seem obvious to some.

If a member of a species acquires new information about something, its morphogenetic field would also make it available – albeit on an unconscious level – to the morphogenetic fields of other members of the same species. Telepathy would be just one, partially conscious, expression of a very common biological phenomenon of so-called morphic "resonance" between fields. This resonance would presumably take place outside the defined boundaries of time and space.

Now, by the same token, paranormal CORTs would have to be explained by morphic resonance between the field of the previous personality and that of the present one. What can we think of this? It was Alan Gauld who addressed this issue in a review of one of the volumes of Stevenson's series *Cases of the reincarnation type* (Gauld, 1985).

Gauld's main point is, that there is no reason to believe that the morphogenetic field of a deceased adults – as most previous personalities were when they died – would particularly resonate with that of a young child[25].

If the adult and child are not biologically related, there can be no special resemblance between the two and there is no reason to suppose that the resonance would be strong enough to create the cases that we are trying to interpret here. The paranormal information that a particular child shows about a particular deceased adult is such that a special linkage would have to exist between their two biological fields.

There is no ground for assuming that there is such a linkage, unless, perhaps, if the two organisms would be very closely related genetically. We have already seen that most subjects in CORTs do not have a genetic relationship to the previous personalities.

Influence from a Discarnate Personality

Charlie A. Hall discusses Emanuel Swedenborg's[26] views on claimed memories of previous lives in an online paper titled *Rebirth and Reincarnation*:

He tells us that we are in unconscious association with spirits who influence us in an inner way. On the communication of spirits with people on earth, he says in his *Heaven and Hell,* #256:

Angels and spirits are not allowed to speak to a person from their own memory: only from the person's memory. Spirits and angels have a memory just as people do.

If a spirit talked to a person from his own memory, the person would not know anything else but that all he thought then were his own thoughts, when they were actually the spirit's. It is like remembering things that the person never actually heard or saw. I have been shown by experience that it is like this.

---

[25] Similar arguments may be formulated against the so-called Archetypal Synchronistic (or Synchronistic Archetypal) Resonance of Jeffrey Mishlove and Brendan C. Engen.

[26] Emanuel Swedenborg (1688-1772) was a Swedish scientist, philosopher, mystic, theologian and psychic. He wrote books about his contacts with the spirit world and continues to have a considerable spiritual following.

It was from this experience that some of the ancients got the belief that after several thousand years they would return to their former life, and to everything they did in it, and also that they had already returned from before. They concluded this because they occasionally had something like a memory of things that they had never seen or heard. This happened because spirits flowed from their own memory into the ideas of their thought.

This approach of trying to explain CORTs by way of some kind of influence from a discarnate personality, ranging from an interference known as overshadowing to total possession, is popular among people who believe in survival after death but for some reason reject the concept of reincarnation. For example, Spiritualist and anti-reincarnationist James Webster claims that the hypothesis of a "visiting spirit" could explain all paranormal CORTs.

A famous and well-documented case of possible possession by a discarnate personality is that of Lurancy Vennum (Stevenson, 1974; Smith, 1975). In 1878 the 13-year-old Mary Lurancy Vennum from Watseka, Illinois repeatedly went into a state of trance during which she was possessed by a whole series of "spirits". Dr. E. W. Stevens investigated Lurancy and advised her to look for a guiding spirit among all the visiting spirits so that order could be created out of chaos.

When she tried to do so, a certain Mary Roff "appeared" who was prepared to fulfil this function. Mary Roff had died in Watseka at the age of 18, when Lurancy was only 15 months old. Mary Roff had taken "possession" of Lurancy and apparently dominated the child for three months: Lurancy talked, acted and seemed to remember things as if she was Mary Roff. Lurancy even went to live with Mary's parents, where everything was familiar for her, and where she met relatives, friends and acquaintances. Also, she was capable of recalling things that did indeed correspond to Mary Roff's life.

The main difference between this authenticated case of possession and cases of reincarnation is that Mary disappeared after three months because Lurancy had been "completely cured". This means she no longer showed any characteristics belonging to Mary and could return to her own house. Later, Mary did occasionally return, with Lurancy's permission, so that she could talk with her parents (See Zorab, 1986).

Thus, we see two distinct personalities between whom there is no continuity, in contrast to CORTs. The main argument against the possession hypothesis for paranormal CORTs is that there is no alternation of personalities. This would be something we could expect if there was a strong influence by a discarnate spirit (Andrade, 1980). Guy Lyon Playfair (2004, & 2006) and Archie Roy (2004) were two experts on possession and "overshadowing" (influence) by discarnate spirits who do not exclude the possibility of reincarnation as being a special form of possession. The cases of reincarnation in young children that we have examined to date do not fit the possession pattern.

Furthermore, there seem to be almost no cases of apparent split or secondary personalities in this context, only children whose general psychological functioning appears to fall within the accepted range of behaviour generally referred to as "normal"[27]. Any possible dissociation almost never reaches the level of the creation of an alternative personality.

Similarly, subjects in cases of reincarnation usually show ignorance about changes that have taken place in buildings and in association with people known in the past since the previous personality died. It is also hard to think of a motive for a discarnate entity to possess a child in such a way that the latter comes to believe he was the discarnate entity in a past life and is the child in his present life. Also, why should discarnate spirits fool only *children* into believing that they are their reincarnations? (Tucker, 2005.)

The reader should note that we do not exclude the possibility of possession per se. There may actually be a continuum between normal reincarnation and a special kind of postnatal reincarnation, suggested by cases like that of Jasbir (Stevenson, 1974). Jasbir, an Indian boy of three, appeared to have died from entirely exogenous smallpox, and, having revived, claimed to have been a person named Sobha Ram. Jasbir gave sufficient detail about the latter to enable identification to take place, but evidently being aware that he was describing events in a previous life of his own.

Titus Rivas studied a similar case in Hungary and Spain, together with Mary Rose Barrington (1926-2020), Peter Mulacz and Zsolt Banhegyi, that of Iris Farczády (Barrington, Mulacz, & Rivas, 2005). In the 1930s, the Hungarian teenage girl Iris (who had been a Spiritualist medium), or someone manifesting through her, suddenly claimed she was Lucía Altarez or Altares from Madrid, giving (partially unverified) details

---

[27] An exception being, of course, the presence of posttraumatic symptoms related to traumas suffered during the previous life they recall.

about her life there and demonstrating some unlearned knowledge of the Spanish language (xenoglossy). Rivas had several conversations in Spanish with Lucía (still known as Iris) in 1998.

In 1989, Satwant Pasricha, Ian Stevenson and Nicholas McClean-Rice published a report about an Indian woman, Sumitra, who apparently died and revived. After some time, she claimed to be one Shiva, a person who was murdered in a place about 100 km away. She made 19 statements that the researchers judged paranormal and also showed unusual behaviour that was appropriate for Shiva.

However, this particular possibility of possession or "postnatal reincarnation" (reincarnation that occurs [years] after the original personality was born) is not relevant for typical cases of the kind we are primarily discussing here.

In addition, and like the case for ESP, possession and other forms of influence from discarnate entities cannot account for paranormal birthmarks and birth defects related to the previous life. We would certainly be interested in investigating any instances known to readers, which appear to run counter to our findings.

In conclusion, we both think that among the survivalist hypotheses, the reincarnation hypothesis is the most adequate one for so-called paranormal cases of the reincarnation type, i.e. for CORTS that cannot be explained by normal hypotheses alone.

We do not need to know everything about reincarnation and its mechanisms before we are allowed to draw this important conclusion[28].

The birthmarks and birth defects corresponding to traumatic or fatal wounds would, in this context, have to be explained through the psychosomatic (or *psychokinetic*) impact of memories of traumatic experiences on the person's new (embryonic or foetal) body. These types of effect would be similar to *maternal impression* as described above, the crucial difference being that the physical phenomena would be caused by the reincarnating entity itself rather than by anyone else.

In this sense the effect is internal or *intrasomatic* rather than external.

Parallels may be drawn to psychogenic intrasomatic alterations of the person's own body during one lifetime, ranging from the effects

---

[28] Charles Darwin did not know much about the exact mechanisms behind heredity either, but this does not mean that Darwin's explanation of the origin of species became scientific only after the discovery of the structure of DNA by Crick and Watson.

of hypnotic suggestion on a person's skin to so called stigmata among certain Catholic saints, such as St. Francis, who concentrated on the suffering of Christ (Stevenson, 1997a, 1997b).

Personalism vs. Impersonalism

This brings us to an important question related to reincarnation: what within a person is it that reincarnates?

Although this is a profound question that many Indian, Tibetan and other sages have tried to answer, basically we need to distinguish between two philosophical currents: personalism and impersonalism.

Personalism states that the entity that survives death and is reborn into a new organism is in fact the same entity that thinks, feels and strives during this present life. The "I," *experient* or *conscious subject* of the previous life is the same as the person who recalls this previous life during his new incarnation. Thus, the experient of the past incarnation and the present one would be identical. The personal experient considered as a personal experient has not changed, but only his or her experiences and memories of those experiences have changed over time. The fact that the person inhabits a different body now, or functions at a certain psychological level due to his interaction with an immature brain, does not imply that it is not the same person.

Impersonalism declares the conscious subject, personal experient or "I" to be nothing more than a convention or illusion. According to impersonalism, as there was really no constant conscious subject during the past life there can be no identity with the (illusory) present conscious subject of this life either.

In fact, both subjects would be mere illusions or conventions and nothing would exist that supports the continuation of life, thoughts, feelings or foresight as part of a total spiritual person. Persons according to impersonalism would not be "selves" in physical bodies, but merely "minds" connected to bodies. To be more precise: there would really be no (substantial) "selves". Therefore, at rebirth only certain memories, personality traits and skills would be "recycled" during the formation of a fundamentally new person. In a sense, the theory of reincarnation would be remarkably similar to the materialist theory of extinction after death in that the person as such would irreversibly be destroyed.

As far as we know, within reincarnation research, Dr. Jürgen Keil explicitly holds this view and quite a few others may have been influenced by it.

Titus Rivas wrote a Master's thesis of Philosophy on the problem of personal identity in relation to survival after death. He concluded that the impersonalist view of a conscious subject as nothing but an illusion is untenable, as the concept of illusion makes sense only if illusions are seen as real *subjective* phenomena. They must "objectively" (i.e. really) exist as subjective phenomena, as their existence itself can not be denied.

We can only really *have* an illusion if we are *real* (rather than illusory) conscious subjects or experients. It does not make sense to hold that a person undergoes only the *illusion* of his own conscious existence, as the presence of any real illusion shows that the conscious subject (or *experient*) experiencing the illusion must really exist as well. Similarly, the fact that a certain impression is illusory means that we get a wrong idea of what it stands for or refers to, not that the impression itself does not exist. Thus, illusions cannot be non-existent themselves, and neither can the subject undergoing an illusion be merely illusory (Compare: Valicella, 2002).

Rivas quotes with approval the Bohemian philosopher and mathematician Dr. Bernhard Bolzano who, in his book *Athanasia*, showed that the subject of normal psychology must be substantial and indivisible and that it cannot be explained on the basis of any divisible psychological or physical composition of elements.

There is a plurality of mental processes integrated into one's consciousness. As the reductionist philosopher Daniel Dennett rightly states, there is *no single spot* in the brain on which all the different neuronal information would be integrated. There is a conscious subject or "I" who sees, thinks, feels, wants, etc. all at once (Robinson, 1991).

This feeling and functionality can be explained only by a substantial personal soul that is not composed by lower subconscious or non-conscious elements, as such a composition would never create the *unity* of consciousness. If some aspect of our being (identified by many as our personal soul) cannot be composed or created by other things, and it cannot be affected by the dissolution of any thing, including the brain or body; it cannot be destroyed by material processes and must therefore be immortal.

In fact, this is the classical substantialist proof for indivisibility and, thus, also for survival of the personal experient as such, considered in its identity as a personal experient. It was formulated by a whole line of Western philosophers, including Plotin, Augustine, Descartes, Leibniz and Bernhard Bolzano, but also in various formulations by Indian thinkers of so-called logical realism of the pluralist Nyaya philosophy, of Jainism, and of the Dvaita and Visistadvaita schools of Vedanta[29].

A whole Spiritualist movement exists; Kardecism, also called Spiritism, accepts personal reincarnation. It is based on the writings of Hippolyte Léon Dénizarth Rivail, better known by his pseudonym Allan Kardec (1804-1869). Don Morse (2000, p. 292) writes about it: "It differs in that with each incarnation, the spirit retains its individuality and spirits always evolve".

For Titus Rivas, personalism is an essential part of his reincarnation hypothesis. (See Appendix C for an English article by Rivas about personalism within reincarnation theory.) In his view, *the very same conscious subject, experient or personal soul who was called Lugdi in one life is called Shanti Devi in its next life.* Thus, the body is not essential for personal identity and life after death must be just as personal as life on earth (Rivas, 2004).

Jim Tucker also seems to support a personalist interpretation of reincarnation, as is demonstrated in his book *Life before Life.* The same goes for Erlendur Haraldsson who explicitly rejects the impersonalist bundle (or anatta)-theory in favor of personal reincarnation in *I Saw a Light and Came Here* (Haraldsson & Matlock, 2017).

It is important to note that a *personal self* should be distinguished conceptually from its *personality*. A personality may be seen as an acquired pattern of psychological structures, attitudes and skills of a personal self. A personality is dynamic and changes over time, and, in certain pathological cases, a personal self may possess several personalities simultaneously though it can be conscious only in one personality at the time. Thus, changes of personality and even dissociation are fully compatible with the notion of a substantial personal self (Braude, 1995).

---

[29] In other schools of Indian philosophy such as Advaita, the Atman is supposed to be immortal but transpersonal rather than personal, in that it would be identical to God. Titus Rivas' position is closer to that of the Dvaita and Visistadvaita currents. However, in practice, transpersonalism can go hand in hand with a belief in a type of personal reincarnation of the so-called jivatman, a personalized manifestation of the supposed transpersonal Atman.

According to Rivas, in the context of reincarnation we should expect certain changes of personality through the processes of death, rebirth and childhood, but this does not mean those changes imply a new or different personal self. We would remain ourselves just as much as we remain ourselves in the course of a single earthly lifetime.

These notions are different from the concepts of *personality* and *individuality* proposed by Stevenson who follows C. J. Ducasse in this respect. For Stevenson, what survives death and reincarnation is not the entire personality but an individuality of which the personality is a manifestation. Within the theory posited by Titus Rivas, it's one and the same personal self that survives death and reincarnates, and what changes continually is its personality. In this sense, the concept of individuality becomes unnecessary and is replaced by that of the personal self itself.

What is sometimes presented against the thesis that the conscious subject is indivisible, such as data from multiple personality cases or split-brain experiments, falls short of demonstrating that when a person's psychological functioning becomes somehow disintegrated or dissociated, the conscious subject will be divided as well (Braude, 1995). Consciousness (in the sense of subjective awareness) is a private and personal phenomenon, which cannot be established externally. Therefore, any behaviour shown by a person could in principle be caused by both conscious and non-conscious psychological processes.

Only if it were possible to show conclusively that a particular type of behaviour could be caused only by consciousness, would it be reasonable to claim that if two such types of behaviour occurred separately at exactly the same instant, the original consciousness would have been replaced by two separate streams of consciousness (Pinto et al, 2017).

Moreover, in scenarios where mind functions appear divided, most split-brain patients normally act in an integrated manner and yet some of them are able to perform complex actions like playing the piano, which involve both hemispheres. If the conscious mind of such a patient were in reality replaced by two conscious minds, in effect creating two separate people or subjects, it would be very difficult, even impossible, to explain.

In other words, the claimed literal divisibility of the conscious soul *remains a logical impossibility*. A less literal interpretation of it in terms of the creation of a new stream of consciousness cannot be demonstrated experimentally, and existing empirical data are clearly incompatible. Rivas stresses that personalism remains coherent and that there has been no conclusive empirical evidence against it. He also points to the fact that this hypothesis is in accordance with the subjective view of the children in CORTs, which, though not conclusive in itself, still is a reflection of his theory. These children believe that they themselves, not just an arbitrary other deceased person whose memories they seem to recall as their own, lived the previous incarnations, survived physical death, and returned to live in another biological body.

Titus Rivas acknowledges that there are also other forms of personalism in the context of reincarnation research, such as the one proposed by Geoffrey Read who believes that personal reincarnation is a consequence of the individuation of the psyche (Hewitt, 2003). In general, the approach taken by Rivas to reincarnation is not determined by cyclical notions, but a positive concept of personal evolution (Rivas, 2005a, 2005b; Tucker, 2005; Stevenson, 1987; Gerding & Van der Put, 2001).

James Matlock's theory

It characterizes James Matlock in his book *Signs of Reincarnation* more than anything that he rejects a substantial personal self rather resolutely. Instead, he prefers to talk about a mind, psyche, and consciousness, defining the term "person" as a living, "embodied" human being. This means, for instance, that "persons" in Matlock's definition cannot survive death, and that post-mortem survival is, therefore, limited to the (conscious and subconscious) mind. This implies that a reincarnated child cannot be the same "person" as the one whose life the child remembers. It could suggest that Matlock does not believe in a personal kind of reincarnation. A child with past life memories would not literally be a reincarnation of a deceased person, but it would have non-physically inherited, so to speak, that person's psyche, while still being another person.

Matlock terms his model the theory of a processual soul, with the word "processual" immediately suggesting that the theory has a background of an anti-substantialist process-philosophy built around processes rather than ontological substances. This seems to suggest that the theory is close to the anatta-doctrine of Buddhism, but Matlock stresses that he really does accept a personal kind of reincarnation, albeit of the personal mind or consciousness that used to belong to someone else and not of a substantial Cartesian soul. For example, he states that we become "another person" with each incarnation.

In our view, this seems rather incoherent because it's hard to imagine how someone from the past, who is not the same person as someone in the present, still can change into that other person. We would assume that the body is either an intrinsic part of our personal identity or it is not, but not both at the same time.

Parallel Lives

Some cases of hypnotic reincarnation research show an inconsistency between the year of death at the end of the previous life and birth in the present life. A subject would have been born in one life before dying in his previous incarnation.

This problem is sometimes explained away through an exotic notion known as "parallel lives". According to this idea, someone could be incarnated on earth in many physical bodies simultaneously, because linear time as we experience it would just be an illusion[30].

However, the idea of previous life seems a typical ad hoc explanation and mainly serves the purpose of saving the value of certain cases collected during sessions of hypnotic regression or related techniques. No serious, unequivocal evidence for it has been found in spontaneous CORTs. Sometimes, a child seems to recall a previous life that ended shortly after he was born, but this usually occurs in countries where registration of birth and death is still not very accurate. Even if such (very rare) claims were substantiated, they could be explained more easily by a form of "permanent possession" of a child's body by another deceased personality after the child was born, than by real parallel incarnations.

Binary Soul Doctrine

A recent and rather original addition to theorizing within the fields of survival and reincarnation research comes from Peter Novak (2003) who defends the so-called Binary Soul Doctrine (BSD). According to this theory, personal mind is composed of two distinct parts that may

---

[30] This would also explain why some regression subjects seem to "recall" future lives. Unfortunately, none of these purported "memories" have ever been verified.

be identified as an individual conscious spirit and an unconscious soul. A person's conscious part or *spirit* would reincarnate without recollections of its previous life, whereas the unconscious portion or *soul* would contain memories of its past incarnation. Only if a person's mind were exceptionally well integrated would it be possible consciously to recall a previous life.

Original as that may sound, the data presented here clearly seem to falsify Novak's BSD. Contrary to what his theory predicts, these children had usually not been exceptional in terms of psychological integration. In fact, in some cases such as those of Bishan Chand and Sujith, they had habits that would conventionally be regarded as signs of a lack of psychological maturity, such as a drinking habit or drug addiction. For this and other reasons, Titus Rivas does not regard the BSD as a serious threat to his own, more conventional spiritual personalism.

Objections Against the Reincarnation Hypothesis

Some additional objections/arguments have been formulated against the hypothesis of reincarnation by several critics, they are:

1. The psychocultural need to believe in reincarnation could create the cases in a conscious conspiracy between parents and children, neighbours and strangers.
2. There are factual inconsistencies that appear in even the strongest cases.
3. The possibility of connections between present and past life families cannot always be ruled out.
4. There can be various incentives for wanting to be thought of as being reborn.

These boil down to an interpretation of cases of reincarnation as nothing more than an artificial cultural phenomenon rather than a spontaneous natural one. One of the most compelling arguments is to say, "they were self-reinforcing communal fantasies, proving nothing more than a society's desire to believe". However, such a statement shows a lack of considered facts. Nothing we have seen points in that direction, in fact, if anything it tests levels of tolerance and credulity far more often than any society's desire to believe. Many people within both more developed societies and less educated areas are filled with disbelief and varying amounts of scepticism, until an acceptable level of proof is shown.

Also, if the phenomenon of children remembering previous lives were a purely cultural creation, similarities between cases found in different cultures and countries would be superficial at best. Collaboration between children of the ages most commonly associated with the recollections is non-existent, and highly unlikely to exist, as they do not have a common language let alone the means to communicate their experiences to other children. Moreover, we find a lot of differences between what a community believes in and what the children's recollections indicate. For example:

> If the innumerable Druze cases were motivated by the desire to reinforce belief, why did the average separation between death and rebirth equal eight months when dogma insists the interval should be nil? (Shroder, Pp. 173).

Demographical Argument

Several authors stress that there are many more people alive today than, say, 100 years ago, which would seem to make the reincarnation hypothesis incoherent in that not all people could have been reincarnated.

This would be important only if reincarnation could exclusively occur immediately after death, i.e. if there does not exist any type of discarnate realm between incarnation and also if humans could never have been members of other animal species. David Bishai (2000) of the *Johns Hopkins School of Public Health*, Department of *Population and Family Health Sciences* has dedicated a whole article to these issues.

Summing up, we conclude that these counter-arguments are not really as important as they may seem.

6

RECURRENT FEATURES OF REINCARNATION

~

Arriving at the best interpretation by eliminating alternative hypotheses is one approach – yet it's a somewhat negative approach.

Alternatively, we can examine another approach, which we see as a positive one. It consists of highlighting recurrent aspects or features of known CORTs that can, in our view, be sufficiently explained only by applying the hypothesis of reincarnation.

Let us look at such aspects:

Remarkable Uniformity

Though cases are found in different countries and contrasting cultures, remarkable uniformity has been observed from case to case, not necessarily in specifics but certainly in structure. The age of recall, age of forgetting, mode of death, emotional expressions, and longing for the relatives of the former life, etc., are some of the examples in which we find similar information in different countries.

Another similarity is that solved cases, with documented records before any attempt at verification, are not fundamentally different from other solved cases that lack such records (Stevenson & Schouten, 1998).

Most of the subjects we have described started to talk about their previous life when they were between two and five years old. The age children usually are when they start speaking about a previous life seems to be one of the most consistent features of all spontaneous CORTs in children. It is found in all unsolved Dutch CORTs among children and in the (thus far only) solved Dutch CORT that did not refer to one and the same family, that of Christina.

The average age when the subject started his or her recalls and recognitions related to an alleged past life in a total of 514 cases studied by Dr. Rawat is 37 months. Dr. Stevenson reports thirty months in both Indian (235) and a sample of American (79) cases (Stevenson (1987), Pp. 103). There are rare cases in which memories of a past suddenly emerged in the subject at an advanced age.

Similarly, almost all subjects stop talking about a previous life, sometimes within a period of a few months, although a few continue to recall new things for two or three years more. Some subjects like Shanti Devi and Swarnlata could recall a great deal about their past life for many years. (Shanti talked to Dr. Rawat until just four days before she died at the age of about 62 years; Swarnlata spoke to him in 1999 when she was about 53).

In some Dutch CORTs, subjects also seemed to retain their memories much longer than average. So we may conclude that the variations in terms of recollection are probably relevant to the intensity of the recollection and the manner in which it was subsequently reinforced by the reliving of the experiences and the investigation.

It's quite possible that they could do so only because they had constantly been asked about their memories and they did not have new imaged memories. On the other hand, in the unsolved Dutch case of Angela, studied by Titus Rivas, the subject soon stopped mentioning her previous life altogether after she had started talking about it when she was about three years old. If a lack of reinforcement (by discussing or having people interested in any aspect of it) contributed to the diminishing of the recollection that might partially explain why more cases are not apparent.

Profuse Recalls and Recognitions

In some cases we find an abundance of correct recollections of events and recognition of people and places related to the previous personality. In Dr. Rawat's collection we have 10 CORTs in which the number of these recalls and recognitions exceeded 50 and in two cases the figure exceeded 100.

Knowledge of Private Information or Secrets

As we have seen above, Shanti Devi (at the age of nine) could demonstrate the special sexual position adopted by Lugdi and her husband in order to conceive since Lugdi was suffering from arthritis.

A boy in Turkey (studied by Dr. Stevenson) correctly stated that his wife of the past life had a mole on her thigh. Similarly, a boy in India (studied by Dr. Rawat) surprised everybody by saying that his wife had a mole on her thigh. Raghunath (also studied by Dr. Rawat) could also satisfy Mahpool, his past-life wife, on the basis of intimate knowledge, which he gave to her when she met him alone.

Dr. Rawat has on record 23 cases in which the subject revealed knowledge of some hidden objects, generally money or ornaments, apparently known by him or her in the past life. In Rajasthan, where Dr. Rawat worked for about 20 years, he found people flocking towards the subject as soon as a word reached them about a rebirth – usually of an elderly person; often they were hoping to obtain information about some treasure hidden by the previous personality. He learned that their efforts were sometimes successful.

Unusual Behaviour and Habits

When Rakesh Gaur (whom Dr. Rawat first studied in 1976) was only three or four years old, his parents noted that when it rained heavily during the night he would suddenly get up and murmur: "Oh, Ram! [Oh my God] What a difficult situation my wife and children would be in; it is raining torrentially!"

Titus Rivas has a case in which a three-and-a-half-year-old Dutch girl worried because her past life family did not know where she was located in the present life.

Jenny Cockell, an English woman studied by Mary Rose Barrington, was very concerned, as a young girl, about the fate of the children she recalled having left behind in Ireland after she died while giving birth.

Similarly puzzled were the prosperous parents of a little girl in Sri Lanka when they noticed that she would put a little sugar in the palm of her hand and lick it as she drank the tea. Later, it was found that in the poor family of the previous personality it was the usual way of drinking tea.

In India, the very idea of eating meat is repulsive to Brahmins, yet a little girl born into this family was asking for "pork". Her personal habits were also, to Brahmins, very dirty. She had memories of a past life in an untouchable caste, which would have made Brahmins cringe, as their tolerance of others is limited even now, because remnants of the caste system still exist and they see themselves as superior.

Jagdish Chandra would sometimes roll on the floor dressed in a loincloth, asserting to his family that this was a sort of loosening up before wrestling. This playing at wrestling would have related to the wrestling that went on at the home of Babu Pandey.

In cases of several Burmese children who claimed to remember previous lives as Japanese soldiers, they played at being a soldier. Was their play motivated in part by their recollections of a previous life, and, if so, how many other children have similar motivations based on past incarnations?

Phobias Found in Childhood

Phobias of things such as water and bean curd, were also noticed in some children while many others displayed a marked fear of aeroplanes, lorries, knives, pistols, guns, fire, etc. (the list is extensive).

In the Sri Lankan case of Shamlinie Prema (studied by Stevenson), the parents noticed that "even before she could speak, she showed a remarkable fear of being bathed; she screamed and resisted any attempt to immerse her in water (...). (About the mode of death in her past life she said) that she went to buy bread in the morning (...) the road was flooded. A bush splashed water on her and she fell into a paddy field".

Sangeeta of Ajmer (Rajasthan) was reported to get frightened when any attempt was made to bathe her and particularly whenever she saw a lot of water, e.g. a lake or a river. Usha, the previous personality, had been Dr. Rawat's student and he knew, personally, the tragic incident where a boat capsized and she was one of the victims.

Stevenson has published many cases of phobias and aversions related to the mode of death in the previous life. A notable example is that of Imad Elawar who showed a phobia of large trucks and buses, which corresponded to the fact that Ibrahim was disturbed by the truck accident and death of his cousin and friend Said Bouhamzy from events occurring in a past life. Similarly, Sujith Lakmal Jayaratne was afraid of trucks or "lorries," which corresponded to his own death as Sammy Fernando. We cannot deny that they have these feelings and concerns, and if the cases where they occur are valid, then we must reconsider how to deal with their concerns, or offer suggestions to their families to aid them in coming to terms with their fears.

In the unsolved Dutch case of Kees (pseudonym), the subject had a general phobia of dying that was related to his recalling a traumatic death as a soldier. His parents helped him to get over this phobia by convincing him of the uncommon nature of his death at the end of the past life.

The Dutch girl (of American parents) S. who seemed to recall a previous life during the Holocaust, was afraid of medical doctors and men in general, which may possibly be connected to a generalization of traumatic experiences with Nazi experiments or other "medical" procedures in a concentration camp.

Another Dutch girl, Myriam R., had an aversion to sand related to her memories of dying in a desert storm.

Yet another Dutch girl, Carlijn, recalled a life as a dark-skinned girl by the name of Surea or Suraya who, out of curiosity, had climbed down a hole and was buried with sand, which made it impossible for her to get out. In this life, Carlijn was very afraid of drowning.

A Dutch boy of three had nightmares that seemed to be related to the Holocaust. Every time he woke up from such a dream, he was screaming in terror. The boy recalled a life with another mother and sister and told his mom that they all had to wear a badge in the shape of a star.

Philias (Loves)

There are numerous cases in which the subject expressed strong likings for something apparently related to a past life. Bishan Chand Kapoor showed likings for things that had also appealed to Laxmi Narain, such as meat, alcohol and women.

Imad Elawar longed for the beautiful mistress, Jamileh, whom he claimed to have had in his previous life. Although Kees suffered from a strong phobia due to his memories of dying as a soldier, in early childhood he also expressed a desire to be a soldier again.

A young Dutch girl raised in the Netherlands felt very emotional about her grandfather who had lived in Indonesia, but whom she had never known in this life. At a very early age, she showed a remarkable taste for rice and Indonesian food in general, which was not shared by her brother.

Unusual Craving in the Mother of the Subject for a Particular Food Item During Pregnancy

A subject, whom Dr. Rawat studied in Jodhpur, Rajasthan, India, showed an unusual fondness for spinach. His mother, too, had developed a strong craving for spinach during her pregnancy with him. The previous personality, the subject's own maternal grandfather, had also had the same uncommon liking for spinach.

Dr. Stevenson claimed to have found the same phenomenon in Sujith Lakmal Jayaratne and Gamini Jayasena of Sri Lanka; Bongkuch Promsin and Ornuma Sua Ying Yong of Thailand; and Kumkum Verma and Gopal Gupta of India.

Untaught Skills

In 1996 Dr. Rawat and his wife, Vidya Rawat, studied a boy, Shailendra, of about four years old who could read fluently from books of Hindi and English and from scriptures in Sanskrit. His mother was illiterate and his father undertook no further study beyond middle school.

Dr. Rawat and his associates have records of 38 cases of child prodigies, but of these only six had some memories of a past life and they were non-specific, though this does seem decidedly higher than the average occurrence of these recollections. They have reports of many children who show unusual talents or skills and, at the same time, have a remembrance of a previous personality with a corresponding talent or skill. Bishan Chand of Bareilly played with ease the Indian drums known as tablas (during his visit to Pilibhit) although he had never seen them before. "Playing well on tablas requires discipline and practice," Dr. Stevenson comments (1987, Pp. 58-59). So we can see certain abilities and talents seem transferable between lives and we might therefore wonder if child prodigies have already developed their skills in previous lives. This was recently (2010) stressed again by Brazilian author Gerson Simões Monteiros in a letter to the editor in the magazine *Superinteressante*.

Corliss Chotkin Jr. of Alaska also displayed more than a mere interest in engines. He was never taught, but had some skill in handling and repairing them. The previous personalities of both Bishen Chand and Corliss Chotkin Jr. were reported as possessing similar skills.

Unlearned Words and Languages

Laxmi Kathat uttered words in the Gujarati language, which she could not have learned in a remote village of Rajasthan State – a form of xenoglossy.

Most astonishing is the case of Uttara Huddar of Nagpur, Maharashtra, India. Dr. Rawat first met her in Nagpur in 1976. She was seemingly "under the spell" of the previous personality. This recollection was as a Bengali woman called Sharada who had lived and died in Bengal about 150 years ago. She could speak and write in the Bengali language. Interestingly, her vocabulary contained many almost obsolete words, which were the vernacular during that period but not today. (Uttara's case forms part of a book of 1984 in which Dr. Stevenson has discussed only one additional case of xenoglossy). A substantial number of Sharada's statements have been verified and a family corresponding to them has been traced in the part of Bengal where she claimed she had lived.

We have already mentioned several others cases of xenoglossy, such as the case of Lucía Altarez (Altares) and the hypnotic case of Rataraju studied by Masayuki Ohkado and his associates.

Yet another case was discovered in 2005 by Titus Rivas and Anny Dirven. It concerns a Dutch lady, Jolanda Klaassen, who, as a young girl, showed signs of having lived before in the former Dutch South-American colony of Suriname (Surinam).

At the age of four, Jolanda regarded Suriname as her "promised land" and had spontaneous images of a yard and of red earth. She also felt a strong bond with Amerindian people. At the time, she certainly did not know any Surinamese people.

She soon showed a very unusual propensity for Winti, the Surinamese version of magic that derives from ancient African and Native American traditions. This also seems to be related to a considerable talent for ESP and healing (which is, as we have seen, uncommon among subjects of CORTs).

In general, Jolanda manifested a remarkable speed in absorbing and understanding Surinamese culture and language, the Creole language known as Sranan Tongoe. According to both Jolanda and John, she learnt this language incredibly effortlessly and quickly. She speaks it without the typical Dutch accent of most white people and for this reason she is often asked if she was born in Suriname. Some Surinamese people are so startled by her linguistic skills that they refuse to believe she was not raised in their country. She has even learnt to understand a large part of several dialects. John acknowledges that Jolanda has a general gift for learning languages, but he is certain that this alone cannot easily explain her competence in Sranan Tongue.

On holidays with John in Suriname, she immediately felt at home and she was treated differently from other white people. She often seemed to surpass native Surinamese people in speaking their own language or in her skills of cooking traditional Surinamese dishes and performing various rituals. According to John, she possesses unlearned knowledge about traditional medicine.

In the Netherlands, many people used to tell Jolanda she should have been black. Jolanda formulates this as follows: "The things I like, my taste in music, clothing, perfume, food, and so on, but also my behaviour, opinions, norms, etc." all seemed to be grounded in black culture.

If we take this case seriously, it seems to indicate that Jolanda was a Creole shaman, strongly influenced by the native Surinamese ("Indian") population. In her present life, she has read a lot and followed some courses to enhance her abilities as a healer. Even her attraction to a Ghanaian man may be related to subconscious memories of a Creole life, as much of the original Creole culture derived from Ghana or the Gold Coast, one of the places from where many black slaves were shipped to the Americas.

From all this we can see that past knowledge is transferred from one life to the next. We can only wonder, at the moment, how we might enrich and enhance the education and lives of other children by discovering their past lives.

Prediction of Rebirth

William George, Sr. of Alaska, toward the end of his life, though he had serious doubts about rebirth, entertained a great wish to be reborn. Many times he even declared to his favourite son and daughter-in-law: "If there is anything to this rebirth business I will come back and be your son".

Later, he added: "And you would recognize me because I will have birthmarks like the ones I now have". Then he used to show two prominent pigmented naevi, each about half an inch in diameter, one on the upper surface of his left shoulder and the other on the volar surface of the left forearm about two inches below the crease of the elbow.

Just a few days before his death he gave his son a gold watch, which had been a present from his mother and said: "I will come back. Keep this watch for me. I am going to be your son. If there is anything like that [meaning rebirth] I will do it". Barely nine months after his death a boy was born to his son bearing two pigmented naevi exactly at the locations predicted by William George before his death.

Similarly, Victor Vincent of Alaska, about a year before his death in the spring of 1946 told his niece: "I am coming back as your next son. Your son will have these scars". Then he showed her two scars – one on his back and the other one on his nose on the right side of its base. About eighteen months after his death, the niece gave birth to a son "who had marks on his body of exactly the same shape and location as the scars pointed to by Victor Vincent in his prediction of his rebirth".

Maria Januaria de Oliveiro (commonly known as Sinha or Sinhazinha) on her deathbed promised her good friend Mrs. Ida Lorenz that she would come back and be reborn as her daughter. She further predicted that "when reborn and at an early age when I can speak on the mystery of rebirth in the body of the little girl who will be your daughter, I shall relate many things of my present life, and thus you will recognize the truth". (F.V. Lorenz: *A Voz de Antigo Egito*, 1946, translated by Dr. Stevenson.)

The day after this prediction, Sinha died and about ten months later Ida Lorenz gave birth to a daughter. When this girl, Marta Lorenz, was about two and a half years old she started talking about her past life as Sinha. Later, "Marta went on to make, at various times, no fewer than 120 separate declarations about the life of Sinha and recognitions of people known to Sinha" (Stevenson, *Twenty Cases*, Pp. 185).

Announcing Dreams

In the case of Kumkum Verma, her mother had dreamt about a girl accompanied by snakes before the subject's birth, which turned out to be related to Kumkum's recollections of her previous life.

Shri Nandan Sahay of Uttar Pradesh, India died of a sudden illness at the age of nineteen. His wife was two months pregnant at that time. One night she saw her deceased husband in her dream who told her that he would be born to her but would not take feed from her breast. He also said that he (in his new birth) would have a mark of a scar on his head. The scar mark was found on the head of the boy who was born about seven months later. He didn't take his feed from his mother's breast and even vomited out milk when collected in a spoon from her breast and given to him. At the age of five he told his mother that he was her husband reborn.

In the Turkish case of Necip Ünlütaskiran his mother had dreamt during her pregnancy that a man who called himself Necip announced that he was coming to her. After his birth, the boy who was called Necati at first insisted that his name be changed to Necip. He also recalled a verifiable previous life under the name of Necip Budak. His parents had never heard of this person prior to their son's birth (Stevenson, 1997).

About announcing dreams, Arya Bhushan notes, among other things, that:

> Ian Stevenson, while describing the case of Ma Tin Aung Myo, born on December 26, 1953 in village Nathul in Burma, narrates that Ma Tin's mother, 'Da Aie Tin' saw a Japanese soldier three times in her dreams, and this soldier would tell her that he would come and stay with her family. Ma Tin Aung, as she grew up and was about three or four years old, started remembering and talking of her past life stating that she was a Japanese soldier [...] (Also see: Stevenson, 1980).

And:

> There was [...] case from India, in which a girl died in an accident. Her mother did not want to have another child and got an abortion, whenever there was a pregnancy. Ultimately, the mother saw her dead daughter in her dream, who scolded her for aborting and told her that she should give her an opportunity of being born to her again. The mother agreed to it and a daughter named Rajni was born to her. Rajni, after she grew up, remembered herself as her own dead elder sister from her past life.

Departure Dreams

Sita, a girl of about sixteen years old, drowned in a river. A few months later she appeared in the dream of her mother and told her not to grieve since she was coming soon as a daughter to "Lala" (a shopkeeper from a nearby village). Her brother, who was in service in a distant town, also had a dream with the same message. The wife of Lala was pregnant at the time of the dreams and later delivered a female child.

When Dr. Rawat investigated the case, he found that the girl had some memories related to Sita. According to her parents, she also had some habits and manners of behaviour not found in her siblings that would be similar to those of Sita. Dr. Stevenson has also described several cases in which departure dreams were reported.

Birthmarks and Birth Defects

In numerous cases birthmarks and birth defects have been found on the body of the subjects corresponding to the wounds on the body of the previous personality. Dr. Stevenson's latest work, *Reincarnation and Biology*, in two volumes presents and discusses such cases from all over the world. Dr. Rawat had 51 CORTs of birthmarks and five of birth defects in his collection of cases. In addition to the case of Neera we have already described, we will show some other CORTs with these characteristics:

The Case of Radha

Sohani, a girl of fifteen from Jhadali (a village in the Pali district of Rajasthan, India) had come to her maternal aunt's village Saradhana on a casual visit in December 1971. One day when she was cutting some tree-branches and leaves for some cattle she fell and suffered a fatal head injury, caused by a pointed stone about two inches above her forehead. She died within five minutes.

A few days later, the maternal aunt Phundi dreamt of Sohani telling her that she was coming to "Juri". Juri was a relative of Phundi and lived in the same village of Saradhana. About nine months later, in August 1972, a girl was born to Juri. The girl was named Radha.

When Radha started talking she soon declared that she was Sohani of the village of Jhadali.

Once when asking for more vegetables and not getting them she threatened her mother, Juri: "Give me more or I will go to my village Jhadali". Subsequently, she made several verifiable statements relating to Sohani's life, including the manner of her death. She also described having lived a short life as a bird – "Kamedi" – prior to her birth as Radha. While this is the first example of a recollection of a life other than as a human that we have mentioned as an example, it is not the only one we have encountered.

Dr. Rawat met Radha and her various relatives in Saradhana and Sohani's relatives in Jhadali first in 1981 and later in 1986. In Jhadali, Sohani's mother Hanja gave the details of Radha's recollections of her past life as Sohani and told Dr. Rawat that she addressed her as "Ya" (mother) when she saw her for the first time. She also told Dr. Rawat that Radha's face strongly resembles that of Sohani. "Her hair and lips are exactly of the same sort," she emphasized.

The most important feature of this case is that Radha bears a birthmark, clearly still visible in 1986, when Dr. Rawat photographed her. It is in the same spot where Sohani is reported to have suffered the fatal blow, i.e. about two inches above her forehead.

The case of Suwa Bilat

Dr. Rawat interviewed a number of people at Kanecha and other villages where people knew of the case as first hand witnesses. A 75 year-old, who helped at the delivery of Suwa, told his assistant Vidya Rawat that the body of the newly born baby bore a number of red marks (birthmarks).

Suwa Bilat was born on November 11th, 1953, in a village called Kanecha about 17 kms towards South-West of Beawar (Rajasthan, India). Dr. Rawat received information about him in 1985 when Suwa was already 32. He still bore several birthmarks; at least four of them could be well seen. One was on his right thigh, and ones on both the left and right hand. The most prominent one was on the back of his neck.

When Suwa was two years old he used to get very upset and enraged on seeing two particular individuals named Moti and Nimba passing along a street in front of Suwa's house. When asked about this unusual behaviour, the child used to say that those people had murdered him and that he would take revenge. "His eyes seemed to become red hot and he used to fetch some rod or stick and tried to rush towards them murmuring abuses," said Ganga, Suwa's older sister.

This incident occurred when Dr. Rawat met her in a distant village called Rawatmal in order to verify the information obtained in Kanecha. She was about seven years older than Suwa and used to act as a sort of baby-sitter for him. Suwa spent most of his childhood with her. So she knew more about Suwa's behaviour in childhood than anyone else.

A former landlord in the area was also interviewed about whom it was told that on hearing about Suwa's recalling a past life, he had called him at his residence and had questioned him. From police records, Dr. Rawat verified that in the early hours of March 28, 1952, Maida (the previous personality) was in fact murdered by two of his brothers – Moti and Nimba.

Other cases

A case of a peculiar type is that of a boy Mukul Bhasava of the village of Soyat Kalan, M.P., whom Dr. Rawat studied in 1986. This boy was born with a penis without a foreskin. He recalled a past life as a Muslim and also remembered how he was circumcised.

In eight cases there were two birthmarks, in two cases three birthmarks were noticed, and in three cases there were even more than three birthmarks on the body of the subject. In two cases "internal birthmarks" (i.e. presence of a physical ailment corresponding to some ailment suffered by the previous personality) were found.

In 1998, Satwant Pasricha reported ten cases of birthmarks and birth defects in Northern India.

Their correspondence with the supposedly matching wounds on the concerned deceased person was independently verified, mostly from the medical records. Two subjects had major birth defects. One was born without his right hand and right forearm; another had a severe malformation of the spine (kyphosis) and prominent birthmark on the head. The remaining eight subjects had birthmarks corresponding to gunshot wounds, knife wounds, burns and injuries in a vehicular accident. The birthmarks and birth defects closely corresponded to the injuries of the concerned deceased people. In Pasricha's view, the hypothesis of reincarnation seems best to explain the features of these cases.

Another prominent parapsychologist who has studied birthmarks in relation to reincarnation is Dr. Erlendur Haraldsson. He has published reports about cases in Sri Lanka (Haraldsson, 2000a, 2000b), of which the case of Purnima has become well known.

Arya Bhushan has also written about birthmarks:

In one [Indian] case, Dr. Stevenson saw two children Ramoo and Rajoo, born as twins, each having birthmarks across their abdomen as streaks of increased pigmentation, running more or less horizontally and spaced irregularly. These according to the twin's mother, were present at the time of birth, giving an appearance as if their bodies had been cut. These twins, when about three years old, gave a vivid account of their previous lives, also as twins. In that life, they had been murdered and their bodies had been tied with ropes and dropped in a well, from where they were recovered four days later. All these facts were found to be correct in a detailed investigation and the two children recognized their brother, mother and other relations from their past life (Also see: Stevenson, 1975).

Titus Rivas encountered a few unsolved cases in the Netherlands with birthmarks that might be related to the cause of death at the end of the previous life.

In 2002 he was approached by Mr. E. J. V. from Alkmaar, a 68-year-old pensioner. Mr. V. told Rivas that from the age of two he had been having visual memories of a previous life. He remembered being a four or five-year-old toddler playing in the sand, in front of a round open cabin at the edge of a forest. There was no one in the cabin and he was suddenly attacked by a tiger that grabbed him by his neck and lifted him up in the air. He still was able to scream, but that is where the memory ends.

Mr. V. did not share these images with anyone until he was married. When he did, someone suggested to him that he should look for a birthmark on his neck. It turned out that he actually showed a dark birthmark near the spot where the tiger would have grabbed him.

Experimental Birthmarks

Interesting, as well as important, are cases in which "experimental" birthmarks are reported. These subjects bore some marks that corresponded with marks deliberately placed on the body (mostly without using violence) of a dying or recently deceased person, whose life the subject recalled.

Mrs. V. Singh of Ajmer, Rajasthan (India) had drawn a mark (a spot) on the right knee of her father's corpse. A few months later when she was pregnant, she dreamt of her father announcing his return as her son on a particular day.

Although it was not the due date given by the doctor, a boy was born on that very day. Mrs. Singh reported to Dr. and Mrs. Rawat that instead of first looking at the face of the newly born, she looked immediately at the right knee of the child, and sure enough there was a mark there. (The mark was still visible after seven years when Dr. Rawat studied this case in 1984).

In March 1999, Dr. Rawat and Mrs. Vidya Rawat researched a case in Kathmandu, Nepal, in which an elderly man bore a big black mark on his right temple that corresponded to the mark his mother had supposedly made on the last of her six children who had died one after another as young infants.

Similarly, after two deaths of her infant sons, Bhagirath's mother had sprinkled a few drops of hot oil on the stomach of the last dead child. Her next son, Bhagirath, did survive. He was still alive at the age of 48 when Dr. Rawat last met him in 1992. Black round marks were clearly visible on his stomach. Dr. Stevenson has presented reports of about a dozen similar cases in his *Reincarnation and Biology* (Pp. 803-809).

The Faggot Approach

If we collate the different types of evidence, the combined cases point in the direction of rebirth. Looking for common features in order to strengthen a hypothesis can be likened to binding sticks together in a faggot or bundle of sticks. Each individual case (or stick) may have its weaknesses but, when accumulated, their combined effect provides strong evidence.

Titus Rivas believes that based on these cases, the patterns found both in CORTs and in CORTs without "paranormal" elements becomes decidedly more impressive.

We think we can also use this approach to establish whether unsolved cases fit in the general pattern of verified paranormal CORTs. This way, one could include unsolved cases when testing specific hypotheses about processes involved in reincarnation and in recalling past lives.

The Case of Rozemarijn

Titus Rivas in the *Journal of Scientific Exploration* published a recent example of the application of the reincarnation hypothesis used for strong cases to unsolved cases. His article describes three Dutch unsolved CORTs, one of which is that of the girl Rozemarijn (pseudonym). In the spring of 2001 a friend of Rivas, Ms. Anja Janssen from Nijmegen, told Rivas that she knew a married couple in Molenhoek whose daughter had memories of a previous life. Titus Rivas met all the family members, both parents and their four daughters, in May of 2001. His team included Mrs. Anny Stevens-Dirven, who also interviewed them by phone and asked them numerous questions via (normal) mail on several occasions in 2001 and 2002.

The girl who claimed to remember a previous life was called Rozemarijn. She was aged seven when Rivas met her. Both of her parents had some belief in reincarnation before the case developed, yet they were not interested in publicly stating such a belief. During our investigations they were both very keen on providing a precise wording of their statements even if this meant that the case would seem weaker from a scholarly point of view.

Rozemarijn's father seemed quite eager to know our motivation for conducting the investigation before he would participate in it. Finally, Rozemarijn's father admitted he did not value scholarly research as much as meditation as a way to finding truth. We have no reason to suppose that the case was fabricated to promote a particular belief in reincarnation. Instead, both parents just seemed interested in sharing their experiences and also were relatively supportive in terms of a possible verification of their daughter's statements. It is also important to note that Anja Janssen was mistaken about the daughter who would have had memories of a previous life. She thought it was the youngest daughter who was only three when Rivas first met the family. If Rozemarijn's parents had created it as a story, it is very strange that they did not choose their youngest child as its central character.

Rozemarijn's mother had an announcing dream in the eighth month of her pregnancy with her daughter. She saw a strange "Pictic" woman in her forties, barefoot and dressed in fur, who held deer antlers in her hand. It seemed that this woman told her telepathically that she was going to give birth to a daughter and that she should call her "Deer". She also told her the child had had a difficult past life. This experience made the parents choose a Celtic name for their daughter, not to be confused with her pseudonym Rozemarijn, which is derived from a Celtic divinity who was associated with deer and the world between death and rebirth.

During the first two years of her life, Rozemarijn was a silent child but very quick in her motor development. She also seemed a bit boyish, both physically and psychologically. When Rozemarijn was about two or three years old, she spontaneously told her parents about a previous life as a (male) sailor. She commented on the waves in a swimming pool saying that she used to see waves, which were much higher, "as tall as a house".

She also told them that life at sea could be very strange. Sometimes there had been a storm all night and the next morning everything was completely silent. Often Rozemarijn would draw a sailing-ship and she claimed that the passenger-ship she had sailed on had been called the *Vurk*.

Aboard, she had many tasks, including watching the sail and pennants and being on watch, but also caring for the passengers. She also described where on the ship the adult passengers and the children were sleeping at night, and stated that they did not have beds or hammocks, just a pillow and a blanket. They urinated somewhere on the floor, because there was not any sanitation. There were dead cows aboard from which they cut pieces of meat, which they ate, raw.

Sometimes there were knife fights among the sailors onboard, but she said (that in her past life) she could not stand rudeness and aggression. Also, there was an accident in which a friend of hers fell from a mast and broke his back. There was a large rudder on the ship.

She also mentioned the word "moekille" (Dutch spelling), a pointed walking stick that was also used as a weapon. Her own name was Peer and she, in that life was a lean man with a black beard. The ship sailed to la Garoonya or Karoonya (English Spelling) to pick up poor families and take them to a harbour with palm trees, on an island. She also mentioned the name India in this respect. There were mountains in the background and a few small shops. The poor families weren't slaves and they were fair-skinned. Sometimes the ship moored illegally. On the island she sometimes slept in filthy huts, but the inhabitants were very nice, relaxed and easy-going.

When she was seven her memories seemed largely intact, but she felt too embarrassed to talk about them with strangers such as Titus Rivas. She told her parents that she had been at least 95 years old when she died and had remained fit for most of her life. She mentioned dry biscuits, which they had been eating aboard the ship. She commented: "We were healthy men".

A remarkable skill that might be related to her memories of a life as a sailor was an unlearned agility in climbing. She showed this skill from a very young age and never suffered from fear of heights. She could not swim however, though she was convinced she could. According to her parents she also showed "toughness" uncommon in girls of her age.

Athanasia's team established that in the nineteenth and early twentieth century la Coruña (which phonetically is very close to la Karoonya) used to be an important harbour for immigration to the Spanish colonies sometimes referred to as *las Indias*, including Cuba, an island with palm trees. The (white) Galician immigrants were so poor that they were known as "Galician slaves" (escravos galegos).

The word moekille can be related to makila, originally a Basque pointed walking stick, which was also used as a weapon. The makila had become known in the Galician region of La Coruña through the pilgrimages to Santiago de Compostela. The names Peer and Vurk may, with some imagination, be seen as distortions of the Spanish name Pedro and Barco or Barca (ship). Note that the Spanish "b" and "v" are indistinguishable so that a "b" may sound somewhat like a "v" to people who do not speak the language.

In our view, these features taken together strongly suggest a paranormal process rather than cryptomnesia or childish fantasy.

A strange link exists between Christine's announcing dream about a shamanistic priestess and La Coruña. The city of La Coruña, or part of it, was originally founded by the Celtic people of the Brigantes and known as Brigantia. Many elements of Galician culture are derived from this Celtic heritage. Furthermore, the divinity that was worshipped at Brigantia, named Briga, was a fertility goddess, and she is therefore thematically related to the male Celtic god Rozemarijn's real name was based upon.

Titus Rivas thinks it is a matter of theoretical economy or "parsimony" to interpret this and other unsolved CORTs in a similar way to other classical cases. This principle of parsimony states that you should not choose a new theory for a phenomenon if you already have a satisfactory theory for similar phenomena.

Also, the apparently paranormal features in the case of Rozemarijn strongly suggest that the reincarnation hypothesis is the most fitting interpretation of them.

The Indian Case of IA

Dr. Satwant Pasricha studied the unsolved case of IA, an Indian boy from Kanoi, Uttar Pradesh, who was born in 1982. His parents were Sunni Muslims and his father worked as a mid-level government employee.

Almost immediately after IA's birth, his mother noticed that he had severe malformations of his fingers and toes that did not run in his family. One of his fingers had to be amputated because it repeatedly became infected.

Pasricha writes:

> When IA became able to speak he said that he was from a place called Dapta Balia, and he described his life and death there. He said that he had been a dacoit, as bandits are called in India, and his own gang members had tortured and killed him.
>
> When IA was about two years old, he went out of the house and walked down the road. His mother caught up with him and asked him where he was going. He said that he was going home where 'his' mother and daughters lived. His mother protested that she was his mother. IA then explained that he was from Dapta Balia, where 'his' family lived.

IA explained in detail how to reach Dapta Balia, a village about 95 km from Kanoi. He also explained that he had been the leader of a band of dacoits and described how he and his gang had looted a village and agreed to divide the booty on the following day. Normally the leader of a band of dacoits would receive half the loot and the other half would be shared by the other gang members. IA said that the other members of his gang suspected him of deceiving them while dividing the loot. Therefore, they tied him up, tortured him by chopping his fingers and toes, and left him to die.

After learning of his statements, his maternal grandfather had gone to Dapta Balia, where he learned about a dacoit who had been killed there.

IA also showed a range of unusual behaviour that seemed related to his previous life, such as worries that he should get his daughters married and a wish to regain the stolen treasure he claimed to have buried at Dapta Balia.

He also wished to exact revenge on his former gang members and when he was three to four years old he played at being a dacoit, imitating a gun with a branch of a tree and organizing his playmates into a gang of which he was the leader. Also, he sometimes showed repentance for having killed so many people as a dacoit.

Even more remarkably, he behaved like a Hindu:

> Considering himself a Hindu, and one of fairly high caste, IA refused to eat meat and to say Namaz (Moslem prayers) until he was eight years old. He grumbled at finding himself in a Moslem family, and until later childhood, he would not join other family members in their annual month of fasting (Ramadan). On the contrary, he never missed an opportunity to participate in Hindu festivities.

As IA's parents were Muslims, they did not believe in reincarnation, but were impressed by the boy's detailed knowledge of the geography of Dapta Balia, which astonished them as being quite beyond his normal knowledge. They did not, however, approve of the boy's rejection of Islam.

Dr. Pasricha started investigating the case in 1998 and was joined by Ian Stevenson in 2000. In the meantime, Pasricha's Research Assistant, Ashraf Valli, made enquiries at Dapta Balia and the surrounding villages. He could not verify IA's statements.

Dr Pasricha comments:

> Although IA's statements remain unverified, we ask readers to consider the case as a whole. The malformations are not its only feature, although bleeding and repeated infections suggest recent wounds; we have not found this feature reported in the literature of congenital anomalies of the hand.
>
> The malformations require some explanation, but so does IA's unusual behavior. Among such behavior we count his rejection of his family and his concern to return – as he saw his situation – to Dapta Balia, in order to recover his buried treasure and marry off his daughters. We might regard these attitudes as expressions of childish fantasies. We cannot, however, say this of his rejection of Islam and strong preference for Hinduism.
>
> It remains conjecturable [...] that the murderous cutting of limbs that IA described somehow influenced his embryonic development.

The Dutch Case of Y. K.

In 2003, Titus Rivas and Anny Dirven studied the unsolved Dutch case of Y. K., a boy who talked about two previous lives from the age of one year and eight months to the age of four.

Later on, Y. K. told his mother about his memories in fragments. Since he was still very young, he sometimes lacked the necessary vocabulary to explain what he was talking about. His mother intentionally avoided asking him leading questions and just responded to what he was telling her.

Y. K. seemed to have memories of two previous incarnations. The first one concerned a life "in the snow". He told his mother that in this life his eyes and those of his family resembled stripes rather than normal eyes. This specific memory evoked a lot of tenderness and joy in the boy. He also told her that they did wear shoes, but that these were very different from the shoes he was wearing now. They were thick "bags" made of animals. Sometimes, these shoes were not sufficient to be able to plough through the snow, and they had to put what seemed like big and flat tennis rackets underneath. Y. K. knew these aids, which his mother used to put under his shoes for him, weren't actually tennis rackets. Sometimes they used a sled, but this happened only rarely.

He also recalled that the food was different and resembled a thick porridge.

About his clothing he recalled that they made their own clothes out of animal skins. They sometimes chewed the skins to make them softer.

When Y. K. had become older, between the ages of three and three and a half he also seemed to recall a second life. He lived in a small house, which his family had made from big rocks. They filled the cracks with horse dung. It wasn't a real house, because it contained only one room with everything in it.

They had a horse and a dog, which were allowed to walk about freely. His surroundings reminded his mother of a forest, as he talked about a lot of bushes and trees. They were poor, but they did have enough to eat. His father often left them to go to work for long periods of time.

He remembered that his mother from that life, a beautiful woman with long black hair, at first was very cheerful and sang, danced a lot and often made jokes, but after a while, they were struck by what they described as "the great sadness". This concerned the death of his older brother. He had been horse riding and banged his head against a thick branch. Y. K. witnessed this accident and his mother carried his brother inside. His brother was still alive, but he died in the evening. When his father had returned from work they buried him together.

After this event, that life was "no fun" anymore. His mother was continuously sad and neglected her younger son. Y. K. told his mother that from then on, the good life had never returned.

Rivas and Dirven asked Dr. Antonia Mills whether these memories could be related to the culture and life of Native Americans. She answered them that the first account reminds her of Inuit culture, or what they used to call Eskimo culture.

According to historian Pieter van Wezel, Y. K.'s second account seem to refer to a life in Asia.

Explanatory Value

The strength of a hypothesis also depends on its explanatory value for certain problems and complexities, which currently accepted theories are unable to solve or clarify. The hypothesis of reincarnation provides explanations for puzzling problems such as:

- Phobias and other seemingly unexplainable psychological problems of childhood
- Skills not learned in the present life
- Unusual intellectual, literary musical and artistic gifts
- "Abnormalities" within child-parent relationships
- Differences between members of monozygotic twin pairs
- Gender identity confusion
- Birthmarks and birth defects
- Uniqueness of the individual, etc.

In 1915, Sri Aurobindo wrote: "It's a luminous key which we can fit into many doors of obscurity".

The theory of reincarnation may shed light on many mysteries.

7

CONCLUSION

How Strong is the Growing Evidence?

~

How strong is the scientific (i.e. scholarly) evidence for reincarnation? Can or should we accept it?

At the start of his journey in 1960, Dr. Stevenson stated: "Reincarnation (is) the most plausible hypothesis for understanding the cases of this series". Then he quickly added: "This is not to say that I think they prove reincarnation. Indeed, I am quite sure they do not".

He further stated: "My investigation of apparent memories of former incarnations may well establish reincarnation as the most probable explanation of these experiences".

He did not hope to "prove" reincarnation and seems to have arrived at where he expected himself to be. After studying thousands of cases all over the world and spending a lifetime (more than 37 years) in analyzing, he writes: "No case is perfect; all have flaws. (...) Nevertheless I believe that reincarnation is the best interpretation, although by no means the only one, for the stronger cases without birthmarks or birth defects". In the list of stronger cases, he would "probably count only about 50".

They are, however, not the only ones for which reincarnation seems to me to be the best interpretation. In this category I include also those numerous cases in which the subject had one or more than one unusual birthmark or birth defect that corresponded closely to a wound (or wounds) or other mark (or marks) on a deceased person whose life the subject remembered or with whom others identify him or her.

Even after putting "about 50" plus other "numerous cases" in the category of cases for which the best interpretation is reincarnation, Dr. Stevenson does not say that these cases "prove" reincarnation or that the reincarnation theory is now worthy of being "accepted," although he does speak of a "rational belief" in reincarnation on the basis of them.

Why? Perhaps because, "No case is perfect. All have flaws".

What is a perfect case? In 1960, after describing the "Criteria for the ideal case" he asked, "Do we have any cases, which meet the criteria proposed? I think we do have a few … " (The *Indian Journal of Parapsychology*, 1960, Vol. 2, No. 4, Pp. 152-155.)

In a paper to the Fifth Annual Convention of the Parapsychology Association in 1972 he imagined a case that he considered the "perfect case" of the reincarnation type. The criteria were changed and he wrote, "In conclusion, I wish to emphasize that I do not have such a "perfect case" and have more hope than expectation of finding one". Referring to this he writes in 1997: "We can imagine the perfect case (Stevenson, 1973) but I do not expect to find it, and I doubt whether my successors ever will". (*Reincarnation and Biology*, Pp. 2065.)

Let us discuss the necessity of there being (or of our finding) a "perfect case" in order to prove or accept a phenomenon. Almost every textbook on Principles of Sociology carries a dictum by Aristotle: "Man is a social animal". In order to "prove," or "accept" it, is it necessary for us to discover some – or even a single – "perfect" social animal? Can we find him anywhere? Similar would be the fate of our search if we set ourselves to finding out a "perfect" man from a physiological or psychological perspective. As a parody of what Dr. Stevenson has said, we may say: "No man is perfect, all have flaws".

Even in the absence of perfection, existence is to be accepted. Moreover, what do we mean by a "perfect case"? Would Dr. Stevenson expect all others to agree with his characterization of a "perfect case"? Let us repeat that, in 1960, after describing the "Criteria for the Ideal Case" (The *Indian Journal of Parapsychology*, Vol. 2, No. 4), he asked, "Do we have any cases which meet the criteria I have proposed? I think we do have a few". (Pp. 152-155).

Indeed, it's one's privilege to imagine differently at different times. We think that the pursuit of a "perfect case" is futile if not entirely meaningless. It is true that taken individually each case would seem weak and would not provide us any "proof". If we have a large group of cases displaying some recurrent features, then the principle of the bundle of faggots may well be applied, for it is the combined effect, which creates the greatest strength of proof.

In the eighteenth century (1766), the German philosopher Immanuel Kant wrote about ghost stories, "Although I doubt each one taken by itself, when they are considered as a group, I have some belief in them". Just over 150 years ago, Whately (1858) gave an interesting example, "If any one out of a hundred men throws a stone which strikes a certain object, there is but a slight probability, from that fact alone, that he aimed at that object; but if all the hundred threw stones which struck the same object, no one would doubt that they aimed at it". (Quoted by Dr. Stevenson, 1987, Pp. 159).

The combined strength of a large group of cases from diverse sources is, as said before, like a so-called *faggot of sticks*: individually taken, every stick may have some weakness somewhere but, when many sticks are bound together, their strength increases manifold. (We may also compare this to the method of structuralism defended by Lévi-Strauss.)

Similarly, the evidence from a single case of the reincarnation type may not carry much weight, but, when combined together in a large body of thousands of cases, it becomes almost compelling. In 1960, Dr. Stevenson, while reviewing reports of the 44 cases previously published (with the exception of one), said that these were, in his opinion, "quite sufficient to establish reincarnation as a plausible theory". (The *Indian Journal of Parapsychology*, Ibidem, Pp. 150). In 1966, after investigating about 200 cases and presenting thorough reports of 20 of them he wrote, "The evidence favoring reincarnation as a hypothesis for the cases of this type has increased since I published my review in 1960" (Stevenson, 1966, Pp. 386). In 1974 he made a significant statement: "There is an impressive body of evidence, and it is getting stronger all the time. I think a rational person, if he wants, can believe in reincarnation on the basis of evidence". (Quoted by Alton Slagle in his *Reincarnation: A Doctor looks beyond Death*, New York Sunday News, August 4, 1974.)

Still, it should be conceded that reincarnation is not "proved" in the way theories in physics and chemistry are proved. It would, indeed, always remain a matter of personal judgment, and our judgment in such matters depends on the amount of exposure to "evidence", the strength of our own preconceived notions and what we think would constitute a "proof" (See Mary Rose Barrington's paper "What is Proof?" revised in 1999).

On the basis of all the impressive evidence that has been collected, only a glimpse of which could be presented here, both of us – one from an Eastern culture and the other from a Western culture – believe that the reincarnation hypothesis may now be taken as scientifically (in the sense of scholarly) "acceptable" if not "proved" to the satisfaction of all. This is our (rational) belief. At the same time we stress that all the readers should independently make their own assessment and judgment, preferably on the basis of empirical data of the kind we've presented in this book and of sound rational argumentation. Or as Dr. Stevenson (1997b) formulates it: "Each reader should study the evidence carefully [...] and then reach his or her own conclusion" (pp. 112-113).

Finally, a word about *falsification* of the reincarnation hypothesis. It is sometimes claimed that a particular theory or hypothesis may be called scientific only if it can be falsified by new evidence. The theory of reincarnation cannot generally be falsified, but it is specifically falsifiable as the most suitable hypothesis for paranormal Stevensonian CORTs, since we could imagine a child with paranormal memories of a life as a person who, at that very moment, is still alive and conscious. It is doubtful if the principle of falsifiability is really as important for science as claimed, but it is certainly remarkable to note that the reincarnation hypothesis for paranormal CORTs even fulfils this rather severe criterion.

The Reincarnation Hypothesis as a Working Hypothesis.

The empirical study of reincarnation does not end with the evidence for its existence. On the contrary, the reincarnation hypothesis should stimulate researchers to study many questions related to reincarnation, memories of previous lives, and personal development or evolution through the course of more than one life.

An influential traditional concept in this context is that of "karma" (or its plural: "karmas"), a law (or laws) of nature linking deeds in one life to the circumstances of another one. The study of karma is closely linked to that of reincarnation in the mind of the general public, but in fact it is one of the most complex or subtle aspects that may or may not[31] be involved in actual cases of reincarnation. We are referring here to so-called *external* (or exterior) karma, in terms of external

---

[31] Or it may be involved, but only in unexpected ways.

circumstances and events, not to "internal karma" which is the (rather unproblematic) concept of psychological continuity within someone's own mind in the course of several lifetimes[32].

As it stands, the results of reincarnation research certainly do not justify blaming a person's negative fate in this life on his or her actions in previous lives. In other words, these results are compatible with a notion of real injustice.

Dr. Ian Stevenson published multiple observations about numerous aspects of cases, which might teach us something about various mechanisms, such as mechanisms involved in memory and amnesia concerning previous lives, talents related to skills in previous lives, the influences of images of fatal wounds that ended the previous life appearing on the present body, etc. In a paper written in 2000 he considered the importance of his findings for various questions about human personality and related subjects.

Dr. Erlendur Haraldsson published articles that compare the psychological development of children who remember previous lives with those who do not (Haraldsson, 1997; Haraldsson et al., 2000).

Dr. Jamuna Prasad, who passed away in 2003, developed methods to study personal evolution and karma, which he describes in his *New Dimensions in Reincarnation Researches* (1993). His findings constitute the basis of further investigations at the Dr. Shail Kumari Reincarnation and Spiritual Research Institute. Prasad's heir Harish Chandra Srivastava is working on a book entitled *Beyond the Gateway of Death*.

Arya Bhushan states about Prasad's special interest: "A small pilot study [...] was carried out [...] to determine the role of sanskars (inner cultural traits) in human behaviour. An attempt was made to see if the personality make up in the previous life had significant influence on the behaviour and personality qualities in the present life.

Six authentic cases of reincarnation, which had been studied by Dr. Stevenson, were taken up for this study and the personality make up of both the previous and the present personalities were examined, with the help of a personality questionnaire, by interviewing several informants for each case. The results obtained were very encouraging

---

[32] Some apparent instances of external karma (such as a repetition of events from the previous life in the present one) might, in actual fact, be expressions of internal or interior karma, in the sense that a person might subconsciously attract certain characters or re-create circumstances, based on memories, desires or fears, rather than being affected by an external natural force.

and it was felt that the study should be extended over a wider geographical area".

About innate faculties Von Ward writes:

> Confronted with [...] stories of an inherent genius in languages, mathematics, or music, one immediately asks the how and why questions. Parents say: "He or she was born with it". Since we know mathematics and music at that level require considerable knowledge and practice, that's the only possible answer. Self-evident from infancy and beyond those possessed by their parents, the skills and understanding cannot be explained by environmental or genetic influences.

Von Ward states that there is no normal theory, which offers a satisfactory explanation for such extraordinary skills. Calling such skills "innate faculties" does not explain why they exist.

He goes as far as claiming that during our childhood all of us are prodigies, if we look systematically at all the untutored and inexplicable behaviors of most children.

> All children seem to have some knowledge and skills well before she or he could have learned them as a result of external influences. (Paul Von Ward. *The Soul Genome*, Pp. 15 & 18.)

Titus Rivas recently published an article about possible organic (neurological) and psychological factors involved in recalling and forgetting previous lives (amnesia), in the Dutch journal *Spiegel der Parapsychologie* (See Appendix B for an English summary). He also designed a personalistic model of childhood as a kind of functional "rehabilitation period" after reincarnation that does not depend on the ultimate disintegration of personality (and loss of personal psychological structure) after death that seems to be popular among several other researchers in the field.

Another question concerns the re-interpretation of so-called behavioural genetics in the light of reincarnation. Remarkable psychological similarities among family members in terms of behavioural or personality traits could to a (very) large extent be explained by a matching or "resonance" process that unconsciously or consciously attracts a discarnate entity to specific people with similar psychological characteristics and leads to reincarnation into their family. Such a process of matching might also explain (possible) remarkable psychological similarities between the child and certain genetically unrelated people who are close to the child's present family.

In 2005 we jointly published an article about a possible connection of memories of an intermission period between two incarnations and prebirth memories in young children, with Near-Death Experiences (NDEs), in the *Journal of Religion and Psychical Research* (See Appendix A for extracts of this article). In 2015, Titus Rivas, Anny Dirven, and Elizabeth and Neil Carman wrote an article for the *Journal of Near-Death Studies* concentrating on externally confirmed paranormal aspects of pre-existence memories in young children.

In general, we wish to stress the convergence of data of both (and other) fields of the study of survival after death and personal evolution.

This convergence was also found in an analysis – of 35 Burmese subjects with intermission memories – carried out by Poonam Sharma and Jim B. Tucker (2004), who conclude: "The similarities indicate that the intermission reports by children claiming to remember previous lives may need to be considered as part of the same overall phenomenon – reports of the afterlife – that encompass NDEs".

Another question is the reincarnation of non-human animals. If animals, like people, are spiritual beings then it may be expected that they pass through several incarnations as well. Perhaps, one day, there will be more attention paid to possible cases indicative of the reincarnation of individual animals (Ellis, 2003; Sheridan, 2004).

More generally, reincarnation research has important implications for the empirical study of the interaction between the mind and the brain.

Reincarnation research should be recognized as a serious scientific endeavour. It should also be realized that after the plausibility of reincarnation has been established, we have to concentrate on the exploration of all that it involves and everything that it implies.

APPENDIX A

~

Extracts from "The Life Beyond: Through the eyes of Children who claim to remember previous lives" by Kirti Swaroop Rawat and Titus Rivas, published in *The Journal of Religion and Psychical Research*, Vol. 28, Number 3, 126-136, July 2005.

Shanti Devi about the Life Beyond

Shanti Devi narrated considerable details about the interval between the moment of Lugdi's death and her subsequent rebirth.

Mr. Nahata interviewed Shanti Devi on February 22, 1936. The relevant portions (translated from Hindi) are as follows:

> Question: Tell us: what did you experience at the time of death?
> Answer: Smoke. Three men wearing yellow clothes. I went with them till the Third plane. To the fourth I went alone.
> Q: What did you see there?
> A: There are saints (Sadhus) at all the three places.
> Q: What did you see on the fourth place?
> A: Krishanaji was sitting on a throne. (The suffix -ji expresses veneration.)
> Q: What else was there?
> A: In front, there was a saint.
> Q: Did he have any beard or long plaits of hair?
> A: He had a white beard. There were many saints.
> Q: What else were there?
> A: Krishanaji had a paper in his hand and was reading from it.

Q: What was he reading?
A: I don't know about other thing, but I know he read out –
House Number 565 (The Number of the house Shanti Devi is
residing these days is 565)
Q: What happened then?
A: I returned to a black cell.
Q: Were those three people with you while returning?
A: No.
Q: What was there on your way?
A: Staircases of Gold and silver.
Q: Did you remain hungry in the dark cell?
A: No, I didn't feel any hunger or thirst.

A hypnotic test was conducted on April 13, 1936. The hypnotist was
Mr. Jagdish Mitra. Dr. Indra Sen was present during the sitting. Prof.
Begg took notes. The relevant portions from Prof. Begg's report are as
follows:

Girl: Lugdi is dead. Now Lugdi is getting up from her bed.
Hypnotist: Whether Lugdi is getting up or her soul? The body
is already dead.
Girl: Yes, the body is on the bed. Her soul is getting up. Four men
wearing yellow underwear are standing. They have thrones also.
And there are three saints in blue, black and white clothes. (I
must admit that this portion of what Lugdi said was not clearly
audible to me).
Girl: Now Lugdi has reached God. She had a chit [official
document of an agreement] in hand. She is showing the chit to
God. Bad people are crying.
Hypnotist: What is Lugdi doing now?
Girl: Now Lugdi is coming down stairs of gold and silver now.

Mr. Sushil Bose interviewed Shanti Devi on July 25 and 26 1936. His
monograph, entitled: *A case of Reincarnation* was published in 1952
and is in English.

The relevant portions from his monograph are as follows:

Question: Do you remember how you felt at the time of death?
Answer: Yes, Just before death I felt a profound darkness and

after death I saw a dazzling light. Then and there I knew I had come out of my body in a vaporous form and that I was moving upwards ... I saw that four men in saffron robes had come to me .... All the four seemed to be in their teens and their appearance and dress were very bright .... They put me in a cup and carried me .... It was about nine or ten inches wide and rectangular in shape.

Q: Did you not ask them anything about the river?

A: When asked they said that those who aspired for a higher life sincerely, but who had committed fleshly wrong in this life, were dipped in the river before moving any higher. They took me to the fourth place.

Q: Is there any place to live there at night?

A: No, there are no houses or dwelling places. All is open space .... Arriving on the fourth place I saw that there are still more saints, brighter in appearance than those on the third plane. And in the midst of them, seated on a huge dazzling throne was lord Krishna [one of the most popular Hindu gods]. He was showing each person a record of his activities on earth, good and bad, and accordingly what would be his condition in the future.

Q: What happened then?

A: Then those people, who had carried me, took me to a place like a staircase where it was very bright. I was seated there.

Q: Is there anything like darkness or light there?

A: No, nothing like light or darkness. It was all full of light. It was all day and light, very mild, and smoothing and enlivening light.

Q: Did you have a sense of time? Can you say how long you stayed there?

A: No, I can't say how long I remained there. I had no feeling of time.

Q: Did you feel there was any higher plane above the one where you were?

A: Yes, I observed and felt there was a higher place but I can't say thing about it. I ... in the fourth plane, near the throne of Lord Krishna, I saw one with a long beard.

Q: What finally happened?

A: After remaining on the staircase for a long time I was taken to a dark room, from all sides of which a very bad smell was coming out. I was made to lie down in a clean place there.

Q: Did you feel any pain at the time of death? Did you see anything at that time?

A: I did not feel any pain. I simply passed into a state of unconsciousness, and at that very moment I saw very brilliant light.

Along with Dr. Stevenson and Dr. Pasricha, Dr. Rawat interviewed Shanti Devi at her residence in Delhi on February 3, 1986. The interview was in English. The relevant portions are as follows:

Shanti Devi: Before my death, I saw dazzling light... Very dazzling. Four people, very handsome boys, with large yellow garments. They came with a square shaped vessel and sort of roomal [handkerchief] or whatever you call it. All of a sudden, light came out from the body that I was and they put this light into that vessel and took me up, up and up...
Then again these four people came and put me in the vessel. Then they descended me a very bright staircase and then I came in a cell – dark cell.
Dr. Rawat: Who was looking to your action in this life as Lugdi Lord Krishna or Chitragupta? [In Hindu belief, the recorder of the vices and the virtues of men. Chitragupta is the judge who sends men to heaven or hell.]
Shanti Devi: Chitragupta.

Later, on October 30, 1987, when Dr. Rawat again interviewed Shanti Devi (this time, alone), she mentioned a river and the appearances of the souls present on the fourth plane, in addition to the various details she had given previously. This interview was recorded on a videocassette:

Shanti Devi: They took me up. There was a river. It was quite clean and pure like milk.

About the appearance of the souls she said: "they were like flames in lamps".

From the accounts given above, some salient features emerge:

No pain at the time of death.
Experience of profound darkness at the time of death. Seeing a dazzling light.
Coming out of the (physical) body in vaporous form.

Coming of three or four young people wearing saffron or yellow robes.

Put in a square or rectangular vessel. Feeling of going up and up. Seeing an extremely beautiful garden on the way up. Coming across a river.

Passing through three planes, ultimately taken to the fourth. Absence of an open space on the fourth plane.

Absence of any sense of time at the fourth plane. Presence of Saints on all the four planes.

Presence of a bright (Godly) entity on the fourth plane.

Reading of a review of the actions performed in earthly life on the fourth plane.

Reading of a review of the actions performed in earthly life by this godly entity.

Put on a staircase of silver (and gold), which was very bright, for descending back, by the same people who took her up.

Coming down to a dark cell.

No feeling of hunger or thirst in the black cell.

Frederick H. Holck (1978) has found numerous examples of experiences similar to NDEs in religion and folklore. He discovered four similarities between the new wave of NDEs and previous reports:

The experience of leaving one's body accompanied by the sense of having a "spiritual" body.

A meeting or reunion with departed friends and ancestors.

An experience with a light of dazzling brightness.

Discovering a dividing line or border between both worlds of experience.

In the reports of Shanti Devi's narration we do not find any mention of a "meeting or reunion with departed friends and ancestors," but we do come across her experience of leaving her body in a vaporous form, and of crossing "this" world and ascending to the world "beyond". The experience of a "light of dazzling brightness" has been stressed unambiguously. Her experience of "Darkness" immediately after death may be compared with the experience of a "dark tunnel" narrated by some subject having a close brush with death. Similarly, the return to the "dark cell" before birth may signify entering the womb or the mother.

Cases studied by Dr. Ian Stevenson

Dr. Ian Stevenson found more recent cases of memories of an intermediate state or intermission period between lives, which include memories of an afterlife. Here are a few examples of cases studied by Ian Stevenson that remind us of NDEs (all taken from his book *Reincarnation and Biology*.)

Celal Kapan, a Turkish boy, described events that occurred immediately after he died in the previous life, such as the transport of his body in an ambulance and a doctor pronouncing him dead. He also mentioned the washing of his dead body and its funeral.

A Thai boy, Chanai Choomalaiwong, claimed that he did not know who shot him because he was shot in the back and lost consciousness before he died.

"Afterwards, though, I felt my soul leaving the body. I could see myself lying on the ground. My legs were still twitching. My blood was running on the road".

Santosh Sukla, a girl from India, said that after dying she was taken by four people to a river and was immersed in it. She cried, and then she was taken to a village with many fruit trees and gardens. She saw a person there wearing yellow clothes and sitting on a wooden bed. She sat down, against a pillar and remained there for some time.

There were many people around, and they used to pick the fruit and eat them; but she just watched these people. Then she was asked if she would like to eat some fruit; she accepted and they gave her some. She remained there for a year, after which she was reborn.

A Burmese girl, Ma Par, claimed to recall a life as a British airman whose plane had crashed. She said that she had been buried together with the pilot of the crashed aeroplane. After her death she thought of her family in England and went to see them. However, the "King of Death" did not permit her to stay in England and she returned to Burma, the country where she was killed. She visited England once more, but was again pulled back to Burma and "ordered to be reborn".

Sunita Khandelwal, another Indian girl stated: "I went up. There was a baba (holy man) with a long beard. They checked my record and said:

'Send her back.' There are some rooms there. I have seen God's house. It's very nice. You do not know everything that is there". On another occasion Sunita remarked: "When I fell from a small height, I got a mark, but when I was thrown down from the great height [meaning from God's house] I got no mark".

Peter and Mary Harrison mention several cases in their book *Children that time forgot* about British cases of the reincarnation type. For instance, Nicola Wheater recalled that she fell asleep and died. After that, she saw God in Heaven. She described him as being very beautiful though she did not recall the clothes he was wearing. She added that he was much nicer than you can see on religious pictures.

Dutch theologian Joanne Klink describes similar cases in the Netherlands in her book *Vroeger toen ik groot was*. One example concerns an adopted five-year-old Dutch girl who claimed she used to live in France. She told her grandmother: "I was with the angels in the sky and I looked down upon the earth. I saw you in the garden and have chosen you as my grandmother. I flew to the earth, walked into a house and looked around".

Titus Rivas also studied Dutch cases with intermission memories. Here are a few examples:

Sietske, a Dutch girl, told her mother, crying, that she had dreamed that she had sat on the back of a motorcycle and was run over by a truck. She was put in a "bag" in the back of the car, and afterwards she was put in a "box". Finally she was buried in the "garden".

Kees (pseudonym), a Dutch boy who was already studied by Dr. Klink, explained to his mother that when you die, an angel comes to take you to God, who is pure "goodness," the "Big Light" and "humour". It was very difficult to describe the other world. It did not fit on any slide and could not be drawn with crayons. He added that he had had his own spot near a beautiful blue waterfall, which streamed over and under a flowerbed, and there were wonderful fruits hanging from the trees nearby, which tasted better than all the Mars Bars and candy of the world taken together. Kees had not felt like reincarnating and resisted the angels who tried to convince him that it would be for his own good. They practically pushed him – though they did so lovingly – back to earth, as it was time for him to get to work again. The angels told him: "You know, when you go to earth, you will be accompanied by assistants". He would be protected after he returned. The "Big Light" told him: "To make a good life is your own responsibility".

Christina (pseudonym), a Dutch girl, recalled a life that ended in a fire. A lady in white told her that she had died and took her through the burning house. Christina was shown several possible mothers and asked to pick one of them. She chose a woman with blond hair who was typing at an office. The lady told her that in that case she had to wait a bit longer. The woman's appearance corresponded to that of her mother years before she got pregnant with Christina.

Pre-existence

Recently, Western researchers like Sarah Hinze and Elisabeth Hallett and webmasters such as Michael and Toni Maguire have realized that memories of an intermediate state may also occur without conscious recollections of a previous life. Usually, such memories are termed "prebirth experiences" or "memories of a spiritual pre-existence".

For instance, Toni Maguire claims that as an infant she recalled "buildings and fields. I remembered guides and angels. I would lie around and think about what had been arranged for my life and what I had to do. I specifically recalled standing in front of a huge, white book in heaven. The book was very thick with pages and all the pages had gold trim around the edges. The book sat on a white, marble bookstand or maybe I could describe it as a church pulpit. Light shined out of the book and pulpit the same as it did out of everything else I remembered seeing in heaven. The book lay open as I approached and stood directly in front of it. I noticed the pages were blank. I was taken to it by a guide who stood to my left and gave me some directions about how to proceed. "Look into the pages" my guide instructed. I then looked down at the pages and the blank sheets began to display parts of my future life on earth. I watched as if it was a movie being played for me. As another life change was about to occur, the page would turn again and begin the next part of my life in movie form on that page. I saw a little accident at my grandparent's barn where I took a fall and many other things".

Spiritual Pre-Existence

Titus Rivas and his colleague Anny Dirven found several Dutch cases of a spiritual pre-existence. In the summer of 2003, Mrs. Henny van Sleeuwen from Rosmalen approached them with claimed prebirth memories as a child, which she still retained as an adult:

> I was in a big white room with a white bed. I was lying in the bed and was very ill. I don't know what was wrong with me. I couldn't move any part of my body except for my eyes. Next to my bed there was a nun watching over me. She wore white clothing and a nun's hood, like the ones nuns used to wear. Everything was white and bright. On the other side of my bed there was a door. The door opened and a young woman or girl, about 18 years old, looked inside and entered the room for a little while. She was about 1.60 m tall and slim and she had dark blond curly hair, a brown coat with large buttons and a small pair of spectacles. The nun lifted up my head, so that I could look better at the woman, and, after doing so, I said: 'Yes, this is the woman I want to have for my mum.'
>
> Suddenly I was waiting somewhere and it took quite a long time before I heard or saw anything. There was some kind of long cylinder in front of me. I was ready to go to a new life, but I had to wait to get permission, probably from God, though I'm not sure. There was an all-embracing, invisible voice that could be felt as some sort of energy. This voice was the "boss". It said: 'Are you sure you can deal with it?'
>
> 'Yes, I can', and I nodded my head confidently.
>
> Once more, the Voice asked me: 'Are you completely certain?' Yes, I said, and nodded again. Nothing happened yet. A few moments later, the Voice said: 'Are you absolutely sure that you can deal with that?' I probably thought about what they showed me of the life I'm having now, though I can't remember what exactly I was shown. Again, I told him: 'Yes, I'm certain, I can handle it.' I suppose that I knew what I had to face in this life, though as a child I had already forgotten.
>
> In this life, when I was about 7 years old, I told all this to my mother and she said: 'I really had such a coat, camel-coloured with very large buttons and long curly dark blond hair, and a pair of small spectacles, when I was about 18.' So she recognized everything and I normally couldn't have known any of this".

Henny also said her life has been very tough, especially because of a handicapped father whose condition has been deteriorating over the years and also because she lost her mother at an early age.

Concluding Remarks

One of the main tenets of survival research is that the data clearly seems to be convergent. Dr. Joanne Klink concurs: "It is very remarkable, that these messages from children correspond with messages from people who had near-death experiences and were clinically dead".

APPENDIX B

Amnesia: The universality of reincarnation and the preservation of psychological structure by Titus Rivas

~

Abstract

In this paper, two questions are addressed: *Is reincarnation a universal process?* and *to what extent is our psychological structure preserved from one life to another?* The first question is answered affirmatively and the author gives a plausible explanation for the absence of conscious memories of previous lives in most people due to organic and functional factors of amnesia. About the preservation of psychological structure, the author concludes that we have reason to believe that structure is completely preserved, although much of it latently, in a dispositional form. Attention is also given to the consequences of the foregoing for our views on childhood and to the question whether amnesia concerning previous lives is functional.

Introduction

Researchers such as Ian Stevenson, Jamuna Prasad, K.S. Rawat and others have studied cases of the reincarnation type, which contain information, emotional and motivational patterns, and skills that most probably are not satisfactorily explainable by any so-called "normal" hypothesis. Of the parapsychological hypotheses put forward to explain such cases, reincarnation certainly appears to be the most plausible (Rivas, 1993, 2000). Thus, at least some people can be said to have reincarnated into a new physical body after they died.

Now, we will have to ask ourselves how probable it is that not only such children as are studied in veridical cases of the reincarnation type (including the ones never reported), but also most if not *all* of us have lived before. This problem may be termed the question of the *universality of reincarnation*. Another question is whether the memories and personality structures that turn out to have been preserved in verified cases of the reincarnation type are exceptional not only on the conscious level but also subconsciously.

In other words, is psychological (cognitive, emotional, motor, etc.) structure destroyed after death or at the moment of reincarnation? Or should we suppose that what we find to be actively present in consciousness is not all there in the person's mind as a whole. I would like to call this question the problem of the *preservation of psychological structure*.

Personalism Versus Impersonalism

Before I try to answer both of these questions, I will first have to clarify what I mean by "reincarnation". My own conceptualisation of reincarnation is personalistic. I hold that the mind is not some impersonal or collective category, but the life of a constant, substantial *self*. In Western philosophy my position can be linked with that of such philosophers as Descartes, Leibniz, Bernhard Bolzano, T.K. Österreich and John Foster.

There can be no mind without a self. The self is the ontological substance, which is the condition for mental life. This goes for any mind, both animal and human, and even for any possible extraterrestrial and discarnate minds. We simply cannot coherently conceive of a mind that would not be linked to a subject. Here I will not go into the extensive literature about the problem of self in Western and Eastern philosophy of mind. Suffice to say that my position opposes the Buddhist notion of anatta and other such impersonalistic conceptions.

The self is what I conceive to be the personal agent that is the subject of all of psychological life or *experient*. Thus, it is also the entity that reincarnates and remembers its previous life. The person who remembers what he or she experienced in a previous life is exactly the same person as the one who originally experienced what is now being remembered. It is only within this personalistic context that the questions of the universality of reincarnation and the preservation of psychological structure make any sense. This shows that the philosophical problem of personal identity cannot be disregarded if we dig deeper into the topics related to reincarnation.

1. Universality of Reincarnation

How universal is reincarnation? I am aware that there are many doctrines, both religious (exoterical) and esoterical, which answer this question in pertinent ways. Now, as empirical researchers and theorists, we cannot trust any such doctrines. This is because they are usually based completely on authoritarian statements of "gurus" who claim to possess perfect knowledge. In the West, there are also some examples of such influential gurus as H.P. Blavatsky, founder of the Theosophical Society, and Rudolf Steiner of the Anthroposophical Society.

Similarly, many so-called spiritualistic or spiritist movements have clear ideas about what souls reincarnate and even within what kind of time span and geographical region. The claims of such gurus are as absolute as they are inconsistent with one another. Instead of believing in any of them, it is therefore necessary to deal rationally with this problem of universality and to stay independent as scholars, rejecting the purported self-evident truths of all such diverse "revelations".

By these words obviously I do not intend to offend any religion or its adepts, but I just stress the important truism that rationally unfounded dogma should not enter scientific theory. Let us consider what can be said about the universality of reincarnation on a rational basis.

Most people don't remember a previous life, at least not consciously. If we were to identify the number of people who have reincarnated with those who consciously remember their former lives, we would in fact be identifying past experience with the conscious recollection of it. In general, this is unwarranted, as we all know regarding our present life.

Consciously, we cannot remember everything we have experienced, and if we consider every moment that we have lived through, we see that only a tiny fraction of our experience can be recalled consciously.

This is why we have to conclude that the fact that most of us cannot consciously remember a previous life does not necessarily mean that they don't exist, but may also mean that a process has occurred, which is psychologically known as amnesia, the loss of conscious memory. We may have forgotten what we have experienced rather than not have had any previous life at all. The question of universality depends, therefore, on the question of how plausible it is that amnesia is the real reason why most of us don't seem to remember anything of our psychical past before the physical conception of our bodies.

Let's look at the main types of amnesia that are known to exist and see whether it seems convincing that any of them are the cause of our widespread conscious ignorance about our personal previous lives.

1.1. Types of Amnesia

According to Baddeley, Wilson, and Watts (1995) amnesia can be either *organic,* i.e. based on brain disorders or lesions, or *functional,* i.e. based on psychodynamic factors (such as defense mechanisms). In a book titled, *Handbook of Memory Disorders,* Daniel Tranel and Antonio R. Damasio published a paper called *Neurobiology: foundations of human memory.* They stress the fact that several parts of the brain are involved in organic amnesia. Damage to the lateral parts of the temporal lobes for instance, is linked to problems in retrieving factual knowledge. Damage to the hippocampus is involved in amnesia concerning new factual knowledge. And lesions of the basal ganglia and cerebellum are related to impairment of motor skills. Finally, damage to the nonmedial system can significantly compromise previously acquired information. "When the damage is bilateral, in fact, retrograde memory may be severely compromised for a wide array of knowledge. Patient Boswell, one of the few well-studied cases with extensive bilateral nonmedial temporal destruction, lost nearly all capacity to retrieve knowledge about his past. Outside of a few shreds of general information regarding his hometown, and his former occupation, he can recall virtually nothing regarding important events of his past life – for example, he cannot remember details about his spouse, his children, places he has lived, or his educational history. Even the few pieces of information that he does retrieve cannot be placed correctly in the context of his autobiography". (page 39) It is clear that if organic factors are to explain the blankness of most of our conscious minds regarding previous lives, they must be similar to the ones involved in the kind of general retrograde amnesia as the one that patient Boswell suffered from. On the other hand, possible amnesia about previous lives might also be functional.

This is defined in J.F. Kihlstrom and D.L. Schacter's "Functional disorders of autobiographical memory" (in the same book, page 337) as "memory loss that is attributable to an instigating event or process that does not result in injury or disease affecting brain tissue but nevertheless produces more memory loss than would normally occur in the absence of the instigating event or process". The most likely candidate for a range of functional amnesia as would be necessary to explain our blankness about real previous lives, involves the so-called dissociative disorders, such as multiple personality and fugue. Just as in the case of organic general amnesia, a person may lose virtually all access to his retograde memory, though in that case through purely psychological factors. Gregory and Smeltzer (1983, page 291) state, "Less often, there may be generalized amnesia (for the entire previous life, including loss of knowledge of personal identity and in rare cases, even loss of the ability to use language or understand the function of common objects)". With this in mind, we are able to conclude that retrograde amnesia about previous lives may in principle be caused both by organic and by functional factors.

1.2. Amnesia and Past Lives

Let us now elaborate on our insight that amnesia about previous lives might be caused both psychogenically and somatogenically. What specific organic and psychological factors could be involved?

1.2.1. Organic Factors

From near-death experiences (NDEs) we know that the cessation of brain function near brain death in itself does not seem to cause loss of memory for the discarnate mind. On the contrary, the psychological functioning of a person who experiences an NDE is generally enhanced, and especially memory of the present life is enlarged (see for example: Morse, 1990). People are often presented with a kaleidoscope of all kinds of experiences of their current life when they approach their physical death. This would unequivocally imply that possible amnesia couldn't be linked to brain death. In other words, the only possible source of organic amnesia concerning previous lives would not involve the previous but the *present* brain.

Now, could it be the case that organic memory loss is caused by brain damage in the present body? Perhaps brain damage could play some role in those individuals who actually show the overt signs of it. But they are only a small minority within the totality of the human population. Thus, brain damage cannot be a plausible explanation for amnesia in people without any physiological abnormalities, i.e. the majority of us. The conclusion therefore is that if organic amnesia occurs in this context, it probably has to involve a developmental neuroanatomical or neurophysiological factor, not a lesion or any other form of damage. After reincarnation, the psyche has to interact with a brain that is not yet fully developed. After birth the brain matures just like other organs of the body, and it is conceivable that during the first period of childhood, insufficient brain development might impair retrograde memory of previous lives (a theory which may already be found in some writings by Allen Kardec, and of the movement for Krishna consciousness).

In that case, retrograde amnesia would be the result of the specifically human characteristic of a long period of anatomical and physiological maturation. Our brains and bodies are far from fully developed at birth and need a growth period of at least about two decades to be completed. By the way, this is generally linked by biologists to the need for an extremely complex apparatus (the brain) to interact with our higher mental faculties. Ironically, if we accept the hypothesis that it is the incomplete cerebral development of man that makes us forget as infants what we experienced in our previous lives, it would mean that such organic retrograde amnesia is the price we pay for our higher mental functioning during physical life.

Now, the hypothesis of organic amnesia concerning former incarnations would, surprisingly enough, apply to all people, including those children and adults who do, in fact, remember their previous lives. This is because all of us have (seen from a relative perspective) started this life with underdeveloped brains; not one of us – and this applies to all subjects in veridical cases of rebirth as well – is born with a fully developed brain. So the "underdeveloped brain-hypothesis" can adequately explain amnesia in all people, but it cannot at all explain why some people would consciously recover their memories of their past lives, such as children in paranormal cases of the reincarnation type (CORTs) (Stevenson, 1970). For this, we need another hypothesis.

It is clear that this hypothesis cannot mean that the brains of subjects of CORTs are substantially different from those of other people. Not because this would have been proven empirically not to be the case, but simply because memory of a previous life would, in principle, have to be neuroanatomically possible for any child with enough cerebral development to produce coherent speech. In this respect, all children without physical handicaps are the same. Thus, it is probably not a cerebral difference then, but a psychological one, which must be responsible for the disappearance of amnesia in some children after their brains have developed enough.

A neuropsychological experiment could be carried out on children who remember previous lives. Assuming they are not afraid of such an investigation and are willing to cooperate with it, they might voluntarily be subjected to safe, harmless tests that would show what regions of their brains are active while they remember a previous life and whether these regions are anomalous in any way. The modern techniques of brain scanning are a lot safer than the older ones so that such a test can be done without any real risk and should not be seen as immoral, i.e. as long as the child itself does not object to it.

Please note that postulating physiological factors does not amount to accepting a physicalist account of memory. In this case, it is a matter of applying dualist interactionism and the *transmission* or *filter* theory of the brain's somatogenic influence to the manifestation of non-physical memories.

1.2.2. Psychological Factors

Within psychological factors we can distinguish between functional causes of amnesia, which would be the result of external pressure from the present environment, and the outcome of inner psychological processes stemming from the previous life itself. External pressure would always involve an environment hostile to children's recovering memories of their previous lives. Through some kind of natural "aversion therapy" children would learn from their parents that it is nonsensical, dangerous or even evil to be talking about their previous life.

They might internalize this negative attitude and thereby repress their memories. If this is indeed an important factor, we would expect that many children prematurely lose their memories in countries and (sub) cultures, which are opposed to the idea of reincarnation or at least to remembering past existences. This is a theory that can be tested on a large scale only by carrying out extensive research in Western countries. The prediction would be that we would find many cases in the West wherein there would indeed be some memory, but not enough to make verification possible. Also, we should expect – starting from this model – that in circles in the West, in which reincarnation has become a more respectable concept, we would find relatively more verifiable cases of memories of a previous life. Naturally, it would already seem that this factor is present and must play an important part.

Internal psychological factors would include the absence of strong motives to remember a previous life. The hypothesis that such factors would play a role in amnesia, would predict that people with, for instance, strong personalities or minds trained in meditation and similar techniques and people with special reasons to remember their past (such as traumas or unfinished business) would be over represented within the population of subjects who remember previous lives (See: Matlock in Haraldsson & Matlock, 2017)[33]. That this is indeed the case is indicated, among other things, by the relatively high occurrence of memories of a life ended by a violent death, which could be seen as traumatic (Stevenson, 1987). Erlendur Haraldsson (2005) found that many children who remember previous lives show striking psychological similarities to people who suffer from Post Traumatic Stress Disorder (PTSD) (Also see: Haraldsson & Matlock, 2017). Other factors, such as personality types, have also been studied in this respect by Dr. Ian Stevenson (1987, pages 210-217).

1.3. Conclusion

It is possible to formulate a model including specific factors, both organic and functional, that could account for widespread amnesia about previous lives.

1.4. Reasons for Postulating Universality

Showing that a plausible account can be offered for amnesia about past lives is not the same thing as proving that amnesia really applies to every person who does not remember any former existence. However,

---

[33] Rather surpisingly, Haraldsson and Matlock (2017) found that past life memories might be better retained into adult life than normal memories from preschool years.

I would like to point out three strong reasons to suspect that this plausible account really corresponds to how things are, in this respect:

(1) Many children who remember previous lives also exhibit partial or almost total amnesia having grown up. In other words, remembering a previous life is as vulnerable to amnesia as remembering anything else.

(2) In my opinion this is the main argument: if we look at nature, things hardly ever occur as mere exceptions. It is, by analogy, much more plausible, and, apart from that, even more parsimonious on a theoretical level, to assume that reincarnation, which occurs at least in thousands of cases, is the rule rather than a freak of nature.

(3) Sometimes memories of previous lives show up long after childhood, spontaneously or (in exceptional verified cases) only through hypnosis. Thus, it is seen that amnesia in childhood does not equal non-existence of memory. Therefore, I conclude that reincarnation is indeed a universal process and that the absence of memory should be explained by amnesia as I have tried to do above, not through the absence of previous lives.

2. Preservation of Psychological Structure

The hypothesis I have described above – that our brains are underdeveloped at birth, which explains amnesia in all of us as infants – has consequences for the next question: that of preservation of psychological structure. One of its implications is that when children remember previous lives, they do so after they have temporarily forgotten them. And this, in turn, means that the organic amnesia must have been a question of the impairment of retrieval, not of destruction. If memories can be recovered, they must have been there in the first place. Similarly, we should expect the same for all types of psychological structures, such as personality traits, skills, and factual knowledge. CORTs do, indeed, show the active preservation of such elements. We should, therefore, expect that the entire psychological structure is in some form preserved within the mind as a whole, albeit (to some extent) only on a subconscious level. There is no reason to believe that any part of the mind is lost forever after death or after reincarnation, just because it was developed during a previous physical life. This conclusion seems to harmonize remarkably well with the viewpoints of Dr. Jamuna Prasad where he writes that any act invariably produces its effect in our inner nature (Prasad, 1993, p. 31). These effects he calls "samskars" or "vasanas," terms he borrowed from the Upanishads, without adhering uncritically to these scriptures.

3. Causes of Amnesia During the Intermediate State

Apart from the organic and functional factors that explain amnesia about previous lives, several traditions also mention specific factors that would occur in the state between death and reincarnation when the soul dwells in some other dimension. For example, according to ancient Greek mythology, the river Lethe would wash away all memory of earthly life (Bartelink, 1969). Similarly, other traditions talk about special types of food, offered by spiritual beings, which would induce amnesia but could also be denied. I do not claim that it is impossible that there are factors of this nature that might explain a part of the amnesia so common in many people. However, I do hold that, for the time being, we do not need any such exotic causal factors as long as we can explain amnesia by organic and functional causes alone. This is simply a matter of theoretical parsimony, a virtue not to be underestimated in science.

4. Consequences for Our Views on Childhood

In principle, the conception of the universality of reincarnation leads us to posit that all children, not just those who actively remember past lives, are reincarnated souls. Two aspects may be distinguished in this context. On one hand, the fact that adults temporarily lose the fullness of their memories, personality and skills, might fill one with horror and sadness. However, there is obviously a great consolation: reincarnation implies survival of bodily death and, in this context, childhood is usually comparable to a successful *rehabilitation* process. Parallel to neurological maturation, people can recover and even expand their psychological potentials of the previous life, which they had before their functional regression due to brain underdevelopment. On the other hand, we may also conceive the fact that we reincarnate as a kind of natural rejuvenation process. This positive notion implies that childhood is not only a period of limitation and of dependence on others, but is often a period of recovering strength, particularly, (I should add[34]) in the West.

Thus, whereas reincarnation may at first seem to be basically a humiliating phenomenon, if we take a closer look, it usually turns out to be an interesting, moving and continuously recurrent stage continuously recurrent stage, meaning, as long as somebody continues to reincarnate, which does not imply we always do or have to, within the enormous, constructive process of our personal evolution, in which nothing should be expected to be lost forever.

5. Amnesia is in Itself Dysfunctional

In contrast to the doctrines stating that amnesia regarding past lives is a positive, functional process, I hold that its consequences have often been rather nasty. On the other hand, there might be some positive effects of forgetting a previous life. For instance, it might help a reincarnated soul to adapt to its present existence and social environment. However, the sum total clearly seems to be very negative. First of all, if people do not remember that they have lived before, they lack the security and consolation that such memories offer in the sense that they are immortal and cannot be destroyed by physical death. Especially in Western culture, this has had, and still has, disastrous consequences. Moreover, to forget the whole of one's autobiographical history before birth amounts to a tremendous range of alienation. If we knew more about who and what we have been in the past, we would know better who and what we really are now, and where we stand. It might also enhance our interest in life, our passion for it in the positive sense of this word, our love for ourselves, our dignity, our love and respect for all of our fellow beings. I feel strongly that we would benefit if we could remember our previous lives at will. This accords with recent findings presented by Haraldsson and Matlock (2017), which suggest

---

[34] I mean that in many other parts of the world, child labour still is a common phenomenon.

that having (real) past life memories has mainly positive consequences for the well-being of the people concerned.

In this context, I want to propose the following experiment in children who remember previous lives. They could be hypnotized, not so much to broaden their memory of the past existence, as to consolidate it for the rest of their lives (as long as the children are willing to participate).

I'm talking about (post) hypnotic suggestions that they would remember everything at will forever[35]. If we believe, as I do, that remembering a previous life is, as such, a very positive, even transcendent phenomenon, this is a way that we might use to preserve conscious memory in people who have already been shown to remember their past life. At a later stage, if this plan works for children who remember previous lives, we could try, on that basis, to devise a specific posthypnotic (auto) suggestion that could consolidate important memories of the present life for their conscious use in all of our next incarnations.

Paradoxically, this may even help to overcome posttraumatic phenomena that derive from a previous life. Such phenomena do not depend on conscious memories, but they can be dealt with more easily after they have reached consciousness.

---

[35] This does not include the *involuntary* posttraumatic memory of traumatic events.

APPENDIX C

Rebirth and Personal identity: Is Reincarnation an Intrinsically Impersonal Concept?

by Titus Rivas

~

"You should know that in my previous life I was already the very same person I am now!"
~ Kees, a Dutch boy with previous life memories

Abstract

Some Westerners associate the concept of reincarnation with the loss of personal identity. This is an oversimplification resulting from a strong influence of the Buddhist anatta-doctrine on contemporary Western spirituality. The notion of reincarnation can indeed be reconciled with a personalist philosophy. Spiritual personalists may benefit a lot from reincarnation research. Rather than giving up on their personalism, they could extend it to the notion of a truly personal evolution over several lives on earth.

Introduction

Some spiritualists, Swedenborgians, Christians, Muslims and others appear to regard reincarnation research as a threat to a realistic and positive perspective on personal survival after death. It seems that in their view, reincarnation theory could be compatible only with an impersonalist stand on personal identity. Accordingly, reincarnation would imply that death is followed by a radical disintegration of personality, or loss of self. Only certain memories, personality traits and skills would be "recycled" during the formation of a fundamentally new person. In a sense, the theory of reincarnation would be remarkably similar to the materialist theory of extinction after death in that the person, as such, would really be irreversibly destroyed. The consolation offered by reincarnation for the eternal loss of a person would be very bleak indeed, adding a new bizarre dimension to life rather than taking away the apparent absurdity of death. However, this particular concept is not the only rationally conceivable perspective on reincarnation.

Impersonal rebirth

Most Buddhist views about personal identity can be summarized by the Pali term "anatta," which literally means "no soul" (Sanskrit an-atman). There used to be a minor Buddhist movement that accepted some type of personal survival after death (known as Vatsiputriya or Pudgalavada), but nowadays most Buddhists consider this school as little more than an outdated early sect. (However, there are a few Buddhist scholars who believe that the original teachings of the Buddha were not impersonalist). The Buddhist teaching of anatta has, to a considerable extent, influenced contemporary Western spiritual theory. This doctrine teaches that there cannot even be a real personal identity during a physical lifetime as there is no constant, substantial self. In this ontological anti-substantialism, Buddhism is quite close to the fashionable so-called process-metaphysics in the West, of scholars such as Alfred North Whitehead. The (mainstream) Buddhist position on personal identity implies that reincarnation cannot be a personal process, as there never is a real substantial self in the first place. For a Buddhist, rebirth is ultimately just as non-personal as any human life itself.

Forms of substantialism

As popular as process-metaphysics may be, substantialism is not rejected by all serious contemporary philosophers. In general, substantialism is the theory that there are one or more things in reality, known as substances, which cannot be reduced to events or processes. Substances in this ontological (rather than chemical) sense remain constant in their ultimate, irreducible and un-analysable identity with themselves (their essence), although they may change in their temporal properties or actions (their existence). For substantialists, substances are the ontological realms within which events or processes take place, whereas supporters of process metaphysics deny that we need any such substantial ground for events and processes. Traditional examples of things or entities that are believed to be substances are: a God or gods, human beings or animals in general, subjective experients or selves, physical atoms, matter, or the universe.

Both in the East and in the West, a great many educated people, including the author of this paper, continue to endorse some form of substantialism, as they believe that the reasons for it remain more valid than the arguments offered for process-metaphysics. Generally speaking, there are three major ontological positions that involve a notion of a substantial self. One of these is the holistic type of personalism, which holds that a person is an indivisible whole consisting of a body and mind or personality. Except for the possibilities of a literal resurrection of the "total person" (which is part of the creed of Jehovah's witnesses; see: Morse, 2000, Pp. 267) and of (divine) emancipation of the emergent soul from its body (William Hasker, personal communication), this holistic or emergentist personalism typically seems incompatible with personal survival after bodily death, let alone personal reincarnation. Holistic or emergent personalism is related to the Aristotelian view, see Morse (2000, Pp. 203): "For Aristotle, as the soul is an intricate materialistic part of the body, when a person dies, the soul dies as well". A second type of substantialism also accepts that there is a substantial self, but claims that this self is ultimately not personal, but transpersonal. This theory is often expressed by the equation Atman (soul) = Brahman (God), and it amounts to the assumption that our real Selves – which would go beyond our individual personalities – would all be identical and consist of one single divine spiritual essence or soul (noetic monism). The theory is typical for certain currents within Hinduism such as Advaita. It is compatible with a notion of "personal" reincarnation, in that both the transpersonal Atman and the individual personality dependent on it (jivatman) may be assumed to survive death and be reborn. Certain Western authors, such as Aldous Huxley, clearly have been influenced by this transpersonalist type of substantialism. More recently, echoes of this theory can be found in the literature of channelling, e.g. in the books about the entity named "Seth," channelled through Jane Roberts. A third type of substantialism amounts to the theory that there is a plurality of ultimately irreducible individual souls rather than just a single divine one. There is a personal conscious subject, self or "I" who sees, thinks, feels, wants, etc. The physical body is not part of the real person in this spiritual sense and personal identity of the personal self cannot be affected by bodily death. Also, as the personal self is substantial, even radical inner change (of its existence) will never be able to disintegrate it (in the essential sense) into more than one personal experient.

Spiritual personalism

Within Indian philosophy, this position, which may be termed spiritual personalism, is supported by the Dvaita interpretation of Vedanta and other pluralistic currents such as Jainism or the logical realism of Nyaya-philosophy. Within European or, more generally Western, thought it is defended in the Monadology of Leibniz and in Athanasia by Bernhard Bolzano, and also by major Christian and modern thinkers such as Augustine, Descartes, Oesterreich (1910), John Foster (1991), the Jewish mystical movements of Kabbalah and Hassidism (Morse, 2000) (and the present author) (Rivas, 2003a, 2005). Don Morse (2000) even traces it back to Socrates and Plato: "Socrates stated that the soul was substance and could not vanish but merely changed form. He stated that all substances are indestructible, but their forms can change". (Pp. 200) and "Plato said that the soul is neither created nor destroyed. Every soul has been here forever and will exist for eternity". (Pp. 202). Applied to the context of previous lives, spiritual personalism can make sense of rebirth only if it is conceived of as a truly personal phenomenon. There is even a whole spiritualist (or, perhaps more accurately, spiritist) movement, Kardecism, which accepts personal reincarnation and is based on the writings of Hippolyte Leon Denizarth Rivail, better known by his pseudonym Allan Kardec (1804-1869). Don Morse (2000, Pp. 292) writes about Kardecism: "It differs in that with each incarnation, the spirit retains its individuality and spirits always evolve". It is important to note that a personal self should be distinguished conceptually from its personality. A personality may be seen as an acquired (existential) pattern of psychological structures, attitudes and skills of a substantial personal self, which (essentially) always remains identical to itself. A personality is dynamic and changes over time, and, in certain pathological cases, a personal self may possess several personalities simultaneously though it can be conscious only in one personality at a time. Thus, changes of personality and even dissociation are fully compatible with the notion of a substantial personal self. In the context of reincarnation we will expect certain changes of personality through the processes of death, rebirth and childhood, but this does not mean that those changes imply a new or different personal self. We would remain ourselves just as much as we remain ourselves in the course of a single earthly lifetime. During one life we start off as children and, after about two decades, we normally become adults, which we remain until, as a consequence of reincarnation, we become children again, though hopefully at a somewhat "higher (dispositional) level" of personal evolution.

The reader will not be surprised to learn that spiritual personalism is also the author's position.

Other positions reconcilable with some kind of personal reincarnation

Recently, a fourth approach to personal identity is proposed by Peter Novak (1997). It was partially adopted by Donald Morse (2000) during the development of his own personal theory of survival after death (Chapter 15). However, Morse acknowledges, "There are certain aspects of the theory that are difficult to reconcile with existing beliefs" (Pp. 331). Novak defends what might be termed a kind of mental dualism, which he traces back to ancient theories of the kind found in the Gnostic literature. A personal mind would be composed of two distinct parts that may be identified as an individual conscious spirit and an unconscious soul. In a sense, we might also term this position "spiritual holism" in that a person would be non-physical and consist of two clearly distinguishable spiritual components. The difference with mind-body holism lies in the idea that after death the two parts of the personal mind may both survive separately and ultimately reunite. A person's conscious part or spirit would reincarnate without recollections of its previous life, whereas the unconscious portion or soul would contain memories of one's past incarnation. Yet another, fifth approach was recently presented by Geoffrey Read. It is, in fact, an exponent of process-metaphysics in that it does not accept the validity of the concept of ontological substances. However, Read is convinced that human survival and reincarnation are personal, due to the "individuation" of the psyche: "the higher [more complex] the species of the developing organism, and the longer it survives, the less the likelihood of the associated psyche being replaced by another. In short, this psyche is now in command of a new organism. We say that it has reincarnated". (Hewitt, 2003, Pp.351). Summing up, apart from holistic personalism and other non-reincarnationist positions, only Buddhist anatta-doctrine and its Western counterparts (with the exception of Geoffrey Read's specific brand of process metaphysics) are by definition incompatible with any type of personal rebirth. Therefore, it is incorrect to assume that the idea of reincarnation would automatically have to imply destruction of a personal soul or ultimate loss of personal identity. If we accept that we are spiritual entities, which are not identical with our bodies and irreducible to ultimately impersonal events or processes, personal reincarnation turns out to be a coherent notion. The author is a supporter of the third position (traditional spiritual personalism), but accepts that personalism concerning reincarnation may also manifest in other ways.

Empirical support for impersonalism or personalism?

The main empirical evidence for reincarnation consists of cases of young children who claim to recall their previous lives (Stevenson, 1987; Rivas, 2003b). It is sometimes assumed that this type of case shows the validity of the anatta-theory of rebirth. The children involved would never completely retain their previous personality, which would demonstrate that only fragments of a personality are reborn and integrated into a whole new psychophysical "person" as defined by Buddhism. On the other hand, personalists may point out that the children themselves clearly claim to be spiritually identical to the people whose lives they seem to remember. It would seem far-fetched to believe they are correct about the accuracy of their imaged memories and, at the same time, radically misinterpret their origin. Similarly, memories of an intermission period between two incarnations suggest that there is a continuity of individual consciousness ranging from one physical life to another (Rawat & Rivas, 2005).

Empirical findings should primarily be interpreted within an ontological context rather than the other way around, because the categories used in our empirical theories ultimately depend on a more general, metaphysical analysis, which precedes empirical research. This metaphysical analysis may, in principle, be corrected by logical argumentation, but never by "raw" empirical data, and as such, data can make a theoretical difference only after it has been categorized ontologically. Thus, all empirical data collected by reincarnation researchers can in principle be covered by both impersonalist and personalist conceptualizations of rebirth. The question of which theory should be regarded as the right interpretation has to be treated as part of a more general problem of personal identity within the philosophy of mind, rather than tackled ad hoc in the special context of reincarnation research.

Once we accept the philosophical, analytical arguments in favor of anatta, no amount of empirical data will be able to falsify them conclusively. Similarly, for a personalist, it is possible to interpret the fact that infants seem to have a relatively reduced level of mental functioning in the following way. Their immature brains cause their personal souls to regress to a less complex mode of activity.

This interpretation would reconcile the personalist notion of a substantial psyche with what only seems like a psychological disintegration or loss of personal identity. In other words, the minds of babies appear to disprove that they are reincarnated personal souls in infant bodies, but following the personalist interpretation, this would be the only temporary effect of the immature brains with which those minds are interacting.

Purported empirical evidence against the indivisibility of the conscious subject, such as data from multiple personality cases or split-brain experiments, falls short of demonstrating that when a person's psychological functioning becomes, somehow, partially dissociated, the conscious subject will be divided as well. Consciousness (in the sense of subjective awareness) is a private and personal phenomenon, the presence of which cannot directly be established by others. Therefore, any behavior shown by a person could, in principle, be caused both by conscious and non-conscious psychological processes. More importantly, the literal, ontological (rather than functional) division of a non-holistic, irreducible conscious subject is not a coherent notion, because one of the main aspects of the concept of such a substantial self is precisely that it is elementary and indivisible. In other words, either the "self" is an impersonal or emergent phenomenon and therefore it could be split or destroyed, or it is a (non-emergent) substance, in which case any evidence for its supposed ontological divisibility (or destruction) must *a priori* be interpreted differently. Empirical data cannot be conclusive here because, as stated above, the real debate about personal identity and the substantiality of the self is not an empirical but a philosophical (ontological) issue that can be decided by analytical argumentation alone.

The same[36] can be said for the traditional concept that may be found, according to Dr. Antonia Mills, among Native Americans and Tibetans[37] (and some Western adepts of the so-called New Age movement) that aspects of one personality may be reborn in different bodies simultaneously. Dr. Jürgen Keil (2010) claims to have found a real case of this type in 2006, in which two Turkish children would have given "fairly detailed information" that would link both of them to the same previous life. However, Keil does not provide any specific items of this case. Therefore, we do not even know whether the information may be considered "probably paranormal" or whether it can easily be explained normally. According to Kirti Swaroop Rawat, there have been several children in India who all claimed to be the reincarnation of Mahatma Gandhi, and Stevenson informs us that in Turkey there have been several subjects who stated that they had been John F. Kennedy in their previous life. In such cases, the parents are motivated to "coach" their child into believing that he/she used to be a celebrity. Only if such social factors can convincingly be excluded, could we even start to examine these extravagant claims more closely. Also, these cases are atypical in most respects in that the children lack the usual emotional and behavioral characteristics of average subjects in CORTs.

More generally, we should not only realize that, to date, not a single shred of convincing evidence for the claim of multiple simultaneous reincarnation has been published, but also that such an interpretation of data is simply irreconcilable with the notion of a substantial soul.

---

[36] This and the following paragraph were added in 2010. It was not part of the original article.

[37] The Tibetan notion was reflected in the popular movie *Little Buddha* by Bernardo Bertolucci.

In other words, within a substantialist framework, any evidence for a paranormal process in such cases could never be explained in terms of a real fragmented rebirth of elements of a soulless bundle of psychological characteristics. It would have to be something else.

Similarly, Buddhists commonly accept evidence for consciousness after death and before rebirth. Tibetan Buddhists have even developed a theory of several so-called Bardos (intermediate states), which shows that they do not so much reject data that suggests personal survival as reinterpret it in the light of anatta-doctrine.

In other words, it is possible to agree on the evidential strength and scope of certain empirical data in the field of reincarnation research, and, at the same time, to disagree fundamentally about the ontological framework needed to interpret these findings.

It is sometimes supposed that general consensus is the main criterion by which to judge the maturity of a specific scholarly field. This criterion is certainly misguided in this particular case, and both impersonalist and personalist theoretical traditions within reincarnation research could further be developed in a sophisticated spirit of mutual tolerance and friendly empirical cooperation. For instance, data about the evolution of personality traits, skills, capacities, attitudes, etc., in the course of more than one physical lifetime, can be gathered and shared despite fundamental theoretical differences. The same data that would show an evolution of impersonal karma according to most Buddhists may also be used within a spiritual personalist theory of a truly personal evolution (Prasad, 1993; Rivas, 2005).

Conclusion

Spiritual personalists may benefit a lot from reincarnation research. Rather than giving up on our personalism, we could extend it to the notion of a personal evolution over several lives on earth. Losing one's present physical body and adopting a new one may be accompanied by changes in one's psychological functioning, but this should not be confused with an ultimate disintegration or loss of personal identity.

APPENDIX D

The Analytical Demolition of Epiphenomenalism Fragments of the article *Exit Epiphenomenalism* by Titus Rivas and Hein van Dongen, published in 2003 in the *Journal of Non-Locality and Remote Mental Interactions*.

~

Epiphenomenalism

Epiphenomenalism holds that all mental phenomena, processes or conditions are nothing more than epiphenomena (by-products) of cerebral processes. Hereby one does not intend to say that the mental could not exist apart from the physical (although this is indeed implied by it), but that the mental does not have any influence on reality. The subjective mind does exist, but it is not "efficacious," i.e. it cannot be the cause of anything, neither within its own mental dominion, nor within the physical world. For this supposed mental incapacity people have created illustrative images, like that of the steam whistle of a locomotive. The sound of the steam whistle constitutes a real phenomenon, but it does not influence the functioning of the locomotive; it is only an epiphenomenon of it. In a similar way, there are conscious experiences that are inevitably caused by cerebral processes. Just as the steam whistle does not influence the functioning of the locomotive, neither does consciousness influence the cerebral processes by which it is produced".

Arguments against the internal consistency of epiphenomenalism

Several arguments have been formulated according to which epiphenomenalism contradicts itself. All of these arguments are structured as follows: Epiphenomenalism does itself mention consciousness, while denying, for example, its efficacy. This implies that consciousness in one way or another has had an effect upon epiphenomenalism's argumentation and upon the ideas on which it is based.

The argument from the knowledge of contents of consciousness

The first and crudest form of the argument mentioned above states the following: Some epiphenomenalists are talking about all kinds of contents of consciousness, such as, for example, the experience of colours or sounds, and, at the same time, they hold that none of these contents would have any impact on reality. How is it possible then that those very same epiphenomenalists talk about contents of consciousness? This version of the argument, however, can still be refuted by epiphenomenalism. While talking about the contents of consciousness, one does not have to be talking, according to epiphenomenalism, about the contents themselves, but in fact only about the specific physiological substrates that constitute the supposed cause of any kind of subjective experiences.

A proposition such as "I see the colour red" would thus be caused completely by the supposed physiological correlate of the content of the consciousness concerned. That there would be such physiological substrates for any conscious content that exists, is a basic principle of epiphenomenalism: All subjective experiences would be caused by cerebral structures or processes.

The argument from the origin of the concept of consciousness

Where did our concepts regarding subjective experiences come from? S. Shoemaker[38] holds that it is qualia, which are the cause of the existence of a belief in the existence of qualia. Following Shoemaker, one could maintain that people would think, talk and write about the concept of consciousness because they formed this concept on the basis of consciousness. Thus formulated, the argument is still not strong enough. First, according to epiphenomenalists one could still well imagine a conceptual representation of consciousness within a system that does not possess any consciousness itself, but only an innate concept of consciousness. Secondly, talking about consciousness does not in itself prove anything regarding the presence of such consciousness, because one could also program a computer in such a way that it would produce verbal output about the concept of consciousness.

The argument from wondering about consciousness

Elitzur states that consciousness does not have to be the cause of a concept of consciousness, but it does have to be the cause of the fact that "people are bothered by problems of consciousness". However, if it is possible that there is an innate concept of consciousness, which is not excluded by Elitzur, then the emotional interest concerning the strange concept of consciousness could be explained away as a subjective epiphenomenon of a purely physiological phenomenon. Physiological substrates of wondering about the supposedly innate concept of consciousness would lead to an experience of wonder and interest.

---

[38] S. Shoemaker (1975). 'Functionalism and qualia'. *Philosophical Studies*, 27, 291-315.

The argument from the justification of the concept of consciousness

We know three authors who, completely independently from us, have reached the following version of the logical argument against epiphenomenalism; they are: Michael Watkins[39], Dennett[40] and John Foster. Responding to an essay by Jackson of 1982[41], Michael Watkins wrote a short article in the journal *Analysis.* Jackson had defended in his essay the existence of epiphenomenal qualia, which are completely impotent, i.e. qualitative aspects of subjective experience. To this, Watkins reacted in the following way: "Beliefs about qualia cannot be justified on the basis of qualitative experiences since those experiences do not cause those beliefs. The only evidence we have of qualia is our direct experience of them". Daniel C. Dennett published in 1991 his *Consciousness explained* after the formulation by Watkins and also after a first formulation of this argument by one of us, Titus Rivas.

Although starting from a different philosophy of mind, functionalism, he shows in a similar way that epiphenomenalism is incoherent or internally inconsistent, and that for that reason it does not deserve any serious philosophical attention. On page 403 he says literally: "So if anyone claims to uphold a variety of epiphenomenalism, try to be polite, but ask: "What are you talking about?", and on page 405 he concludes: "There could not be an empirical reason, then, for believing in epiphenomena. Could there be another sort of reason for asserting their existence? What sort of reason? An *a priori* reason, presumably. But what? No one has ever offered one – good, bad, or indifferent – that I have seen".

According to Stokes (1991)[42] John Foster stated, in a discussion of the subject, that if epiphenomenalism is valid, anything said by its proponents about mental events would lose its meaning as there could be no impact of such events on their own thought and words. In other words, the supposed validity of epiphenomenalism is self-defeating.

---

[39] Michael Watkins (1989). The Knowledge Argument Against the Knowledge Argument. *Analysis, 49,* 158-160.

[40] Daniel C. Dennett (1991). *Consciousness Explained.* London: Penguin Books.

[41] F. Jackson (1982). Epiphenomenal qualia. *Philosophical Quarterly, 32,* 134.

[42] Douglas M. Stokes (1991). "The Case for Dualism" ed. by J. Smythies & J. Beloff (Review). *The Journal of the American Society for Psychical Research, 85,* 388-393.

These philosophers make the point perfectly in our opinion. In order to clarify this, we will present our own independent formulation:

(1) Epiphenomenalism uses the concept of consciousness, as it states that there is such a thing as consciousness, which has got properties that are not physical, etc.

(2) Epiphenomenalism thus holds that its concept of consciousness refers to a real part of reality, namely to the (presumably) epiphenomenal but irreducible world of mental experience.

(3) We have to be aware that even if the concept of consciousness had been innate, the reality to which it refers – consciousness – could be established only through introspection, i.e. by establishing that there are such things as conscious experiences. Epiphenomenalism starts from the reality of consciousness and it is based on the (introspective) evidence for the existence of conscious experiences. There may be an innate concept of consciousness or not; in any case, epiphenomenalism uses subjective experiences as a touchstone for such a concept. After all, it is absurd to think that the reality of something might be established on the basis that we have a concept of that entity (take for example the case of the unicorn). The only valid reason for supposing that there really are conscious experiences is, therefore, the introspective observation that there are such experiences. If nobody introspectively observed subjective experiences, there would be no reason to suppose that there really would be such a thing as consciousness. Epiphenomenalism is forced, therefore, to find its unconditional acceptance on an introspective contact with that very same consciousness. Such a contact, however, equals a causal effect by consciousness upon the conceptualization processes of the one that contemplates his or her subjective experiences through introspection. By the way, it is not necessary to conceive of the impact of consciousness during this process as a conscious "act". It suffices to conceive it as a "factor," comparable to the causal status of an object perceived during the process of perception. In this respect, we might rephrase Berkeley by saying: *percipi est movere* (to be perceived is to move). This view clearly contrasts with that of David Chalmers (1996) who seems to believe that a real entity can make a difference for our knowledge without, at the same time, exerting a causal influence[43]. Chalmers seems to overlook the fact that in order to have a realistic concept of something,

---

[43] However, since 1996, Chalmers seems to have become more open-minded about psychogenic causation.

that entity must somehow be represented in memory (be it mental or neural), which means that the non-causal influence on knowledge postulated by him must, in the end, have a really causal effect after all. (4) Thus, epiphenomenalism internally contradicts itself. It states that there would be a valid reason to postulate mental experiences, but proclaims, at the same time, that these experiences are completely unknowable, by denying them any causal impact. The inevitable conclusion, therefore, is that epiphenomenalism should be disqualified for good.

A possible defense by the epiphenomenalists would, at first sight, be that in this analytical argument we would encounter a dubious kind of "justificationism," as not all theoretical entities must be justified directly by observations. Is it not enough that the entities would make a difference for the predictions that follow from the hypothesis? Perhaps this defense may seem to set the epiphenomenalist free from the need of founding his or her certainty that there really is such a thing as subjective awareness. However, the contrary is true. Even if we would take the case mentioned seriously, this would still lead us to the conclusion that consciousness needs to make an impact, even if only indirectly, on the predictions about reality, and that influence would not be reconcilable with epiphenomenalism either.

Epiphenomenalism turns out to be a kind of obscurantism: an erroneous representation of (part of) reality in favour of conceptions that are considered indubitable, i.e. of physicalism, and of the irreducibility of the subjective mind. We might say that it is a "refuge" for those physicalists who are not blind to their own subjectivity. The argument described above shows clearly that physicalism can no longer believe that it is safe from radical dualistic attacks.

Implications of the disqualification of epiphenomenalism

The disqualification of epiphenomenalism is, as we have just seen, inevitable. Now, we will give some attention to the consequences of the disqualification of epiphenomenalism. Ray Jackendoff[44] stated in 1989, confronted by our version of the argument from the justification

---

[44] Author of *Consciousness and the Computational Mind*, MIT Press, Cambridge, 1987. In this book he defended the hypothesis of the so-called Non-Efficacy of Consciousness.

of the concept of consciousness, that it might be wise to reconsider the reality of subjective experiences. Dennett has an even more extreme position. Starting from his own formulation of our analytical argument, he concludes that no one is conscious, at least not in the common, "mysterious" and qualitative sense of the term. Both authors conclude, in other words, from the irreconcilability of physicalism and dualism, that the concept of consciousness should be eliminated, i.e. sacrificed to the protection of indubitable physicalism. In fact we might qualify this as a contemporaneous form of blind and unfounded dogmatism.

The disqualification of the materialistic identity theory

On the other hand, it is interesting to note that both Daniel Dennett and Ray Jackendoff no longer opt for the materialistic identity theory, but directly for reductionist materialism, which denies the existence of the subjective mind. This is so, because the identity theory also holds that only the so-called "objective" side to the subjective mind, i.e. the brain (or part of it), would have an objective impact on reality. However, this is impossible, as we have already seen, because for the justification of postulating a subjective mind, it is necessary to believe that subjective mind is efficacious *qua* subjective mind, and not only in the so called "objective," physiological sense, as identity theory would have it. Therefore, as we are not going to imitate the opportunistic denial of consciousness, we will have to look for another variant with regards to psychogenical causality within dualism, unless we would go for idealism, which is a conception we will not discuss in this paper.

The disqualification of parallellism

Various authors stress that parallellism and epiphenomenalism have a lot in common. Both positions state that for each and every subjective experience there is a physiological correlate. The difference is, however, that this correlate, according to epiphenomenalism, is the substrate of that experience, whereas, according to parallellism, it would involve only a parallel correlate. Now, parallellism should be disqualified for a reason similar to the one given against epiphenomenalism; it is even the mirror image of our analytical argument. Epiphenomenalism cannot reconcile its certainty that there really is such a thing as a conscious mind with the implied impossibility of knowing the existence of consciousness. Parallellism, on the other hand, cannot reconcile its certainty that there really is a material world with the purported inability of that world to have an impact on the psyche. In other words, on the one hand, there would be no doubt, according to parallellism, that there is a physical world, but, on the other hand, it follows from the supposed parallel and strictly separate causality that the physical world cannot have any influence upon the psyche. Thus there is once again a contradiction: The parallellist claims to know with certainty of the existence of a physical world, while, at the same time, he claims that he is certainly incapable of knowing that same physical world.

Therefore only interactionism is left as the sole possibility. This implies that the acceptance of the existence of irreducible subjective experiences (apart from the existence of a material world), or dualism, logically leads to interactionism.

Interactionism

As it seems, intuition was right. We certainly do count as subjective beings; we doubtlessly have an impact upon ourselves, upon our lives and upon our social and physical environment.

Also, axiology and ethics cannot be reduced to biogenic epiphenomena. In (human) psychology and in ethology and animal psychology, it should, from now on, be clear that consciousness is important for experience and behaviour. Apparently, it is at least a source of conceptualization. Any current or theory within these sciences that would be fundamentally irreconcilable with the existence of psychogenic causality, should be made aware of the untenability of the positions of epiphenomenalism and parallellism. We are not, to paraphrase Huxley, "conscious automata".

Furthermore, in neuropsychology and psychiatry, the point of departure should be that there really are effects of consciousness upon processes in the brain. Cerebral processes are, therefore, not the only internal causes of behaviour and experience, but so is subjective awareness.

A psychiatry that wants to be beneficial cannot limit itself, therefore, to a purely physiological treatment.

Finally, the scientific theoretical status of parapsychology (which, almost by definition, contrasts with physicalism) is no longer an *a priori* problem within the framework of interactionism".

There are three published versions of this paper:

- A Spanish version, "Exit Epifenomenalismo," published in *Revista de Filosofía* of the University of Santiago de Chile, vol. LVII, 111-129, in 2001.
- An English version, "Exit Epiphenomenalism," published in the *Journal of Non-Locality and Remote Mental Interactions*, February 2003, Vol. II Nr. 1.
- An abridged Dutch version, "Exit Epifenomenalisme," published in *Gamma*, September 2009, 16, 3, 58-62

APPENDIX E

Metasubjective Cognition Beyond the Brain

Metasubjective Cognition Beyond the Brain: Subjective Awareness and the Location of Concepts of Consciousness

by Titus Rivas

~

Abstract

Consciousness has irreducible qualitative and subjective aspects that cannot be represented in a physical, purely quantitative system. This implies that an exhaustive conceptual "metasubjective" representation (i.e. a representation of the *defining* properties of conscious experiences) in the brain as an exclusively physical system is impossible. Similarly, individual memories of conscious experiences must contain information about qualitative and subjective aspects as well, since concepts of consciousness ultimately derive from such information abstracted from episodic memories. Therefore, the stored bases from which such individual memories of conscious experiences are reconstructed must also contain elements that cannot be represented in the brain. Both metasubjective concepts and bases of our individual memories of subjective experiences can be stored only in a personal non-physical memory linked to consciousness. There must be a personal mind or psyche that embraces consciousness, metasubjective concepts and bases of episodical memories of one's subjective experiences.

1. Introduction

Conscious experiences are often characterized as qualia, i.e. as entities that are irreducibly qualitative and subjective (Beloff, 1962; Popper & Eccles, 1977; Rivas, 2003a). This is relevant for the status of consciousness within the philosophy of mind. In a completely physical universe, consciousness could exist only if our definition of physicality embraced qualitative and subjective dimensions. This is a major problem, as *being physical* is usually understood as *being non-qualitative* and *non-subjective*. In fact, this classical definition goes back to the notions of so-called primary and secondary properties, based on the doctrines of the Greek atomists such as Democritus and Leucippus and developed by Galileo, Descartes, Boyle, and Locke (1961). Some (so-called "primary") mathematically measurable properties of the physical world such as size, shape, number and momentum are intrinsic to that world, and other (so-called "secondary") apparently non-mathematical aspects, such as redness or sweetness, exist only in our subjective perception of it. The main reason for this basic distinction is that the *phenomenal* or subjective, qualitative way in which a physical object is perceived cannot be an inherent physical property of that object itself. For example, although both a congenitally blind person and a person with normal eyesight may, in principle, have access to the same quantitative information generated by a camera, their understanding of what can be seen subjectively is radically different. In other words, subjectively seeing an object implies more than having physical visual information about that object (Nagel, 1979; Jackendoff, 1987). There is an irreducible conscious visual mode, which allows us to have subjective visual experiences, e.g. of what an object's spatial dimensions and colour *look* like for a conscious subject. These experiences are not part of the object's properties themselves but exclusively of our conscious vision.

Not all philosophers accept the validity of the distinction between primary and secondary properties. For instance, Berkeley (1998) claims that all perceived properties exclusively belong to the mind. Improbable as it may seem, this *idealistic* ontological view is not incoherent (Rivas, 2003a). However, it is incompatible with postulating a real physical world that exists independently of our perception, which is one of the basic assumptions of this paper.

Then, there are also scholars who believe that any type of distinction between appearance and reality is baseless. Anything we perceive would really exist in the world outside. This view makes it impossible to distinguish between illusions or hallucinations and realistic impressions of the physical realm. In contrast, it is almost generally accepted that our subjective normal perception of the physical world is created on the basis of non-subjective neurological processing of physical stimuli. In other words, we do not perceive the physical world outside directly or immediately, but we consciously experience the outcome of neurological perceptual processes, which, in turn, exclusively use mathematical properties of physical patterns that reach the brain through our senses and nervous pathways. Even if the physical world had non-mathematical characteristics, in normal perception we would never be able to perceive them directly as our sensory perception is always mediated by the nervous system.

All this has had important consequences for our understanding of matter (the "stuff" the physical world is assumed to be made of) and consciousness. It has led to the three main fundamental positions within the philosophy of mind:

- "Both the physical world and the realm of consciousness are real and cannot be reduced to one another" or *dualism*. (In this literal sense, certain types of emergentism may also be regarded as forms of dualism.)
- "Only the physical world is irreducibly real" or *materialism*.
- "Only consciousness is irreducibly real" or *idealism*.

2. The reality of consciousness

Some scholars, such as Dennett (1995), claim that what we understand by a conscious mind is really an *abstraction* of complex neurological processing in our brain. In other words, there would be no *irreducibly real* conscious experiences. Others (Rosenthal, 1994) claim that consciousness is really nothing more than the way we experience the brain from the inside. The brain as an objective physical system has no qualitative, subjective dimensions, which thereby would only *appear* to be objectively real by our "first-person perspective". In other words, all of these theorists reduce consciousness to a kind of *illusion* with no ultimate reality or they simply deny the existence of an irreducible consciousness altogether, even in the sense of an irreducibly subjective illusion. All of them concur in their view that consciousness is not a real part of the "objective" world.

Many scholars will not accept the "scientific" reduction of their personal consciousness to something that is ultimately non-conscious or merely illusory. This explains the appeal of a position that does acknowledge the reality of consciousness as more than an illusion even though it also claims that consciousness has no impact on reality or "efficacy" (Jackendoff, 1987; Chalmers, 1996, 2002), a position commonly known as epiphenomenalism. However, this position contains a fatal inner contradiction. If conscious experiences do not have any causal impact upon memory, we cannot possibly have formed a concept of consciousness on the basis of those conscious experiences (Rivas & van Dongen, 2001, 2003; Rivas, 2003b). In other words, we could not have any valid reason to believe that we are conscious beings, whereas this belief is a prerequisite of the very position of *epiphenomenalism*. Therefore, if we acknowledge the reality of consciousness, we also have to accept that our conscious experiences have a *real impact* on the world. In fact, this is also an important argument against the theory that consciousness exists only as an illusion – or identity theory – since, accordingly, conscious experiences would not be part of the real world and, therefore, they would not be able to exercise any real influence either (Rivas & Van Dongen, 2003). In sum, I think that starting from a criterion of coherence, we can choose only between a full-blown acceptance of the reality of conscious experiences and their impact on the world, and a total denial of the reality of consciousness (and its causal efficacy). This is problematic only for those who believe that the world simply must primarily or even exclusively be physical in nature, which is really a matter of convention rather than logical (in the sense of rational) thinking.

Some have tried to redefine the physical world so that it may embrace consciousness. A new definition would have to allow for a real consciousness with an equally real impact on the world. As we have seen, the important problem with this approach is that the distinction between mathematical and non-mathematical properties cannot be regarded as arbitrary, as it is a precondition for the distinction between the qualitative, subjective way we perceive a physical object and the object's reality separate from our phenomenal perception of it. A real physical world with real (rather than just apparent) inherent qualitative and subjective properties would not be a completely *physical* world anymore as commonly understood (Rivas, 2003a). As mentioned above, one of the main premises of this paper is that there is an irreducible physical reality.

3. Memory

3.1. Concepts of consciousness and the brain

Anyone who acknowledges the reality of consciousness implicitly accepts that our concepts of conscious experiences cannot be empty. They must refer to the diverse qualitative and subjective events that we undergo as conscious subjects. Now we may ask in what medium these concepts of consciousness or *metasubjective concepts* are stored. Presupposing the basic (dualist) assumption of the physical reality of the central nervous system, are metasubjective concepts part of a conceptual memory located in the brain?

Let me first explain the term *metasubjective* as it is used in this paper. The word simply means "about subjective experiences" or "about consciousness". So there is no link here with other meanings such as "transcendent" or "belonging to a social or cultural context larger than one's own personal experience". My use of the term is related to the word 'metacognition'. A possible synonym could be "metaphenomenal". However, the word "phenomenal memory" is not a good equivalent, as it implies that a memory is subjective rather than metasubjective (i.e. about consciousness). For instance, a memory of a physical equation may temporarily be "phenomenal" (consciously recalled), but it is not metasubjective (about consciousness).

To complicate things a bit, I'm aware that in the literature of the philosophy of mind, the term *phenomenal concept* is sometimes used to denote what I call here "metasubjective concepts" (Carruthers, 2004). The term can be found in discussions about the irreducible qualities of consciousness or in debates about physicalism. As said, I object to the use of the word "phenomenal" in this sense, as taken literally it seems to suggest that metasubjective concepts would always have to be experienced "phenomenally" (i.e. subjectively), just as "phenomenal" experiences are conscious experiences.

3.2. Storage of metasubjective concepts

In any possible physical memory, concepts are necessarily stored as physical, quantitative patterns. The question, therefore, becomes whether concepts of consciousness can be stored as physical, quantitative patterns. Adequate, sufficient storage of any concept in a conceptual memory must be such that its activation permits cognitive access to its main conceptual dimensions. For example, if we store a concept of bats as flying mammals that use echolocation, all of these three aspects (flying, mammals, echolocation) must be included in the concept as it is stored.

Our scientific concepts of physical entities can contain only information about physical (so-called primary) properties. This should not be a problem for any physical system of conceptual representation, as such a system is, in principle, capable of representing any type of physical entity. The same cannot be said about metasubjective concepts, i.e. concepts of consciousness that also contain representations of non-mathematical properties. In fact, such qualitative and subjective properties (including for example intentionality (Searle, 1983, 1997)) are essential to our understanding of consciousness (Jackendoff, 1987). If we did not have access to these defining conceptual dimensions of our concepts of consciousness, it would be completely impossible to think about consciousness and its manifestations as such.

Can we imagine a physical system that contains *exhaustive* representations of the defining qualitative and subjective dimensions of consciousness?

Note that we're not talking, here, about the presence of consciousness itself in the brain as a physical system, but about the location of exhaustive concepts of consciousness.

To rephrase our question once more: Can exhaustive metasubjective concepts be physical? The answer obviously depends on whether we accept that consciousness possesses non-quantitative aspects or not. As we have already seen above, if we do not, consciousness itself may, in principle, be regarded as a physical phenomenon. If we do, the non-quantitative aspects of consciousness cannot exhaustively be represented quantitatively. *If we could give an exhaustive quantitative description of consciousness, there simply would not be any irreducible non-quantitative aspects to it.* This means that if we accept that consciousness has other than purely quantitative aspects, it is impossible to conceive of an exhaustive physical representation of concepts of consciousness in the brain or anywhere else. An exhaustive representation of metasubjective concepts can, in principle, be realized only in a non-physical medium (Rivas, 1999).

4. Possible objections

Let us take a look at possible objections to my line of reasoning.

Some of these objections were expressed by real opponents, whereas others are only hypothetical.

4.1. Do concepts of consciousness have to be exhaustive?

Some may want to escape from my conclusion by acknowledging that metasubjective concepts cannot exhaustively be represented in the brain, while asserting that we do not need an exhaustive, defining concept of consciousness to be able to use it. We might reconstruct what we mean by diverse metasubjective terms from our immediate subjective experience of the types of consciousness, which they refer to. However, we can never conceptually distinguish between the diverse types of consciousness that we experience if we have not already formed the concepts beforehand. In other words, we cannot understand what a term refers to if there is no defining conceptual representation in our memory linked to that term. We need exhaustive [in the sense of sufficiently defining (added in 2009)] concepts of consciousness, since otherwise we could not use metasubjective terms in a distinctive way.

4.2. Innate concepts of consciousness

Another escape route that might be proposed is that metasubjective concepts are not formed on the basis of consciousness. Instead, they would be innate elements belonging to the blueprint of the human brain. Thus, the brain does not need to abstract information about consciousness but it already possesses all the relevant metasubjective concepts as part of its basic tools.

However, this does not solve the problem either, as any innate concept of consciousness located in the brain would still have to be completely quantitative and therefore lacking several necessary dimensions.

4.3. Quantifiable dimensions of consciousness

Some might object to my analysis, pointing at the fact that consciousness can, indeed, often be quantified. For example, subjects in psychological tests are able to rate the intensity of a conscious feeling in quantitative terms. However, my claim is not that conscious experiences possess no quantifiable dimensions whatsoever, but only that they possess non-quantitative, qualitative and subjective aspects as well.

4.4. Metasubjective concepts and other concepts

Another objection that some might want to raise against my argumentation would be that all concepts *as we subjectively experience them* can exist only in consciousness. This is not specific for metasubjective concepts. So if we believe that non-metasubjective concepts – for example of specific types of physical objects – can be stored in a physical system, but only experienced subjectively through consciousness, what would be the relevant difference between metasubjective and other concepts? However, my point is not that metasubjective concepts are different from other concepts because they would have to be experienced subjectively. My point concerns the *content* of metasubjective concepts. Contrary to other concepts, this content has to include information about the non-physical aspects of consciousness, i.e. information that cannot be represented in a purely quantitative manner. In this crucial respect, metasubjective concepts are very different from other concepts.

4.5. An interactionist alternative to the storage of metasubjective concepts?

A rather sophisticated objection to my analysis runs as follows. There can be no metasubjective information in the brain, but perhaps specific types of consciousness automatically cause specific neuronal changes through some type of psychokinesis. Such changes would not involve information about the specific types of consciousness, but, via natural laws of brain-mind interaction, the changed cerebral patterns would "conjure up" memories of subjective experiences whenever they're activated. The laws of interaction would be similar to the ones governing normal perception in which physical patterns lead to conscious

234

Appendix E

impressions. Metasubjective concepts would, in turn, be abstracted directly from the subjective experiences recalled.

However, the supposed analogy with normal perception is false, because in normal perception the physical patterns certainly do provide specific information about the objects in question reflected in consciousness; whereas, in the supposed case of memory, there would be no informational relation to the subjective experiences (as such) recalled. In this respect, the relation would be causal but not informational, as the non-quantitative *information* about the subjective experiences would not be stored in the hypothetical physical patterns. The information contained in such patterns could exclusively represent the non-subjective, quantitative aspects of the subjective experiences. The subjective, qualitative aspects of the subjective experiences would be recollected solely in consciousness by activation of the hypothetical physical patterns, rather than being represented in the patterns themselves.

By the way, if the supposed physical patterns would merely repeat the (perceptual) physical pattern that caused the conscious experience to be recalled, the hypothetical process would not constitute real memory anymore, as we could not really remember the conscious experience as such. Real memory of a subjective experience presupposes some direct causal relation between the experience (itself) and its recollection, which is absent if the supposed physical memory representation is not caused by the conscious experience but only by its physical precursor. As the subjective experience cannot be represented physically, its non-physical aspects might, at best, cause a non-informational pattern in the brain. Secondly – and this is a conclusive argument against the alternative hypothesis – metasubjective concepts must be based on non-quantitative information about subjective experiences, rather than on hypothetical markers in the brain, which themselves contain no non-physical information. Information that would be present only in the individual conscious memories of subjective experiences cannot be used for abstraction. As soon as the individual conscious memory of one subjective experience would be replaced by the individual conscious memory of another subjective experience, the information contained in the first conscious memory would immediately be lost. Thus, information from one conscious memory could never be compared with information from another conscious memory, and therefore no metasubjective concept based on such a comparison could ever arise.

235

[Also, if metasubjective concepts are never stored in conceptual memory, but always created instantly from specific memories of experiences, how could they ever be used in thought and compared and combined with other concepts?]

The possibility of a mere "working memory" dealing with metasubjective cognition would not count as an alternative for non-physical memory, as such a hypothetical working memory would itself have to be non-physical in order to handle metasubjective concepts! [It does not matter here that working memory would only be temporary.]

4.6. Understanding the nature of metasubjective conceptual memory

Some philosophers who read my manuscript complained that if the conceptual representation of consciousness stored in memory is not physical, we could not possibly imagine what metasubjective conceptual memory would "look like". We cannot make any physical model of it, or simulate its representation in a computer. Also, we cannot understand exactly how a non-physical memory should interact with the brain as a physical system. These thinkers hold that we should not postulate any theoretical entities unless we fully grasp their precise nature and interaction with the rest of the world.

However, in the physical sciences some entities are postulated because their existence seems necessary from a theoretical point of view. There is no reason why this should fundamentally be different in the philosophy of mind or theoretical psychology. If the existence of a non-physical metasubjective conceptual memory logically follows from our analysis, we ought not to avoid postulating it, even if we do not understand its exact nature or functioning.

4.7. Mathematics is part of the mind

Responding to the manuscript of this essay, Dr. Karl Pribram has stressed that mathematics is part of the mind rather than of the physical world. However, it is not my intention to reduce mathematics to anything physical. Within ontology and the (physical) sciences, the physical world is generally described in mathematical terms, but this does not mean that the mathematical should be regarded as physical. Perceptual subjective experiences usually have quantitative aspects and we even derive the quantitative properties of physical objects from our subjective experiences of them. Thus, the idealist claim that even the apparent primary properties of matter exist only in the mind is rationally tenable.

In other words, there is an important asymmetry in the relation between matter and mathematical properties: anything physical possesses mathematical properties, but not everything with mathematical properties is physical.

5. Memories of conscious experiences

My analysis also applies to the building blocks of our episodical memories of individual conscious experiences. Our metasubjective concepts are based on our conscious experiences that are somehow stored in episodical memory. This can work only if, during the process of storage, information about qualitative and subjective aspects of those conscious experiences is not left out. As we have seen already, qualitative and subjective aspects cannot exhaustively be represented in physical memory.

Note that I'm not claiming that individual memories are always retrieved as complete and unchanging entities. I acknowledge that, to a large extent, individual memories seem to be reconstructed continuously and that they may change over time. However, what I am claiming is that the *ingredients* from which individual memories of conscious experiences are recreated must necessarily include representations of the specifically qualitative and subjective dimensions of those experiences.

This is not a mere repetition of my claim that concepts about consciousness must be stored in a non-physical memory. I also claim that metasubjective concepts are abstracted from episodical memories of conscious experiences, and that the building blocks from which those episodical memories are reconstructed must already contain information about the non-quantitative aspects of such experiences. We must be able to recognize the qualitative and subjective aspects of consciousness from our (reconstructed) memories of subjective experiences. Without such recognition, these aspects cannot make any sense to us. For example, without memories of conscious olfactory experiences, we would be unable to form any adequate idea of what it generally means to smell something subjectively.

Glenberg (1997) believes that the classical, sharp distinction between episodic and "semantic" or conceptual memory as two distinct and separate memory systems is untenable. Episodic and semantic memories would all belong to the same system. Be this as it may, metasubjective concepts clearly relate to episodic memories of subjective experiences.

6. Non-physical memory and the psyche

Another question is how the non-physical memory, in which conceptual and episodical metasubjective memories must be stored, relates to consciousness. It seems obvious that we recall only our own subjective experiences. This means that there must be a personal psychical or mental memory, which is related intimately to consciousness. I see this analytical conclusion as a firm basis for a rehabilitation of the *psyche* or personal non-physical mind, which has to include consciousness, but also metasubjective conceptual memories and building blocks of metasubjective episodical memories (Rivas, 2003a, 2005; Bergson, 1908; Bozzano, 1994; Gauld, 1982; Wade, 1996).

This also has an interesting consequence for fundamental theories about telepathy. F.B. Dilley (1990) has tried to conceptualise telepathy as a form of psychically "reading" another person's brain, i.e. a subtype of clairvoyance of the physical world. However, this is inconceivable if telepathy involves metasubjective memories or cognition. In that case, telepathy must consist of a direct interaction between two or more psyches (Rivas, 1990).

7. The brain and metasubjective cognition

Many contemporary psychologists believe that psychological theory should always be "neurologically implementable," which means that their constructs should ultimately correspond to physical events in the brain and accord with its neurological laws. My analysis shows that this basic assumption must be wrong. Conceptual memories and bases of episodical memories of subjective experiences cannot possibly be exhaustively implemented in the brain as a physical system, and yet their role in cognition is clearly very important. This means that a large part of psychological theory can never be translated into neurological terms. Psychology cannot be reduced to neurology (Rivas, 2003a). All of our metasubjective cognitive processes must be *psychogenic* and primarily ruled by specific psychological mechanisms.

As the brain can contain no exhaustive concept of consciousness, it can literally have no idea of what it means to be conscious. Therefore, the brain cannot possibly be the primary source of metasubjective cognition. The brain will often follow the mind, i.e. neurology will often follow psychology.

All of this must hold true not only for human psychology, but also equally for the psychology of individual animals of all other species that possess subjective experiences (Rivas, 2003c).

Regardless of the exact role of the brain in memory processes, it cannot be the location where metasubjective memories are stored. Also, as conceptual and episodical memories about conscious experiences are not located in the brain, brain death certainly does not automatically imply destruction of these memories (Rivas, 1999a, 2000, 2003d; Van Lommel et al., 2001; Parnia et al., 2001; Stevenson, 1987, 1997; Rawat & Rivas, 2005). Storage of metasubjective memory outside the brain during physical life implies that memories can be preserved without a specific physical pattern or "substrate" to account for this. Also, as processes of metasubjective cognition are psychogenic it is *a priori* conceivable that a psyche continues to function cognitively after brain activity has ceased.

Although the brain may – by some kind of natural laws of interaction – facilitate or obstruct storage and retrieval of metasubjective concepts and bases of the reconstruction of individual metasubjective memories in the mind (Rivas, 1999b), such storage and retrieval cannot be embodied in the brain itself. Thus, despite popular materialist doctrine on this issue (Augustine, 1997; Braude, 2003), no amount of somatogenic impairment of our metasubjective memories can ever make them physical or ultimately dependent on our brains.

This article was published in 2006 in the *Journal of Non-Locality and Remote Mental Interactions*, IV (1).

APPENDIX F

A poem by Dr. Kirti Swaroop Rawat,
dating from 2007.

∼

Next in Evolution

If you have developed
Irresistible attraction for
Love,
Music,
Truth, or
Beauty
Be sure
You have grown new wings
Soar high!

REFERENCES

~

Chapter 1

- Alfred, B.F. (1909). *The Transmigration of Souls*. London: Harper &Brothers.
- Carter, C. (2010). *Science and the Near-Death Experience: How Consciousness Survives Death*. Inner Traditions.
- Cook, E.W., Greyson, B., & Stevenson, I. (1998). Do any Near-Death Experiences provide evidence for the survival of human personality after death? Relevant features and illustrative case reports. *Journal of Scientific Exploration, 12*, 3, 377-406.
- C Changzhen Li. (2020). Evidence for Reincarnation: 100 Cases of the Dong People Who Recall Past Lives. Aeon Books.
- Cranston, S. and Williams, C. (1984). *Reincarnation: A New Horizon in Science, Religion, and Society*. Julian Press.
- Frazer, Sir J.G. (1911). *The Golden Bough*. London.
- Germinara, G. & Cayce, H.L. (1999). *Many Mansions: The Edgar Cayce Story on Reincarnation*. New York: Signet.
- Gliedman, J. (1982). *Scientists in Search of the Soul*. Science Digest, July.
- Halbfass, W. (1983). *Karma and Rebirth in Classical Indian Tradition*. Delhi: Wendy Doniger O'Flaherty.
- Humphreys, Chr. (1951). *Buddhism*. Harmondsworth: Penguin Books.
- *Kathopanishad.*
- Lommel, P. van, Wees, R. van, Meyers, V., & Elfferich, I. (2001). Near-death Experience in Survivors of Cardiac Arrest: A Prospective Study in the Netherlands. *The Lancet, 358*, 9298, 2039-2044.
- Lommel, P. van (2010). *Consciousness Beyond Life: The Science of the Near-Death Experience*. HarperOne.
- Parnia, S., Waller, D.G., Yeates, R., & Fenwick, P. (2001). A Qualitative and Quantitative Study of the Incidence, Features and an Aetiology of Near-Death Experiences in Cardiac Arrest Survivors. *Resuscitation, 48*, 149-156.

- Plato. *Phaedrus.*
- *Rig Veda.*
- Rivas, T. (2003). The Survivalist Interpretation of Recent Studies Into the Near-Death Experience. The *Journal of Religion and Psychical Research,* 26, 1, 27-31.
- Rivas, T. (2004). Het geval Al Sullivan: Een BDE met paranormale indrukken. *Terugkeer, 15* (4), 19-21.
- Rivas, T. (2008). Een gesprek met TG over de man met het gebit. *Terugkeer, 19*(3), 12-20.
- Rivas, T., & Dirven, A. (2010). *Van en naar het Licht.* Leeuwarden: Elikser.
- Rivas, T., Dirven, A., & Smit, R.H. (2016). *The Self Does Not Die.* Durham: IANDS.
- Sabom, M.B. (1998). *Light and Death: One Doctor's Fascinating Account of Near-Death Experiences.* Grand Rapids: Zondervan Publishing House, 1998.
- Schweitzer, A. (1960). *Indian Thought and its Development.* Bombay: Wilco Publishing House.
- Smit, R.H. (2003). De unieke BDE van Pamela Reynolds (Uit de BBC–documentaire "The Day I Died"). *Terugkeer, 14* (2).
- Smit, R.H. (2008). Corroboration of the Dentures Anecdote Involving Veridical Perception in a Near-Death Experience. *Journal of Near-Death Studies, 27,* 47-61.
- Smit, R.H., & Rivas, T. (2010). Rejoinder to "Response to 'Corroboration of the Dentures Anecdote Involving Veridical Perception in a Near-Death Experience". *Journal of Near-Death Studies, 28*(4), 193-205.
- Stevenson, I. (1987). *Children Who Remember Previous Lives: A Question of Reincarnation.* Charlottesville: University Press of Virginia.

Chapter 2

- Andrade, H.G. (1979). *Um caso que sugere reencarnaçao: Simone & Angelina.* Sao Paulo: Van Moorsel, Andrade & Cia Ltda.
- Andrade, H.G. (1980). *A Case Suggestive of Reincarnation: Jacira & Ronaldo.* Sao Paulo: Van Moorsel, Andrade & Cia Ltda.
- Atreya, B.L. (1957). *An Introduction to Parapsychology* (Collected Papers on Psychical Research) (second edition, revised and enlarged). Banaras: The International Standard Publications.

References

- Bahadur, R. (1924). Cas apparents de réminiscences de vies antérieures. *Revue Métapsychique, 4,* juillet-aout, Pp. 302-307.

- Banerjee, H.N. (1980). *Americans Who Have Been Reincarnated.* New York: Macmillan.

- Banerjee, H.N. (1979). *Lifetimes: True Accounts of Reincarnation.* New York: Ballantine Books.

- Barrington, M. (1998). *Iris/Lucía – A Stolen Life.* SPR Conference 1998 (Synopsis of Paper).

- Barrington, M. (2000). Hungarian Iris-Spanish Lucía: Update and Provisional Conclusion. *Abstracts from the SPR 24h International Congress.*

- Barrington, M. (2002). The Case of Jenny Cockell: Towards a Verification of an Unusual "Past Life" Report. *Journal of the Society for Psychical Research, 66.2,* 867, 106-115.

- Barrington, M., Mulacz, P., & Rivas, T. (2005). The Case of Iris Farczády: A Stolen Life. *Journal of the Society for Psychical Research, 69.2,* 879, 49-77.

- Bernstein, M. (1989). *The Search for Bridey Murphy.* Doubleday.

- Bissoondoyal, B. (1955). Un enfant se rappelle sa vie antérieure à l'île Maurice. *Revue Métapsychique, 2,* 32-33.

- Björkhem, J. (1943). *De Hypnotiska Hellucinationerna.* Stockholm: Litteraturforlaget.

- Bose, S.C. (1960). *Jatismar Katha / A Book on Reincarnation.* Bihar: Satsang.

- Bowman, C. (1997). *Children's Past Lives.* New York: Bantam.

- Bowman, C. (2001). *Return from Heaven.* New York: HarperCollins.

- Braude, S.E. (2003). *Immortal Remains: The Evidence for Life after Death.* New York, etc.: Rowman & Littlefield Publishers, Inc.

- Dam, H. Ten (1983). *Een ring van licht.* Bressotheek, republished in 2002 as Reïncarnatie: Denkbeelden en Ervaringen. Ommen: Tasso.

- Dam, H. Ten (1990). *Exploring Reincarnation.* Penguin Books.

- Delanne, G. (1924). *Documents pour servir à étude de la réincarnation.* Paris: Editions de la B.P.S.

- Germinara, G. & Cayce, H.L. (1999). *Many Mansions: The Edgar Cayce Story on Reincarnation.* New York: Signet.

- Gershom, Rabbi Y. (1997). *Onmogelijke herinneringen* [Beyond the ashes]. Zeist: Uitgeverij Vrij Geestesleven.

- Gershom, Rabbi Y. (1998). *Onverklaarbaar verdriet* [From Ashes to Freedom]. Zeist: Indigo/Vrij Geestesleven.

- Grubbs, A. (2005). *Chosen To Believe.* Pink Elephant Press.

- Guirdham, A. (1990). *The Cathars and Reincarnation: The Record of a Past Life in Thirteenth-century France.* C W Daniel Co Ltd.

- Hall, F. (1928). *The Soul of a People.* London: Macmillan and co. Ltd.

- Haraldsson, E. (1991). Children claiming past-life memories. Four cases in Sri Lanka. *Journal of Scientific Exploration, 5,* 2, 233.

- Haraldsson, E. (1994). Psychodiagnostische Untersuchungen an Kindern mit "Rückerinnerungen" und Fallbeispiele aus Sri Lanka. *Zeitschrift für Parapsychologie und Grenzgebiete der Psychologie, 36,* 1/2, 22-38.

- Haraldsson, E. (1995). Personality and Abilities of Children Claiming Past-life Memories. *Journal of Nervous and Mental Disease, 183,* 7, 445.

- Haraldsson, E. (1997). A Psychological Comparison Between Ordinary Children and Those Who Claim Previous Life Memories. *Journal of Scientific Exploration, 11,* 3, 323-335.

- Haraldsson, E., & Matlock, J. (2017). *I Saw a Light and Came Here: Children's Experiences of Reincarnation.* White Crow Books.

- Haraldsson, E. and Samararatne, G. (1999) Children Who Speak of Memories of a Previous Life as a Buddhist Monk: Three New Cases. *Journal of the Society for Psychical Research, 63,* 268-291.

- Hassler, D.: *Reinkarnation* at http://www.reinkarnation.de/

- Hassler, D. (2011 früher da war ich mal groß. Und. – Indizienbeweise für ein Leben nach dem Tod und die Wiedergeburt: Band 1: Spontanerinnerungen kleiner Kinder an ihr "früheres Leben".Shaker Media.

- Hassler, D. (2015). *Geh' zurück in eine Zeit: Indizienbeweise für ein Leben nach dem Tod und die Wiedergeburt 2a und 2b.* Shaker Media.

- Hearn, L. (1897). *Gleaning in Buddha Fields.* Boston: Houghton Mifflin.

- Hegener, M. (2012). Leven op herhaling: Bewijzen voor reïncarnatie. Ten Have.

- Jacobson, N. O. (1974). *Life Without Death?* Dell Pub. Co.

- Keene, J. (2003). *Someone Else's Yesterday.* Nevada City, CA: Blue Dolphin Publishing.

- Keil, J. (1994). Kinder, die sich an "frühere Leben" erinnern: Neue Falluntersuchungen und ein Vergleich mit den Ergebnissen von Ian Stevenson. *Zeitschrift für Parapsychologie und Grenzgebiete der Psychologie, 36,* 1/2, 3-21.

- Keil, J. (2010). A Case of the Reincarnation Type in Turkey Suggesting Strong Paranormal Information Involvements. *Journal of Scientific Exploration, 24,* 1, 67-73.

- Klink, J. (1990). *Vroeger toen ik groter was. Vèrgaande herinneringen van kinderen.* Baarn: Ten Have.

References

- Lönnerstrand, S. (1996). *Shanti Devi. Een verhaal over reïncarnatie* (translated from Swedish). The Hague: Mirananda.

- Lönnerstrand, S. (1998). *I Have Lived Before: The True Story of the Reincarnation of Shanti Devi*. Ozark Mountain Publishing.

- Matlock, J.G. (2019). *Signs of Reincarnation: Exploring Beliefs, Cases, and Theory*. Rowman & Littlefield.

- Mills, A. (1994). *Amerindian Rebirth: Reincarnation Belief Among North American Indians and Inuit*. Toronto: University of Toronto Press.

- Mills, A., Haraldsson, E. & Keil, J. (1994). Replication Studies of Cases Suggestive of Reincarnation by Three Different Investigators. *Journal of the American Society for Psychical Research*, 88, 207-219.

- Munshi Subhan Rai (1753). *Khulasa Tarikh*.

- Moura Visoni, V. (2010). How to Improve the Study and Documentation of Cases of the Reincarnation Type? A Reappraisal of the Case of Kemal Atasoy. *Journal of Scientific Exploration*, 24, 1, 95-102.

- Nanninga, R. (2008). Reïncarnatie onder hypnose: de Australische tv-documentaire van Peter Ramster. *Skepter*, 21, 2.

- Ohkado, Masayuki, Katsumi Inagaki, Nobuhiro Suetake, and Satoshi Okamoto. (2009). A Study of a Case Supporting the "Reincarnation Hypothesis," with Special Reference to Xenoglossy, *Journal of International Society of Life Information Science*, 27, 183-185.

- Ohkado, Masayuki. (2010). A Japanese Case of Xenoglossy, in: *Synchronic and Diachronic Approaches to the Study of Language: A Collection of Papers Dedicated to the Memory of Professor Masachiyo Amano*. Tokyo: Eichosha Phoenix Co. – Pasricha, S. (1990). *Claims of Reincarnation: An Empirical Study of Cases in India*. New Delhi: Harman Publishing House.

- Ohkado, M. (2013). A case of a Japanese child with past life memories. *Journal of Scientific Exploration*, 27(4), 623-636.

- Pasricha, S.K. (2008). *Can the Mind Survive Death? In Pursuit of Scientific Evidence*. New Delhi: Harman Publishing House.

- Penkala, M. (1972). *Reïncarnatie en preëxistentie*. Deventer: Ankh-Hermes.

- Prasad, J. (1993). *New Dimensions in Reincarnation Researches*. Allahabad: Jamuna Prasad.

- Puhle, A. (2004). *Lexikon der Geister: Über 1000 Stichwörter aus Mythologie, Volksweisheit, Religion und Wissenschaft*. Munich: Atmosphären.

- Raglan, Lord (1945). *Death and Birth: A study in Comparative Religion*. London: Watts & Co.

- Ramster, P.J. (1980). *The Truth about Reincarnation: Actual stories of Australian Men and Women Who Have Revealed Past Lives under Hypnosis.* Adelaide: Rigby.

- Rawat, K.S. (1996a). Een interview met Dr. Ian Stevenson: reïncarnatie-onderzoek in wetenschappelijk perspectief. *Prana, 97,* 25-28.

- Rawat, K.S. (1996b). Drie gevallen van vermoedelijke wedergeboorte met moedervlekken. *Prana, 97,* 59-62.

- Rawat, K.S. (1997). Shanti Devi's Past. *Venture Inward, March/April,* 18-21.

- *Rig-Veda.*

- Rivas, E., & Rivas, T. (1987). *Wetenschappelijk reïncarnatie-onderzoek* (second edition). Arnhem: Schoon Genoeg.

- Rivas, T. (1992a). Reïncarnatie en psychical research. *Spiegel der Parapsychologie, 31,* 39-45.

- Rivas, T. (1992b). Reïncarnatie-onderzoek in Nederland Geïnduceerde gevallen. *Spiegel der Parapsychologie, 31*(2),104-109.

- Rivas, T. (2000). *Parapsychologisch onderzoek naar reïncarnatie en leven na de dood.* Deventer: Ankh-Hermes.

- Rivas, T. (2003). Three Cases of the Reincarnation Type in the Netherlands. *Journal of Scientific Exploration, 17,* 3, 527-532.

- Rivas, T. (2004). Six Cases of the Reincarnation Type in the Netherlands. *The Paranormal Review, 29,* 17-20.

- Rivas, T. (2004b). *Uit het leven gegrepen: beschouwingen rond een leven na de dood.* Delft: Koopman & Kraaijenbrink.

- Sahay, K.K.N. (1927). *Reincarnation: Verified Cases of Rebirth after Death.* Bareilly: N.L. Gupta.

- Semkiw, W. (2003). *Return of the Revolutionaries.* Charlottesville: Hampton Roads Publishing.

- Sen, I. (1936). *Chitrapat.* Delhi.

- Sen, I. (1937). Shanti Devi Further Investigated. *Proceedings of the Indian Philosophical Congress.*

- Snow, R.L. (1999). *Looking for Carroll Beckwith: The True Story of a Detective's Search for His Past Life.* St. Martin's Press.

- Stemman, R. (2004). *Reincarnation: True Stories of Past Lives.* London: Piatkus Books.

- Stevenson, I. (1960). The Evidence for Survival from Claimed Memories of Former Incarnations. *Journal of the American Society for Psychical Research, 54,* 51-71 & 95-117.

References

- Stevenson, I. (1974a). *Twenty Cases Suggestive of Reincarnation.* Charlottesville: University Press of Virginia.

- Stevenson, I. (1974b). *Xenoglossy: A Review and Report of a Case.* Charlottesville: University Press of Virginia.

- Stevenson, I. (1975a). *Hypnotic Regression to "Previous Lives": A Short Statement.* University of Virginia Medical Center, Division of Parapsychology, Department of Psychiatry.

- Stevenson, I. (1975b). *Cases of the Reincarnation Type, Vol. I. Ten Cases in India.* Charlottesville: University Press of Virginia.

- Stevenson, I. (1977a). Research into the Evidence of Man's Survival after Death: A Historical Survey with a Summary of Recent Developments. *Journal of Nervous and Mental Disease, 165,* 152-170.

- Stevenson, I. (1977b). *Cases of the Reincarnation Type, Vol. II. Ten Cases in Sri Lanka.* Charlottesville: University Press of Virginia.

- Stevenson, I. (1980). *Cases of the Reincarnation Type, Vol. III. Twelve cases in Lebanon and Turkey.* Charlottesville: University Press of Virginia.

- Stevenson, I. (1983). *Cases of the Reincarnation Type, Vol. IV. Twelve cases in Thailand and Burma.* Charlottesville: University Press of Virginia.

- Stevenson, I. (1984). *Unlearned Language: New Studies in Xenoglossy.* Charlottesville: University Press of Virginia.

- Stevenson, I. (1987). *Children Who Remember Previous Lives: A Question of Reincarnation.* (Second edition: 2000.) Charlottesville: University Press of Virginia.

- Stevenson, I. (1997a). *Reincarnation and Biology: A Contribution to the Aetiology of Birthmarks and Birth Defects.* London/Westport: Praeger.

- Stevenson, I. (1997b). *Where Reincarnation and Biology Intersect.* Londen: Praeger.

- Stevenson, I. (2003). *European Cases of the Reincarnation Type.* Jefferson/ London: McFarland & Company.

- Stevenson, I., & Pasricha, S. (1980). A Preliminary Report on an Unusual Case of the Reincarnation Type with Xenoglossy. *Journal of the American Society for Psychical Research, 74,* 341-348.

- Stevenson, I., & Samararatne, G. (1988a). Three New Cases of the Reincarnation Type in Sri Lanka with Written Records Made before Verification. *Journal of Scientific Exploration, 2, 2,* 217-238.

- Stevenson, I., & Samararatne, G. (1988b). Three New Cases of the Reincarnation Type in Sri Lanka with Written Records Made before Verification. The *Journal of Nervous and Mental Disease, 176, 12,* 741.

- Stevenson, I., & Schouten, S. (1998). Does the Socio-psychological Hypothesis Explain the Cases of the Reincarnation Type? *The Journal of Nervous and Mental Disease, 186,* 8, 504-506.
- Sunderlal, R.B.S. (1924). Cas apparents de réminiscences de vies antérieures. *Revue Métapsychique, 4,* 302-307.
- Schweitzer, A. (1960). *Indian Thought and its Development.* Bombay: Wilco Publishing House.
- Tarazi, L. (1990). An Unusual Case of Hypnotic Regression with Some Unexplained Contents. *Journal of the American Society for Psychical Research, 84,* 309-44.
- Weatherhead, Rev. L. D. (1963). *The Case for Reincarnation* (fourth impression). Surrey: M.C. Peto.
- Wilson, I. (1981). *Mind out of time? Reincarnation Claims Investigated.* London.

Chapter 3

- Braude, S.E. (2003). *Immortal Remains: The Evidence for Life after Death.* New York, etc.: Rowman & Littlefield Publishers, Inc.
- Lönnerstrand, S. (1996). *Shanti Devi. Een verhaal over reïncarnatie* (Dutch translation from the Swedish). The Hague: Mirananda.
- Lönnerstrand, S. (1998). *I Have Lived Before: The True Story of the Reincarnation of Shanti Devi.* Ozark Mountain Publishing.
- Sahay, K.K.N. (1927). *Reincarnation: Verified Cases of Re-birth after Death.* Bareilly: N.L. Gupta.
- Stevenson, I. (1960). The Evidence for Survival from Claimed Memories of Former Incarnations. *Journal of the American Society for Psychical Research, 54,* 51-71, 95-117.
- Stevenson, I. (1974). *Twenty Cases Suggestive of Reincarnation.* Charlottesville: University Press of Virginia.
- Stevenson, I. (1975). *Cases of the Reincarnation Type: Vol. I. Ten Cases in India.* Charlottesville: University Press of Virginia.
- Sunderlal, R.B.S. (1924). Cas apparents de réminiscences de vies antérieures. *Revue Métapsychique, 4,* 302-307.

Chapter 4

- Byrd, C. (2017). *The Boy Who Knew Too Much: An Astounding True Story of a Young Boy's Past-Life Memories.* Hay House Inc.

- Haraldsson, E. (2000a). Birthmarks and Claims of Previous Life Memories I. The Case of Purnima Ekanayake. *Journal of the Society for Psychical Research, 64,* 858, 16-25.

- Haraldsson, E., & Matlock, J. (2017). *I Saw a Light and Came Here: Children's Experiences of Reincarnation.* White Crow Books.

- Harrison, P., & Harrison, M. (1983). *The Children That Time Forgot.* Emsworth: Mason Publications.

- Hassler, D. (2014). Ein neuer europäischer Fall vom Reinkarnationstyp. *Zeitschrift für Anomalistik, 14,* 23-44.

- Heald, M. (1998). *Destiny: The True Story of One Man's Journey Through Life, Death, and Rebirth.* Element Books Ltd.

- Leininger, A., Leininger, B., & Gross, K. (2009). *Soul Survivor: The Reincarnation of a World War II Fighter Pilot.* Grand Central Publishing.

- Milligan, W. (2004). The Past Life Memories of James Leininger. *Acadiana Profile Magazine.*

- Rawat, K.S. (1996). Drie gevallen van vermoedelijke wedergeboorte met geboortetekens. *Prana, 97,* 59-62.

- Rivas, T. (1999). De Arnhemse brand van Pasen 1973: herinneringen van Christina uit Malden. *Spiegel der Parapsychologie, 37,* 4, 133-152.

- Rivas, T. (2000). *Parapsychologisch onderzoek naar reïncarnatie en leven na de dood.* Deventer: Ankh-Hermes.

- Steman, B. (2018). *Morgan: Een liefde.* Nieuw Amsterdam.

- Stevenson, I. (1974). *Twenty Cases Suggestive of Reincarnation.* Charlottesville: University Press of Virginia.

- Stevenson, I. (1975) *Cases of the Reincarnation Type: Vol. I. Ten Cases in India.* Charlottesville: University Press of Virginia.

- Stevenson, I. (1977). *Cases of the Reincarnation Type: Vol. II. Ten Cases in Sri Lanka.* Charlottesville: University Press of Virginia.

- Stevenson, I. (1983). *Cases of the Reincarnation Type: Vol. IV. Twelve Cases in Thailand and Burma.* Charlottesvile: University Press of Virginia.

- Stevenson, I. (1997a). *Reincarnation and Biology: A contribution to the aetiology of birthmarks and birth defects.* Westport/London: Praeger.

- Stevenson, I. (1997b). *Where Reincarnation and Biology Intersect.* Westport/ London: Praeger.

- Stevenson, I. (2003). *European Cases of the Reincarnation Type.* Jefferson/ London: McFarland & Company.

Chapter 5

- Almeder, R. (1992). *Death and Personal Survival: The Evidence for Life after Death.* Rowman & Littlefield.

- Almeder, R. (1997). A Critique of Arguments Offered Against Reincarnation. *Journal of Scientific Exploration, 11,* 4, 499-526.

- Andrade, H.G. (1979). *Um caso que sugere reencarnaçao: Simone x Angelina.* Sao Paulo: Van Moorsel, Andrade & Cia Ltda.

- Andrade, H.G. (1980). *A Case Suggestive of Reincarnation: Jacira & Ronaldo.* Sao Paulo: Van Moorsel, Andrade & Cia Ltda.

- Angel, L. (1994). Empirical Evidence for Reincarnation? Examining Stevenson's "Most Impressive" Case. *Sceptical Inquirer, 18,* 481-487.

- Anthony, S. (1940). *The Child's Discovery of Death.* London: Kegan Paul, Trench, Trubner, & Co.

- Barrington, M., Mulacz, P., & Rivas, T. (2005). The Case of Iris Farczády: A Stolen Life. *Journal of the Society for Psychical Research, 69.2,* 879, 49-77.

- Barrington, M., Stevenson, I., & Weaver, Z. (2005). *A World in a Grain of Sand: The Clairvoyance of Stefan Ossowiecki.* McFarland.

- Beauregard, M. (2007). Mind Does Really Matter: Evidence from Neuroimaging Studies of Emotional Self-regulation, Psychotherapy, and Placebo Effect. *Progress in Neurobiology, Vol. 81,* Issue 4, 218-236.

- Beauregard, M., & O'Leary, D. (2007). *The Spiritual Brain: A Neuroscientist's Case for the Existence of the Soul.* HarperOne.

- Bishai, D. (2000). Can Population Growth Rule Out Reincarnation? A Model of Circular Migration. *Journal of Scientific Exploration, 14,* 3, 411-420.

- Bolzano, B. (1970). *Athanasia oder Gründe für die Unsterblichkeit der Seele* (unaltered reprinted edition). Frankfurt am Main: Minerva.

- Bowman, C. (2001). *Return from Heaven.* New York: HarperCollins.

- Bowlby, J. (1980). *Attachment and loss, vol. III.* New York: Basic Books.

- Braude, S.E. (1995). *First Person Plural.* Rowman & Littlefield Publishers.

- Braude, S.E. (2003). *Immortal Remains: The Evidence for Life after Death.* New York, etc.: Rowman & Littlefield Publishers, Inc.

References

- Cain, A.C., & Cain., D.S. (1964). On Replacing a Child. *Journal of the American Academy of Child Psychiatry, 3,* 443-456.

- Carter, C. (2010). "Heads I Lose, Tails You Win," Or, How Richard Wiseman Nullifies Positive Results, and What to Do about It. *Journal of the Society for Psychical Research, 74:* 156-167.

- Chalmers, D. (1995). Facing Up to the Problem of Consciousness. *Journal of Consciousness Studies, 2,* 3, 200-219.

- Chari, C.T.K. (1962). Paramnesia and Reincarnation. *Proceedings of the Society for Psychical Research, 29,* 264-286.

- Chari, C.T.K. (1987). Letter. *Journal of the Society for Psychical Research, 54,* 226-229.

- Damon, W., & Hart, D. (1982). The Development of Self-understanding from Infancy through Adolescency. *Child Development, 53,* 841-864.

- Dennett, D.C. (1991). *Consciousness Explained.* London: Penguin Books.

- Edwards, P. (1996). *Reincarnation: A Critical Examination.* New York: Prometheus.

- Feldman, D.H. (1980). *Beyond Universals in Cognitive Development.* Norwood: Alex Publishing Corporation.

- Feuillet, L., Dufour, H., & Pelletier, J. (2007). Brain of a White Collar Worker. *The Lancet, 370,* 267.

- Foster, J. (1991). *The Immaterial Self: A Defence of the Cartesian Dualist Conception of the Mind.* London: Routledge.

- Gerding, H., & Put, J. v.d. (2001). Rondom geboorte en dood. *Prana, 127,* 28-44.

- Hewitt, P. (2003). *The Coherent Universe. An Introduction to Geoffrey Read's New Fundamental Theory of Matter, Life and Mind.* Richmond: Linden House.

- Haraldsson, E. (1991). Children Claiming Past-life Memories: Four Cases in Sri Lanka. *Journal of Scientific Exploration, 5,* 2, 233-261.

- Haraldsson, E., & Abu-Izzeddin, M. (2002). Development of Certainty About the Correct Deceased Person in a Case of the Reincarnation Type in Lebanon: The Case of Nazih Al-Danaf. *Journal of Scientific Exploration, 16,* 3, 363-380.

- Haraldsson, E., & Matlock, J. (2017).. *I Saw A Light And Came Here: Children's Experiences of Reincarnation.* White Crow Books.

- Isaacs, S. (1945). *Social Development in Young Children* (4th Edition). London: George Routledge & Sons.

- Jones, E. (1920). *Papers on Psychoanalysis.* London: Baillière, Tindall & Cox.

- Pandarakalam, J.P. (2018). Do Reincarnation-Type Cases Involve Consciousness Transfer? *NeuroQuantology, 16* (11), 3043.

- Keil, J. (1991). New Cases in Burma, Thailand, and Turkey: A Limited Field Study Replication of Some Aspects of Ian Stevenson's Work. *Journal of Scientific Exploration, 5,* 1, 27-59.

- Keil, J. (1994). Kinder, die sich an "frühere Leben" erinnern: Neue Falluntersuchungen und ein Vergleich mit den Ergebnissen von Ian Stevenson. *Zeitschrift für Parapsychologie und Grenzgebiete der Psychologie, 36,* 1/2, 3– 21.

- Keil, J. (2010). Questions of the Reincarnation Type. *Journal of Scientific Exploration, 24,* 1, 75-94.

- Keil, H.H.J., & Tucker, J.B. (2005). Children who claim to remember previous lives: Cases with written records made before the previous personality was identified. *Journal of Scientific Exploration, 19,* 1, 91-101.

- Kelly, E.F., Williams Kelly, E., Crabtree, A., Gauld, A., Grosso, M., & Greyson, B. (2007). *Irreducible Mind: Toward a Psychology for the 21st Century.* Rowman & Littlefield Publishers.

- Leahy, R.L., & Shirk, S.R. (1985), in Leahy, R.L. (ed.) *The Development of the Self.* London: Academic Press.

- Lewin, R. (1980). Is Your Brain Really Necessary? *Science* 210, 1232.

- Matlock, J.G. (1990) Past Life Memory Case Studies. In: S. Krippner (Ed.). *Advances in Parapsychological Research.* Jefferson: McFarland. Pp. 184-267.

- Mills, A. (1989). A Replication Study: Three Cases of Children in Northern India Who are Said to Remember a Previous Life. *Journal of Scientific Exploration, 3,* 2, 133-184.

- Mills, A. (1990a). Moslem Cases of the Reincarnation Type in Northern India: A Test of the Hypothesis of Imposed Identification, Part I: Analysis of 26 cases. *Journal of Scientific Exploration, 4,* 2, 171-188.

- Mills, A. (1990b). Moslem Cases of the Reincarnation Type in Northern India: A Test of the Hypothesis of Imposed Identification, Part II: Reports of Three cases. *Journal of Scientific Exploration, 4,* 2, 189-202.

- Milrod, D. (1982). The Wished-for Self-image. *The Psychoanalytic Study of the Child, 37,* 95-120.

- Morse, D. (2000). *Searching for Eternity: A Scientist's Spiritual Journey to Overcome Death Anxiety.* Memphis: Eagle Wing Books.

- Nienhuys, J.W. (1989). Hoop doet leven: de wankele argumenten voor reïncarnatie. *Skepter, 2,* 4.

- Novak, P. (2003). *The Lost Secret of Death: Our Divided Souls and the Afterlife.* Hampton Roads.

References

– Oesterreich, T.K. (1910). *Die Phaenomenologie in ihren Grundproblemen.* Leipzig.

– Pasricha, S., Stevenson, I., & Mcclean-Rice, N. (1989). A Case of the Possession Type in India with Evidence of Paranormal Knowledge. *Journal of Scientific Exploration, 3,* 81-101.

– Pinto, Y., Neville, D.A., Otten, M., Corballis, P.M., Lamme, V.A.F., de Haan, E.H.F., Foschi, N., Fabri, M.(2017). *Split brain: divided perception but undivided consciousness.* Brain, January 2017 DOI:10.1093/brain/aww358

– Playfair, G. L. (2004). *Possession Cases.* SPR-Lecture, Study Day, November 4, London.

– Playfair, G. L. (2006). *New Clothes for Old Souls: Worldwide Evidence for Reincarnation.* London: Druze Heritage Foundation.

– Radhakrishnan, S. (1977). *Indian Philosophy, vol. 2.* London: Allen and Unwin.

– Rivas, T. (1993). Reïncarnatieonderzoek: Op zoek naar de zuinigste toereikende hypothese. *Spiegel der Parapsychologie, 32* (3/4),171-188.

– Rivas, T. (1996). Filosofie van de persoonlijke onsterfelijkheid: Grondslagen voor survivalonderzoek. *Tijdschrift voor Parapsychologie, 64,* 3/4, 27-44.

– Rivas, T. (2000). *Parapsychologisch onderzoek naar reïncarnatie en leven na de dood.* Deventer: Ankh-Hermes.

– Rivas, T. (2003). *Geesten met of zonder lichaam.* Delft: Koopman & Kraaijenbrink.

– Rivas, T. (2004). *Past-Life Interpretations: We need all of them.* SPR–Lecture, Study Day of November 4th, London.

– Rivas, T. (2005a). Reïncarnatie, persoonlijke evolutie en bijzondere kinderen. *Prana, 148,* 47-53.

– Rivas, T. (2005b). Rebirth and Personal Identity: Is Reincarnation an Intrinsically Impersonal Concept? *The Journal of Religion and Psychical Research, 28,* 4, 226-233.

– Rivas, T. (2006). Metasubjective Cognition Beyond the Brain: Subjective Awareness and the Location of Concepts of Consciousness. *Journal of Non-Locality and Remote Mental Interactions, IV,* I.

– Rivas, T. (2020). 'Dutch Children with Past-Life Memories'. Psi Encyclopedia. London: The Society for Psychical Research. https://psi-encyclopedia.spr.ac.uk/articles/dutch-children-who-remember-previous-life.

– Rivas, T., & Dirven, A. (2004). Herinneringen van Célina: een Nederlands geval van reïncarnatie binnen dezelfde familie. *Terugkeer, 15* (2-3), 41-44.

– Robinson, D.N. (1991). Might the Self be a Substance After All? *Theory & Psychology*, *1(1)*: 37-50.

– Roy, A. (2004). *Overshadowing Cases*. SPR-Study Day of November 4th, London.

– Roy, A. (2008). *The Eager Dead: A Study in Haunting*. Sussex Book: Guild Publishing.

– Shroder, T. (1999). *Old Souls: The Scientific Evidence for Past Lives*. New York: Simon and Schuster.

– Sijde, P. van der (1992). Reïncarnatie en parapsychologie. *Spiegel der Parapsychologie*, *31(1)*, 23-29.

– Speece, M.W., & Brent, S.B. (1984). Children's Understanding of Death: A Review of Three Components of a Death Concept. *Child Development*, *55*, 1671-1686.

– Stevenson, I. (1960). The Evidence for Survival from Claimed Memories of Former Incarnations. *Journal of the American Society for Psychical Research*, *54*, 51-71, 95-117.

– Stevenson, I. (1974). *Twenty Cases Suggestive of Reincarnation*. Charlottesville: University Press of Virginia.

– Stevenson, I. (1980). *Cases of the Reincarnation Type: Vol. III. Lebanon and Turkey*. Charlottesville: University Press of Virginia.

– Stevenson, I. (1987). *Children Who Remember Previous Lives: A Question of Reincarnation*. Charlottesville: University Press of Virginia.

– Stevenson, I. (1995). Empirical Evidence for Reincarnation? A Response to Leonard Angel. *Sceptical Inquirer*, 50-51.

– Stevenson, I. (1997a). *Reincarnation and Biology: A contribution to the etiology of birthmarks and birth-defects*. Westport/London: Praeger.

– Stevenson, I. (1997b). *Where Reincarnation and Biology Intersect*. Londen: Praeger.

– Stevenson, I., & Keil, J. (2000). The Stability of Assessments of Paranormal Connections in Reincarnation-Type Cases. *Journal of Scientific Exploration*, *14*, 3, 356-382.

– Stevenson, I., Pasricha, S., G. (1988). Deception and Self-Deception in Cases of the Reincarnation Type: Seven Illustrative Cases in Asia. *Journal of the American Society for Psychical Research*, 82, 1, 1-31

– Stevenson, I., & Schouten, S. (1998). Does the Socio-psychological Hypothesis Explain the Cases of the Reincarnation Type? *The Journal of Nervous and Mental Disease*, *186*, 8, 504-506.

– Swedenborg, E. (1920). *Heaven and its wonders, and Hell*. London.

- Tenhaeff, W.H.C. (1958). *Telepathie en helderziendheid: beschouwingen over nog weinig doorvorste vermogens van de mens* (2e druk). Zeist: De Haan.
- Tucker, J.B. (2000). A Scale to Measure the Strength of Children's Claims of Previous Lives: Metholodogy and Initial Findings. *Journal of Scientific Exploration, 14*, 4, 571-581.
- Tucker, J.B. (2005). *Life before Life: A Scientific Investigation of Children's Memories of Previous Lives*. New York: St. Martin's Press.
- Valicella, W.F. (2002). No Self? A look at a Buddhist Argument. *International Philosophical Quarterly, 24*, 4, 168, 453-466.

Chapter 6

- Haraldsson, E. (2000a). Birthmarks and Claims of Previous Life Memories I. The Case of Purnima Ekanayake. *Journal of the Society for Psychical Research, 64*, 858, 16-25.
- Haraldsson, E. (2000b). Birthmarks and Claims of Previous Life Memories II. The case of Chatura Karunaratne. *Journal of the Society for Psychical Research, 64*, 859, 82-92.
- Pasricha, S.K. (1998). Cases of the Reincarnation Type in Northern India with Birthmarks and Birth Defects. *Journal of Scientific Exploration, 12*, 2, 259-261.
- Rawat, K.S. (1996). Drie gevallen van vermoedelijke wedergeboorte met geboortetekens. *Prana, 97*, 59-62.
- Rawat, K.S. (1997). Shanti Devi's Past. *Venture Inward, March/April*, 18-21.
- Remijnse, M., Rivas, T., Dirven, A., & Maljaars, B. (2003). Drie nieuwe gevallen van herinneringen aan vorige levens in Nederland. *Spiritualiteit* (online Dutch journal).
- Rivas, T. (1998). Kees: Een Nederlands geval van herinneringen aan een vorige incarnatie met herinneringen aan een toestand tussen dood en geboorte. *Spiegel der Parapsychologie, 36 (new edition)*, 1, 43-55.
- Rivas, T. (2000). *Parapsychologisch onderzoek naar reïncarnatie en leven na de dood*. Deventer: Ankh-Hermes.
- Rivas, T. (2003). Three Cases of the Reincarnation Type in the Netherlands. *Journal of Scientific Exploration, 17*, 3, 527-532.
- Rivas, T. (2004). Six Cases of the Reincarnation Type in the Netherlands. *The Paranormal Review, 29*, 17-20.
- Rivas, T., & Dirven, A. (2005). Reïncarnatieherinneringen in Nederland: Vijf klassieke en drie uitzonderlijke gevallen. *Spiritualiteit* (online Dutch journal).

- Rivas, T., & Dirven, A. (2010). *Van en naar het Licht*. Leeuwarden: Elikser.
- Stevenson, I. (1974a). *Twenty cases suggestive of reincarnation*. Charlottesville: University Press of Virginia.
- Stevenson, I. (1974b). *Xenoglossy: A review and report of a case*. Charlottesville: University Press of Virginia.
- Stevenson, I. (1975). *Cases of the Reincarnation Type: Vol. I. Ten Cases in India*. Charlottesville: University Press of Virginia.
- Stevenson, I. (1977). *Cases of the Reincarnation Type: Vol. II. Ten Cases in Sri Lanka*. Charlottesville: University Press of Virginia.
- Stevenson, I. (1980). *Cases of the Reincarnation Type: Vol III. Twelve Cases in Lebanon and Turkey*. Charlottesville: University Press of Virginia.
- Stevenson, I. (1983). *Cases of the Reincarnation Type: Vol. IV. Twelve Cases in Thailand and Burma*. Charlottesvile: University Press of Virginia.
- Stevenson, I. (1984). *Unlearned Language: New studies in Xenoglossy*. Charlottesville: University Press of Virginia.
- Stevenson, I. (1987). *Children who remember previous lives: A question of reincarnation*. Charlottesville: University Press of Virginia.
- Stevenson, I. (1997). *Reincarnation and Biology: A contribution to the etiology of birthmarks and birth-defects*. Westport/London: Praeger.
- Stevenson, I, & Schouten, S. (1998). Does the Socio-psychological Hypothesis Explain the Cases of the Reincarnation Type? *The Journal of Nervous and Mental Disease, 186*, 8, 504-506.
- Tucker, J. B., & Keil, H. H. J. (2013). Experimental birthmarks: New cases of an Asian practice. *Journal of Scientific Exploration, 27*, 269–282.

Chapter 7

- Carman, E.M., & Carman, N.J. (2013). *Cosmic Cradle: Spiritual Dimensions of Life Before Birth*. Berkeley, CA: North Atlantic Books.
- Dr. Shail Kumari Reincarnation and Spiritual Research Institute. (2003). *Depth Research in Reincarnation*. Allahabad.
- Ellis, D. (2003). A Case Suggestive of Reincarnation of Cats? *The Paranormal Review, 28*, 23.
- Haraldsson, E. (1995). Personality and Abilities of Children Claiming Past-life Memories. *Journal of Nervous and Mental Disease, 183*, 7, 445.

References

- Haraldsson, E. (1997). A Psychological Comparison between Ordinary Children and Those Who Claim Previous-life Memories. *Journal of Scientific Exploration, 11,* 3, 323-335.

- Haraldsson, E., Fowler, P., & Periyannanpillai, V. (2000). Psychological Characteristics of Children Who Speak of a Previous Life: A Further Field Study in Sri Lanka. *Transcultural Psychiatry, 37,* 525-544.

- Kant, I., (1766). *Träume eines Geistersehers, erlautet durch Träume der Metaphysik. Werke in sechs Banden, Band I.* (Herausgegeben von published by Wilhelm Weischedel.), republished at Darmstadt in 1983 by the Wissenschaftliche Buchgesellschaft.

- Matlock, J.G. (1990) Past Life Memory Case Studies. In: S. Krippner (Ed.). *Advances in Parapsychological Research.* Jefferson: McFarland. Pp. 184-267.

- Prasad, J. (1993). *New Dimensions in Reincarnation Researches.* Allahabad: Prasad.

- Rawat, K.S., & Rivas, T. (2005). The Life Beyond: Through the eyes of Children who Claim to Remember Previous Lives. The *Journal of Religion and Psychical Research, Vol. 28,* Number 3, 126-136.

- Rivas, T. (1999). Het geheugen en herinneringen aan vorige levens: neuropsychologische en psychologische factoren. *Spiegel der Parapsychologie, 37,* 2-3, 81-104.

- Rivas, T. (2000). *Parapsychologisch onderzoek naar reïncarnatie en leven na de dood.* Deventer: Ankh-Hermes.

- Rivas, T., & Dirven, A. (2004). Herinneringen van Célina: een Nederlands geval van reïncarnatie binnen dezelfde familie. *Terugkeer, 15*(2-3), 41-44.

- Rivas, T., & Dirven, A. (2010). *Van en naar het Licht.* Leeuwarden: Elikser.

- Rivas, T., Dirven, A., Carman, E.M., & Carman, N.J. (2015). Paranormal Aspects of Pre-Existence Memories in Young Children. *Journal of Near-Death Studies, 34*(2), 84-107.

- Sharma, P., & Tucker, J.B. (2004). Cases of the Reincarnation Type with Memories from the Intermission Between Lives. *Journal of Near-Death Studies, 23* (2), 101-118.

- Sheridan, K. (2004). *Animals and the Afterlife.* Escondido: EnLight Publishing.

- Slagle, A. (1974). *Reincarnation: A Doctor looks beyond death.* New York Sunday News, August 4th.

- Stevenson, I. (1960). Evidence for survival from claimed memories of former incarnations. *Journal of the American Society for Psychical Research, 54,* 51-71, 95-117.

- Stevenson, I. (1966). Twenty cases suggestive of reincarnation. *Journal of the American Society for Psychical Research, vol. 26.* Republished as a book in 1974 by the University Press of Virginia at Charlottesville.

- Stevenson, I. (1973). The "perfect" reincarnation case, in: *Research in Parapsychology 1972,* edited by W.G. Roll, R.L. Morris, and J.D. Morris. Metuchen, N.J.: Scarecrow Press.

- Stevenson, I. (1987). *Children Who Remember Previous Lives: A Question of Reincarnation.* Charlottesville: University Press of Virginia.

- Stevenson, I. (1997a). *Reincarnation and Biology: A Contribution to the Etiology of Birthmarks and birth defects.* Westport/London: Praeger.

- Stevenson, I. (1997b). *Where Reincarnation and Biology Intersect.* Westport/ London: Praeger.

- Stevenson, I. (2000). The phenomenon of claimed memories of previous lives: Possible interpretations and importance. *Medical Hypotheses, 54,* 652-659.

- Von Ward, P. (2008). *The Soul Genome: Science and Reincarnation.* Fenestra.

- Webster, J. (2009). *The Case Against Reincarnation: A Rational Approach.* Guildford: Grosvenor House Publishing.

Appendix B

- Baddeley, D., Wilson, B.A., & Watts, F.N. (Eds.) (1995). *Handbook of Memory Disorders.* Chichester, etc.: John Wiley & Sons.

- Bartelink, G.J.M. (1969). *Mythologisch woordenboek.* Utrecht: Het Spectrum.

- Gauld, A. (1983). *Mediumship and Survival: A Century of Investigations.* London: Paladin Books.

- Gregory, I., & Smeltzer, D.J. (1983). *Psychiatry* (2nd ed.) Boston: Little, Brown and Company.

- Haraldsson, E. (1994). Psychodiagnostische Untersuchungen an Kindern mit "Rückerinnerungen" und Fallbeispiele aus Sri Lanka. *Zeitschrift für Parapsychologie und Grenzgebiete der Psychologie, 36,* 1/2, 22-38.

- Haraldsson, E. (2005). *Trauma and Claims of Memories of a Past Life.* Overview of Psychological Studies in Lebanon and Sri Lanka. Bath: The 29th International Conference of the Society for Psychical Research.

- Haraldsson, E., & Matlock, J. (2017). *I Saw A Light And Came Here: Children's Experiences of Reincarnation.* White Crow Books.

- Harrison, P., & Harrison, M. (1983). *The children that time forgot*. Emsworth: Mason Publications.
- Keil, J. (1994). Kinder, die sich an "frühere Leben" erinnern: Neue Falluntersuchungen und ein Vergleich mit den Ergebnissen von Ian Stevenson. *Zeitschrift für Parapsychologie und Grenzgebiete der Psychologie, 36*, 1/2, 3-21.
- Morse, M. (1990). *Closer to the Light*. New York: Villard Books.
- Prasad, J. (1993). *New Dimensions in Reincarnation Research*. Allahabad: Arvind Printers.
- Rivas, T. (1991). *The Logical Necessity of the Survival of Personal Memory After Bodily Death* (lecture). Rajsamand.
- Rivas, T. (1993). Reïncarnatie-onderzoek: Op zoek naar de zuinigste toereikende hypothese. *Spiegel der Parapsychologie, 32*, 3/4, 171-188.
- Rivas, T. (2000). *Parapsychologisch onderzoek naar reïncarnatie en leven na de dood*. Deventer: Ankh-Hermes.
- Stevenson, I. (1970). *Twenty Cases Suggestive of Reincarnation*. Charlottesville: University Press of Virginia.
- Stevenson, I. (1983). *Cases of the Reincarnation Type: Vol. IV. Twelve Cases in Thailand and Burma*. Charlottesville: University Press of Virginia.
- Stevenson, I. (1987). *Children Who Remember a Previous Lives: A Question of Reincarnation*. Charlottesville: University Press of Virginia.
- Stevenson, I. (1997). *Reincarnation and Biology: A Contribution to the Etiology of Birthmarks and Birth Defects*. Westport: Praeger.

This paper was published in 1999, in a more extensive Dutch version in *Spiegel der Parapsychologie, 37*, 2-3, 81-104, as: "Het geheugen en herinneringen aan vorige levens: neuro-psychologische en psychologische factoren".

Appendix C

- Bolzano, B. (1970). *Athanasia oder Gründe fuer die Unsterblichkeit der Seele* (Reprint of book published in 1838). Frankfurt am Main: Minerva.
- Foster, J. (1991). *The Immaterial Self: A Defence of the Cartesian Dualist Conception of the Mind*. London: Routledge.
- Hewitt, P. (2003). *The Coherent Universe. An Introduction to Geoffrey Read's New Fundamental Theory of Matter, Life and Mind*. Richmond: Linden House.
- Huxley, A. (1970). *The Perennial Philosophy*. New York: Harper Colophon.

- Keil, J. (2010). Questions of the Reincarnation Type. *Journal of Scientific Exploration*, 24, 1, 75-94.

- Mills, A. (2000). *Reincarnation and Survival*. Lecture for Esalen Conference on Survival of Bodily Death.

- Morse, D. (2000). *Searching for Eternity: A Scientist's Spiritual Journey to Overcome Death Anxiety*. Memphis: Eagle Wing Books.

- Novak, P. (1997). *The Division of Consciousness: The Secret Afterlife of the Human Psyche*. Hampton Roads.

- Oesterreich, T.K. (1910). *Die Phaenomenologie des Ich in ihren Grundproblemen*. Leipzig.

- Prasad, J. (1993). *New Dimensions in Reincarnation Researches*. Allahabad: Dr. Jamuna Prasad.

- Rawat, K.S., & Rivas, T. (2005). The Life Beyond: Through the Eyes of Children who Claim to Remember Previous Lives. The *Journal of Religion and Psychical Research*, 28, 3, 126-136.

- Rivas, T. (2003a). *Geesten met of zonder lichaam: Pleidooi voor een personalistisch dualisme*. Delft: Koopman & Kraaijenbrink.

- Rivas, T. (2003b). Three Cases of the Reincarnation Type in the Netherlands. *Journal of Scientific Exploration*, 3, 527-532.

- Rivas, T. (2005). *Reincarnatie, persoonlijke evolutie en bijzondere kinderen*. *Prana*, 148, 47-53.

- Roberts, J. (1994). *Seth Speaks: The Eternal Validity of the Soul*. Amber-Allen Publishing.

- Stevenson, I. (1987). *Children Who Remember Previous Lives: A Question of Reincarnation*. Charlottesville: University Press of Virginia.

- Whitehead, A. N. (1982). *An Enquiry Concerning the Principles of Natural Knowledge*. New York: Kraus Reprints.

This paper was published in The *Journal of Religion and Psychical Research*, Vol. 28, Number 4, 226-233, October 2005.

Appendix E

- Augustine, K. 'The Case against Immortality.' *Sceptic* Magazine, 1997, 5, 2.

- Beloff, J. *The Existence of Mind*. Citadell Press, New York, 1962.

- Berkeley, G. *A Treatise Concerning the Principles of Human Knowledge*. Oxford Philosophical Texts, Oxford, 1998.

References

- Bergson, H. *Matière et mémoire*. Félix Alcan, Paris, 1908.
- Bozzano, E. *Cerebro y pensamiento: Literatura del más allá Cima*, Caracas, 1994.
- Braude, S.E. *Immortal Remains: The Evidence for Life after Death*. Rowman & Littlefield Publishers, Inc., New York, 2003.
- Carruthers, P. Phenomenal Concepts and Higher Order-Experiences. *Philosophy and Phenomenological Research*, 2004, 68, 2, 316-336.
- Chalmers, D. *The Conscious Mind: In Search of a Fundamental Theory*. Oxford University Press, New York & Oxford, 1996.
- Chalmers, D. 'The puzzles of conscious experience.' *Scientific American*, The Hidden Mind, 2002, 90-98.
- Dennett, D.C. *Het bewustzijn verklaard* (Dutch translation). Uitgeverij Contact, Amsterdam, 1995.
- Dilley, F.B. 'Telepathy and Mind-Brain Dualism.' *Journal of the Society for Psychical Research*, 1990, 56, 819, 129-137.
- Gauld, A. *Mediumship and survival: A century of investigations*. Paladin, London, 1982.
- Glenberg, A.M. 'What memory is for?' *Behavioral and Brain Sciences*, 1997, 20, 1, 1-55.
- Jackendoff, R. *Consciousness and the computational mind*. MIT Press, Cambridge, 1987.
- Locke, J. *An Essay Concerning Human Understanding*. London: Everyman, 1961.
- Lommel, P. van, Wees, R. van, Meyers, V., & Elfferich, I. 'Near-death experience in survivors of cardiac arrest: a prospective study in the Netherlands.' The *Lancet*, 2001, 358, 9298, 2039-2044.
- Nagel, T., *Mortal Questions*. Cambridge University Press, Cambridge (Mss.), 1979.
- Parnia, S., Waller, D.G., Yeates, R., & Fenwick, P. 'A qualitative and quantitative study of the incidence, features and aetiology of near-death experiences in cardiac arrest survivors.' *Resuscitation*, 2001, 48, 149-156.
- Popper, K.R., & Eccles, J.C. *The Self and its Brain*. Springer, Berlin, 1977.
- Rawat, K.S., & Rivas, T. 'The Life Beyond: Through the eyes of Children who Claim to Remember Previous Lives.' *Journal of Religion and Psychical Research*, 2005, 28, 3, 126-136.
- Rivas, T. 'Telepathy and Mind-Brain Dualism: Comment'. *Journal of the Society for Psychical Research*, 1990, 56, 821, 312-313.

- Rivas, T. *The Logical Necessity of the Survival of Personal Memory after Physical Death.* International Conference on the Survival of Human Personality, Rajsamand, 1991.
- Rivas, T. 'The Efficacy of the Mind in General.' The *Paranormal Review,* 1999a, 11, 34-35.
- Rivas, T. 'Het geheugen en herinneringen aan vorige levens: neuro-psychologische en psychologische factoren. *Spiegel der Parapsychologie,* 1999b, 37, 2-3, 81-104.
- Rivas, T. *Parapsychologisch onderzoek naar reïncarnatie en leven na de dood.* Ankh-Hermes, Deventer, 2000.
- Rivas, T. *Geesten met of zonder lichaam: Pleidooi voor een personalistisch dualisme.* Koopman & Kraaijenbrink, Delft, 2003a.
- Rivas, T. 'Why the Efficacy of Consciousness Cannot Be Limited to the Mind – Letter.', *Journal of Non-Locality and Remote Mental Interactions,* 2003b, II, 2.
- Rivas, T. *Uit het leven gegrepen: Beschouwingen rond een leven na de dood.* Koopman & Kraaijenbrink, Delft, 2003c.
- Rivas, T. 'The Survivalist Interpretation of Recent Studies Into the Near-Death Experience.' The *Journal of Religion and Psychical Research,* 2003d, 26, 1, 27-31.
- Rivas, T. 'Rebirth and Personal identity: Is Reincarnation an Intrinsically Impersonal Concept?' The *Journal of Religion and Psychical Resea*rch, 2005, 28, 4, 226-233.
- Rivas, T., & Dongen, H.v. 'Exit epifenomenalismo: la demolición de un refugio.' Revista de Filosofia, 2001, LVII, 111-129.
- Rivas, T., & Dongen, H. v. 'Exit Epiphenomenalism: the Demolition of a Refuge.' The *Journal of Non-Locality and Remote Mental Interactions,* 2003, II, 1.
- Rosenthal, D.M. 'Identity Theories.', in: Guttenplan, S. *A Companion to the Philosophy of Mind.* Blackwell, Oxford, 1994.
- Searle, J.R. *Intentionality: An Essay in the Philosophy of Mind.* Cambridge University Press, Cambridge, 1983.
- Searle, J.R. *The Mystery of Consciousness.* Granta Books, London, 1997.
- Stevenson, I. *Children who Remember Previous Lives: A Question of Reincarnation.* University Press of Virginia, Charlottesville, 1987.
- Stevenson, I. *Reincarnation and Biology.* Praeger, London/Westport, 1997.
- Wade, J. *Changes of mind: A Holonomic Theory of the Evolution of Consciousness.* State University of New York Press, Albany, 1996.

GLOSSARY

~

Akhara: wrestling arena.

Anathema: in the New Testament it means "accursed", where it clearly suggests separation from God as the penalty. In the early Church and in Judaism contemporaneous with it, it was a penalty conveyed by a decree of excommunication.

Arrack: a coarse liquor manufactured in the East Indies from a large variety of substances, for example fermented rice or coconut juice. Arrack is transparent and the colour of straw and has a peculiar but agreeable taste and contains between 52 and 54% alcohol.

Ashram: spiritual center, usually in India or Nepal, but it can also be used to refer to centers of Western spiritual groups that are influenced by any Indian religion, including Hinduism, Buddhism, Jainism or Sikhism. There even are Christian ashrams.

Babu: a widely used male honorific title, for example by servants who address their male employers.

Babuaji: equivalent of Babu, but with the honorific suffix -ji.

Betel (nut): mildly narcotic nut, which is chewed by millions of Indian men, who stain their gums and teeth with the nut's noticeable red juice.

Bhang: a traditional Indian beverage made of cannabis, milk, and various herbs and spices, which has been popular in India for ages.

Bijou ki barfi: a very sweet dessert made from milk and sugar, typical for the Vaishnev.

Caste: traditionally, a closed group within Indian society whose members are severely restricted in their choice of occupation and degree of social participation. Marriage outside the caste used to be prohibited. Social status was determined by the caste of one's birth and may only rarely be transcended.

Chach(ch)i: Indian word for aunt.

Chhatri: a domed cenotaph (monument to commemorate a deceased person).

Cryptomnesia: subconscious, hidden memories normally acquired in the subject's present life but without the subject's being aware of them.

Cryptomne(s)tic: caused by cryptomnesia.

Diwan: Chief Minister.

ECM: abbreviation of Extra-Cerebral Memory.

Ekadasis: Hindu days of fasting.

Ekka: a horse-drawn cart used for carrying passengers and merchandise.

Extra(-)Cerebral Memory: term of Hemendra Nath Banerjee for possible memories of a previous life.

Extra-Sensory Perception: direct mental perception of the physical world, which does not use the physical sensory apparatus (clairvoyance) or direct mental communication with another mind (telepathy).

Galla: an arrangement for keeping valuables underground.

Ghat: a riverbank particularly used for religious and cultural purposes by Hindus. Religious ceremonies and cremation are common activities that take place at a ghat.

Goondas: bouncers or habitual criminals usually associated with a criminal gang.

Guru: a spiritual teacher.

Informational aspects: the paranormal information a child may have about his or previous life.

Jajaroo: toilet.

Jajman: a land-owning farmer with servants.

Karma: (here) the law of cause and effect; the consequences of our choices.

Katora: within the Chaubey community of Mathura: a type of fried pancake. Outside that community it means a bowl.

Khansama: a cook.

Lambardar: a person who forms an unofficial link between the landowners in his village and the government officials.

Lakh: a unit of 100.000

Lathi: a rattan stick a little over an inch in diameter and 4-5 feet long. Police in India and elsewhere uses them for crowd control.

Maharajah: king.

Malish: a type of massage.

Manioc: a tubular plant similar to our sweet potato or yam.

Maternal impression: the psychokinetic influence of an emotional experience of a pregnant woman upon the body of an unborn child.

Mehandi: a dye sometimes used in a healing ritual.

Metempsychosis: Greek word for reincarnation sometimes reserved for reincarnation between species.

Muttra: alternative spelling for Mathura.

Naevi: congenital naevi or birthmarks are essentially coloured skin markings that develop before or shortly after birth. Benign developmental skin lesions that develop later in life are called acquired naevi. Naevi may be derived from the outside layers of the skin (epithelial naevi) or from the deeper layers (dermal/subcutaneous naevi). Naevi are further classified based on the cell type involved. Melanocytic and vascular naevi are generally the most common types of birthmarks.

Naib Tehsildar: a third-class magistrate.

Narangi ka prasad: beverage, made by crushing some tangerines into juice, then throwing pieces of tangerine into a pot of melted sugar and adding some spices.

Nautch girl: an entertainer of men belonging to a unique class of courtesans who played a significant role in the social and cultural life of India in the 18th and 19th centuries. She represented a delightful synthesis of different cultures and dance forms (the classical and the popular).

The Nautch girl was no ordinary woman of pleasure. She had refined manners, a ready wit and poetry in her blood. She catered to the tastes of the elite who had the time, resources and aptitude to enjoy her company. Her sexual favours were reserved for a chosen few.

Neem tree: an evergreen of the tropics and sub-tropics. It belongs to the family Meliaceae.

Panda: person charged with giving assistance to pilgrims who come to bathe in the holy water of the Ganges or some other sacred river. Pandas provide room, board, and guidance to the pilgrims.

Parantha: a type of fried pancake.

Parval: a common Indian vegetable growing usually in summer.

Peon: a person who is compelled to work for his creditor until his debt is paid.

Phaeton: a light four-wheeled open carriage, usually drawn by a pair of horses.

Philias: conditions, subjects or acts, which someone finds particularly enticing.

Phobias: persistent, irrational fears of certain objects or situations.

Pre-existence: existence before the conception of one's body.

Previous personality: the personality that a child would have been in his or her previous life.

Psychokinesis: direct impact of mind upon matter.

Punarjanma: Sanskrit term for rebirth or reincarnation.

Purdah: practice that includes the seclusion of women from public observation by wearing concealing clothing from head to toe and by the use of high walls, curtains, and screens erected within the home. Purdah is practised by Muslims and by various Hindus, especially in India.

The limits imposed by this practice vary according to different countries and class levels.

Purohit: a priest.

Rabri: a concentrated, sweetened whole milk product, containing several layers of clotted cream.

Rakhi: a sacred thread of trust between brother and sisters.

Raksha Bandhan day: holiday celebrated in India as Brother's Day.

Rebirth: synonym for reincarnation, though sometimes used by Buddhists to denote an impersonalist type of reincarnation.

Riksha: Eastern bike taxi.

Rohu fish: a type of fish often served as a Bengali non-vegetarian dish.

Rupees: Indian currency.

Saree/Sari: Indian dress for women.

Sarong: Sri Lankan dress for men.

Shiva: Indian divinity.

Sceptic: sometimes a cautious, rational person (zetetic) but more often a debunker. Some opponents call debunkers "pseudo-sceptics" as these typically show an attitude, which is almost the opposite of the original "sceptics" from ancient Greece. The Greek sceptics doubted absolutely everything whereas most contemporary sceptics only doubt anything that does not fit into their materialistic, "naturalistic" worldview. In this respect, such "pseudo-sceptics" really are dogmatic.

Tablas: Indian set of two drums, which often accompany the sitar.

Tau: uncle.

Tonga: a carriage drawn by a horse.

Thakerwada: shrine room.

Urdu: Indian and Pakistani language. It is the national language of Pakistan and an official language of UP in India.

Vakil: Indian lawyer.

Wade: A fried patty made of ground dhal (split pulse) and spices.

Xenoglossy: the active, meaningful use of parts of a foreign language, which the subject has never learned through normal means.

Zamindar: Indian landowner.

Zenana: an area where only women are allowed, inaccessible to strangers.

ABOUT THE AUTHORS

~

D r. **Kirti Swaroop Rawat** was born in 1936 in Beawar, Rajasthan, India. He is currently residing at Goyal Nagar, Indore, Madhya Pradesh. He is married to Mrs. Vidya Rawat and has one daughter, Mrs. Bharti Khandelwal, and two sons, Dr. Bharat Rawat and Jai Rawat.

Dr. Rawat holds master degrees in philosophy and sociology from Rajasthan University in Jaipur. He was awarded a Doctorate in Philosophy at the same University with a dissertation about reincarnation, and conducted his own research into cases of memories of past lives in India, Nepal and the Netherlands. For many years, he also worked as a teacher.

He has to his credit many books, articles, poems and stories. Over the years Dr. Rawat travelled widely to give lectures and seminars in India and other countries such as the USA, England, Spain, The Netherlands, Belgium and Nepal. He has also been interviewed by many TV and radio channels such as the Discovery Channel.

Titus Rivas, MA, MSc, was born in 1964, in Nijmegen, the Netherlands, as the son of a Dutch school teacher and a Spanish social worker. He is single, and shares his life with a dog, Moortje, and two cats, Kissa and Mitxi. He is an author, researcher, and teacher of courses about parapsychology, and philosophy.

Rivas studied philosophy and psychology at the Dutch universities of Nijmegen, Utrecht and Amsterdam. He has carried out reincarnation and survival research in the Netherlands and other European countries for the former Foundation for the Scientific Study of Reincarnation, Athanasia Foundation, the International Association for Near-Death

Studies (IANDS), and the Dutch and British Societies for Psychical Research.

For IANDS, Rivas co-authored *The Self Does Not Die*, together with Anny Dirven and Rudolf H. Smit, about confirmed paranormal aspects of Near-Death Experiences.

Rivas has published many books about parapsychological subjects, and also about the philosophy of mind, spirituality, animal ethics and veganism, mental healthcare, and social issues.

Other publications by Dr. K.S. Rawat

1. Paramanovigyan
2. Alaukik Kahaniyan
3. Punarjanm
4. With Titus Rivas: "Reincarnation: The Evidence is Building" (*Writers Publisher, Vancouver, 2007*) ISBN 1-894883-13-6.

Dr. Rawat is also an accomplished poet.

Other publications by Titus Rivas

1. *Parapsychologisch onderzoek naar reïncarnatie en leven na de dood*, Deventer: Ankh-Hermes, 2000. ISBN 90-202-6020-0.
2. *Geesten met of zonder lichaam: pleidooi voor een personalistisch dualisme*, Delft: Koopman & Kraaijenbrink, 2003. ISBN 90-75675-11-9.
3. Onrechtvaardig diergebruik: Essays over dieren, ethiek en veganisme, Delft: Koopman & Kraaijenbrink, 2003. ISBN 90-75675-24-0.
4. With Bert Stoop: Spiritualiteit, vrijheid en engagement (Two Volumes). Brave New Books, 2013. ISBN 97-89402107951.
5. With Tilly Gerritsma: It's Really Rather Normal. Lulu.com, 2013. ISBN 978-1291508574.
6. With Anny Dirven: Van en naar het Licht. Leeuwarden: Elikser, 2010. ISBN 978-90-8954-1468.
7. With Anny Dirven and Rudolf Smit. *The Self Does Not Die*. IANDS, 2016. ISBN 978-0997560800.

INDEX

www.ingramcontent.com/pod-product-compliance
Lightning Source LLC
Chambersburg PA
CBHW021136090426
42740CB00008B/808